THE PEOPLE'S REPRESENTATIVES

Electoral Systems in the
Asia–Pacific Region

Edited by
Graham Hassall & Cheryl Saunders

ALLEN & UNWIN

First published in 1997 by
Allen & Unwin Pty Ltd
9 Atchison Street, St Leonards, NSW 2065 Australia
Phone: (61 2) 9901 4088
Fax: (61 2) 9906 2218
E-mail: frontdesk@allen-unwin.com.au
URL: http://www.allen-unwin.com.au

National Library of Australia
Cataloguing-in-Publication entry:

The people's representatives: electoral systems in the
Asia–Pacific region.

  Bibliography.
  Includes index.
  ISBN 1 86448 258 3.   1002377534

  1. Representative government and representation—Asia.
  2. Representative government and representation—Pacific Area.
  3. Legislative bodies—Asia. 4. Legislative bodies—Pacific Area.
  5. Asia—Constitutional law. 6. Pacific Area—Constitutional law.
  I. Hassall, Graham. II. Saunders, Cheryl.

328.3095

Set in 10.5/12pt Baskerville by DOCUPRO, Sydney
Printed by SRM Production Services Sdn Bhd, Malaysia

10 9 8 7 6 5 4 3 2 1

DATE DUE FOR RETURN

This book may be recalled before the above date

90014

Contents

Notes on Contributors

Satya Arinanto is Secretary of the Department of Constitutional Law and the Secretary of the Associate Dean for Academic Affairs, Faculty of Law, University of Indonesia.

David Bradshaw is Office Solicitor, State Services Commission of New Zealand.

Dai-Kwon Choi is Professor of Law, College of Law, Seoul National University, and Director of American Studies Institute, Seoul National University, Seoul, Korea.

Rajeev Dhavan is the Director of the Public Interest Legal Support Group, New Delhi, India.

Anil Divan is a senior advocate in the High Court of India, and a past President of LAWASIA.

Rohan Edrisinha is a Lecturer in the Faculty of Law, University of Colombo, Sri Lanka.

Yash Ghai is Professor of Law at the Hong Kong University.

Arnaldo Gonçalves is advisor to the Secretary for Economic and Financial Affairs, Macau government.

Graham Hassall is Director of the Asia–Pacific Program at the Centre for Comparative Constitutional Studies, University of Melbourne, Australia.

Xie Manhua is a Lecturer in the Faculty of Law, Zhongshan (Sun Yatsen) University, Guangzhou, People's Republic of China.

Akira Osuka is a Professor in the Law School, Waseda University, Japan.

Jorge Costa Oliveira is Director of the Legislative Affairs Office, Macau.

Ruchi Pant is an Associate of the Public Interest Legal Support and Research Centre, New Delhi, India.

Li Qixin is Dean, Faculty of Law, Zhongshan (Sun Yatsen) University, Guangzhou, People's Republic of China.

Cheryl Saunders is Professor of Law and Director of the Centre for Comparative Constitutional Studies at the University of Melbourne, Australia.

Thio Li-ann is a Lecturer in the Faculty of Law, National University of Singapore.

Ganesh Raj Sharma is a Senior Advocate, Nepal.

Tommy Thomas is a partner at Skrine & Co., Malaysia.

Amir ul-Islam is a barrister and solicitor, Bangladesh.

Jiunn-rong Yeh is a Professor in the Law School, National Taiwan University.

1

Introduction: Systems of Representation in Asia–Pacific Constitutions—A Comparative Analysis

Graham Hassall

THE SIGNIFICANCE OF REPRESENTATION IN THE ASIA–PACIFIC REGION

In the governance of the new and old states of the Asia–Pacific region, effective and efficient electoral processes play a crucial role. But although a smoothly conducted election is often taken for granted and attention is focused on the candidates, the issues and the outcome, the fact is that successful elections can only take place in the context of essential facilitating conditions. These conditions include a recognition by the people and the contestants that the processes and procedures for the election are legitimate. The absence of this sense of legitimacy inevitably results in turmoil, whether during the electoral period, or soon after it, and points to serious weaknesses in the legitimacy of the state itself. Conversely, the successful conduct of elections may mark the emergence of legitimacy for a state, and for a regime.[1]

A second prerequisite for the successful conduct of elections is an adequate legal framework. Electoral laws provide not only for all aspects of the electoral process, but also for dispute resolution procedures that may be required following voting. Where an electoral system is functioning smoothly these laws and procedures rate little mention, and simply provide the framework for the democratic determination of a nation's political leaders. Where weaknesses in the political system are attributed to the constitutional and legal environment, on the other hand, discussion moves away from the political issues and focuses on the system itself. Where difficulties are experienced in the process of electing representatives, the people and the leaders themselves must decide whether the problems are fundamental in nature, or are simple matters that can be fixed through electoral reform. Although problems of a fundamental nature are best resolved through re-examining the constitutional design, the ability to undertake constitutional review requires a maturity in the public sphere that is not always attainable.

Instances of change in the electoral system accompanying a change in constitutional design abound in recent Asian history. In Indonesia, a period of parliamentary democracy and open elections under the 1950 Constitution was followed in 1957 by a return to the (presidential) 1945 Constitution, and the 'guided democracy' of President Soekarno—the precursor to contemporary Indonesia's *Pancasila* democracy. In South Korea, changed electoral laws preceding a presidential election in December 1987 and parliamentary elections in 1988 accompanied the transition from the military rule of General Chun to that of President Roh Tae Woo.[2] In Nepal in 1991 democratic elections were held for the first time since 1959, as a result of the pro-democracy demonstrations that began in 1989 and the 1990 Constitution that replaced the Panchayat system of government.[3] In Cambodia, elections that were administered by the United Nations Transitional Authority in Cambodia (UNTAC) in 1992 and that preceded the new Constitution of 1993 demarcated the new regime from Khmer Rouge control over Kampuchea in the period 1975–78.[4] There are instances, on the other hand, where change in an electoral system occurs without significant change to the overall constitutional system (such as occurred in 1993 in New Zealand—see Chapter 4), just as there are instances of fundamental constitutional change that have less impact on the electoral process; this was the case in the Philippines, where electoral rules changed little before, during and after the martial law period of President Marcos of 1972–86, as expressed in the Philippine Constitutions of 1972 and 1986.[5]

VARIATIONS IN THE NOTION OF REPRESENTATION

Regional constitutional systems display variety in their approaches to democracy and to problems of representation. Their current systems of law and government were for the most part moulded by the collision between colonial power and authority and traditional values, loyalties and customs, so that today they comprise plural legal systems which bear some resemblance to the traditional past, but also reflect their colonial influences. In this case they are hybrid systems, often seeking to bring modern approaches to non-Western communities more familiar with alternative orders premised on discontinuity and pragmatic adaptability. The essays in this book canvass some of the principal issues affecting these systems, and provide useful perspectives on how electoral systems in the Asia–Pacific region are faring at the close of the twentieth century.

In one sense theories of representation are straightforward. Through representation the people exercise their power; representative government ensures that nobody is in a position to exercise absolute power; and the more democratic a system of government is, the greater is the people's involvement in making decisions that affect them—representation functions as an 'intermediary principle' by which democratic systems can be created. Since 'pure democracy' is neither possible nor, necessarily, desirable (the large populations of the countries of Asia suggest that representative democracy will remain far more feasible than direct democracy, no matter what communication and transportation technologies emerge), representation assumes considerable significance. And since 'democracy' and 'representation' themselves tend to be philosophical abstractions or ideals implemented across cultures, the concrete form they take is also of much importance.

In modern usage, democracy is often equated with freedom. But on a more sophisticated level, it refers to all the means by which the power of the people is shaped, restrained, buttressed and exercised. Is there a notion of democracy that is universally applicable? Or are there varieties of democracy, which allow the people to implement their will to greater and lesser degrees? Whereas the Western tradition has given most familiar expression to democratic values, the idea of democracy itself has been elaborated through the experience of diverse cultures, which no single tradition has monopolised.

In the West, the notion of representation has evolved since classical times. Rousseau, however, suggested in *The Social Contract* that representation is now a 'wholly modern' idea which derives from the types of contracts made in the feudal era.[6] Others including Locke and Hobbes also discussed representation in terms of the derivation of authority to govern from the consent of the people to be so governed. In this sense, therefore, the act of choosing representatives is defined in Western theory as part of the core social contract by which the sovereign people transfer their power to the ruler, and impose limits on the ruler's use of this power.

Concepts of representation in non-Western thought admit additional possibilities. Firstly, they allow for representation of groups, not just individual 'citizens'. Secondly, they are more inclined to accept the tenure of non-elected representatives who gain office through means other than election. This variety in the bases of

representation necessitates investigation of the advantages and disadvantages both of methods of selecting representatives apart from
election and of recognising groups as well as individuals within
societies. Some commentators, such as Dhavan and Pant (see Chapter 6), question the appropriateness of borrowing Western models.
If representation is not based solely on the individual citizen,
however, which social, economic or perhaps ethnic groups can
instead claim legitimacy?

THE IMPORTANCE OF SOCIAL AND POLITICAL CONTEXT

The challenges facing electoral systems in the Asia–Pacific region
must be seen in social and political context. At the beginning of
the twentieth century most Asian and Pacific Island states were
subject to colonial powers, their people demoralised, their governments shorn of power and pride. Within decades they had attained
national independence: 'the masses' of the Indian subcontinent
emerged as the states of India, Pakistan, Bangladesh and Sri Lanka;
in Southeast Asia emerged the states of Malaysia, Indonesia, Brunei
and the Philippines; the Vietnamese, Cambodians and Laotians also
reclaimed freedom. Only a handful of states in the Asia–Pacific
region remain confined to colonial status now that the former
colonial empires of the British, Portuguese, French, Germans, Span-
ish and Americans have all but disappeared.[7] The few remaining
colonies in the Pacific Islands comprise French Polynesia and New
Caledonia,[8] and the territories in the possession of the United
States. The Melanesian peoples of the Southwest Pacific gained
independence in Papua New Guinea, the Solomon Islands, Fiji and
Vanuatu; and the Micronesians of the North Pacific, apart from
those on Guam, have all been able to participate in acts of self-
determination. The Polynesians of Tonga, the Cook Islands and
Western Samoa, as well as some even smaller states, have each been
given the opportunity to choose their political status. Living beside
many of these national communities, in both Asia and the Pacific,
are members of large and small diaspora communities—Indian,
Chinese, Polynesian and even Vietnamese—whose impact has gone
beyond the sphere of culture and is evident even in constitutional
arrangements.

Legal traditions and practices in the region must themselves be
considered in the context of the remarkably rapid political and
social change experienced in the region in the twentieth century.
These states now practise sophisticated constitutionalism, with separate organs of power and articulated systems of law. They elect
representatives to legislatures that make law and change law, and
they have access both to courts able to resolve disputes and to

bureaucratic agencies able to administer government programs. The institutions of governance in Asia and the Pacific, however limited in capacity some of them may appear, demonstrate remarkable progress by states and societies that were mostly ruled traditionally by more or less powerful despots and absolute rulers, and that more recently were ruled by colonial overlords.

SOCIAL REFORM

The development of constitutionalism and democracy has been accompanied by positive social reforms. Societies that were traditionally stratified on the bases of class, caste and even slavery are being modified by programs of affirmative action that make opportunities available to the downtrodden, to minorities and to women. Societies in which women traditionally played inferior roles to men now allow their participation in a greater range of activities. There has been expansion, too, in the institutions and values of democracy, and in the requisite qualities of civil societies, including print and electronic media, and there have emerged significant numbers of private individuals well positioned to take an active interest in public life. This social change has been aided by the spread of technology and communications including satellites and, most recently, the Internet. In comparison with former times, the peoples of the Asia–Pacific region are beginning to prosper. Standards of living have risen, life expectancy has increased and quality of life has improved. Formal education systems have emerged where none existed, and opportunities for further study are opening up both domestically and abroad.

TURBULENCE AND CONFLICT

In addition to these positive developments, however, a realistic portrayal of conditions in the region must also recognise a range of destabilising factors that make the region one of ongoing turbulence and conflict. At the current time warfare—whether declared or undeclared, and whether between states or within them—continues to wreak havoc in the lives of the peoples of the Asia–Pacific region, for instance the Tamils' struggle for an independent homeland in Sri Lanka; border disputes in India involving Kashmir and the Punjab; fighting over the status of the former East Timor and the former Dutch New Guinea in Indonesia; ethnic unrest in the Southern Philippines' province of Mindanao; the struggle for democracy in Burma/Myanmar; and the effort to restore civil society in Cambodia following the period of Khmer Rouge rule between 1975 and 1978. Violent political agitation and other forms of social unrest also continue to affect the people of Tibet, Pakistan, Bangladesh, Papua New Guinea, the French Pacific and some regions of China.

The region, like others elsewhere in the world, is also experiencing a crisis in values: whether in the form of corruption in public life leading to instability in political systems; or a decline in traditional religious beliefs resulting in the deterioration of both private and public behaviour; or the emergence of increasingly volatile religious fundamentalism and ethnic chauvinism, which in some cases now threaten the very viability of states. Traditional religions have continued paternalistic attitudes towards 'the masses' by failing to encourage people's involvement in making the decisions that have most impact on their lives. Corruption has taken hold in public offices no less than it has in commerce, and reaches its most extreme form in such places as the 'Golden Triangle' (crossing the borders of Thailand, Laos and Burma)—from where drugs are manufactured and transported to foreign markets—and in the military–bureaucratic alliances that facilitate large-scale monopolistic business enterprises.

These expressions of turbulence and conflict have left their mark on the region's legal and constitutional systems. In a number of countries democracy has become associated with partisanship, cynicism and corruption. It has lost sight of its philosophical roots and succumbed to a form of political theatre around the processes of nomination and candidature, electioneering and solicitation. At times the democratic paradigm has become so weakened as to fall prey to alternative regimes of power, notably military power, and to bureaucratic authoritarianism. Martial law has been imposed on a significant number of countries in the region, on a variety of pretexts.[9] In addition, models of governance have evolved that do not resemble the liberal democracies of the West, but which claim status as democracy in forms required under the prevailing sociocultural conditions.[10] Electoral practices and ideological legitimacy stem from such codes as *Fatung* in Taiwan and *Pancasila* in Indonesia, from socialism in Burma and Laos, from Asian-style Communism in China and Vietnam, and from values of clientelism and patronage in other regional countries. These developments lie at the heart of the important late-twentieth-century debate about the nature and scope of universal democratic moves.

EXAMINING ELECTORAL SYSTEMS

The characteristics by which the structure and operation of an electoral system may be judged include electoral formulae (such as general election, plurality, single transferable vote, proportional representation, indirect elections and electoral colleges), and such other factors as the extent to which votes are translated into seats, the methods for reapportionment, representation of minorities, the organisation of the ballot, questions of intraparty choice (such as primary elections and preference voting), the timing of elections and terms of office, the use of referendums and direct democracy, suffrage, voter registration, compulsory voting, plural voting, election campaigns and finance, and party government and coalitions. It is also necessary to consider elections in their wider context, including regime support and impact on the economy.[11]

Finally, electoral systems must be viewed in the context of constitutional structures that are basically parliamentary or presidential in type—the distinction having implications for the nature of the powers they allocate to the legislative, judicial and executive branches of government.

While it is not possible to explore each one of these important themes, this chapter highlights some of the basic features of electoral design, and some of the issues that have dominated the recent electoral experience of regional countries. The legislature is the primary body affected by elections, and legislatures have either a single chamber (are 'unicameral'), or a dual chamber (with Upper and Lower Houses, such as a House of Representatives, and a Senate). These bodies may be fully elected, or partly elected and partly appointed. Apart from the legislature, the office of head of state is filled through general election in some systems. Singapore established direct presidential elections in 1991.[12] In Taiwan, the head of state was first elected directly by the people in 1996.

ELECTORAL SYSTEMS AND POLITICAL PARTIES

Electoral systems in the region vary between multi-party, limited party and one-party systems of government. In single-party systems such as China and Vietnam voters are given a choice among a range of candidates, but not among a range of parties. In Vietnam under the revised (1992) Constitution, the Communist Party extended the powers of the National Assembly, but the state remains a one-party system without other forms of political pluralism.[13] The few countries in which political parties are non-existent include Tuvalu and Nauru, Pacific Island states in which cliques, rather than parties, compete for political power in the smallest of Parliaments. In Indonesia there are by law just two political parties: the PPP (United Development Party or Partai Persatuan), which groups all former Muslim parties; and the PDI (Indonesian Democratic Party), which groups together the former nationalist and democratic parties.[14] In addition to the two parties there is Golkar, a federation of 260 trade, professional and regional organisations formed in 1964 by senior army officers to establish a loose alliance of sectional interests—farmers, fishers, professionals, factory workers, and the like. Golkar is a government-controlled 'non-party' which nonetheless holds seats in the Parliament. India has a considerable number of political parties, which are identified to voters on polling day by signs that must at the one time signify a party, a candidate and the party program.

Simple plurality

The most basic electoral system is simple plurality, or the 'first-past-the-post' system, which awards a seat to the candidate with the highest number of votes. It is not necessary for the candidate to obtain a set proportion of the vote or to obtain more than 50% (a majority). The use of the simple plurality system in countries where many independent candidates run in each electorate constitutes the open performance of democracy, but returns members who received less than a majority of votes from their constituents. In other words, more constituents will have voted for candidates other than the winner. If such a political community prefers a mandatory view of representation, it would regard such an incumbent as lacking a mandate. For this reason the use of the 'first-past-the-post' system is being questioned; for instance in Papua New Guinea, where the nomination of large numbers of candidates at each election reflects a competitive tribal social system. At general elections in 1992 over 1500 candidates contested 109 parliamentary seats, many of which were secured with less than 10% of the vote. Incumbents frequently enjoy little constituency support and approximately half are returned at subsequent elections.[15]

The election to the office of president in the small Pacific Island state of Belau typifies the problem for the simple plurality system. Under a plurality system, Ngiratkel Etpison won office in 1988 with just 26% of the vote and a mere 31 votes more than his opponent Roman Tmetuchel. A new Presidential Primary Law passed in 1992 required the winning candidate to accumulate an absolute majority. Subsequently, an estimated 85% of registered voters participated in primary elections in September 1992, casting a total of 11 200 votes among three candidates: Johnson Toribong won 3188 votes, Kuniwo Nakamura 3125, and incumbent President Etpison 2084. Nakamura won a run-off election in November between the first two placed candidates. By holding a second ballot between a smaller number of candidates the winner is assured of a greater mandate than initially secured.

The most frequent criticism of the simple plurality electoral system in plural societies is that it is a 'winner takes all' method of selecting representatives. Whereas such a system may suit 'homo-genous' societies, it is less suited to societies comprising a number of ethnic communities (and in which ethnicity is a political factor), since the majority community will win representation every time. The few Asian–Pacific countries that use the 'simple plurality' method generally compensate for the 'winner takes all' outcome through political means. For instance, at independence the Malaysian electoral system was a single-member simple plurality system, but this has been complemented in recent years by multi-member group constituencies (see Chapter 3). The system in practice, furthermore, is tightly organised along ethnic lines by political elites representing the Malay, Chinese and Indian populations. Their alliance, under the banner of UMNO (United Malays National Organisation) has ensured Malay dominance of executive power since the first general elections in 1955, shortly before Malaysian independence, while at the same time offering the leaders of minority communities a role in decision making.[16] Even in Japan, which is a considerably homogenous society, electoral reforms in 1993 added a proportional representation component to its legislature. The Japanese House of Representatives now comprises a mixture of 300 members elected in single constituencies and a further 200 elected in eleven proportional representation constituencies.

Proportional representation

Proportional representation refers to representation of all parties in a legislature in proportion to their popular vote. The system has most appeal when there are more than two major parties and a desire that the legislature include members of these parties in some way proportional to their popularity with the electorate. The simplest method of making the calculation is division of the country into large constituencies that each return several members of Parliament. Those candidates are elected who obtain more than a certain fraction of the vote, and their surplus votes exceeding that fraction are distributed among the other candidates according to the second and later choices indicated on the ballot papers. As a result of this, other candidates, whose votes then reach the required quota, are also elected. This is the method of the transferable vote. Another method provides for the accumulation of votes received by a party that fails to return a candidate in a constituency (which in a majority system would simply have no effect). If the accumulated votes reach a nominated number, candidates of that party may become members of Parliament without a constituency.[17] Taiwan's 125-seat elected legislature is complemented by an additional 36 members appointed from lists of 'at large' candidates, on a proportional representation basis among the major parties. Vanuatu's electoral system includes an element of proportional representation 'so as to ensure fair representation of different political groups and opinions'.

Preferential voting

In preferential voting systems voters rank each of the candidates in order of preference, and one MP is elected for each electorate. Such a system is useful when the winner is required to receive more than 50% of the vote. If no candidate receives more than half the votes cast in the electorate, then the second preferences of the lowest polling candidate are transferred to the other candidates. This process of transferring preferences continues until one candidate has more than half the votes and is elected. The system can be organised in various ways—with voters ranking their preferences for every candidate, or for only as many candidates as they wish. Those who support minor parties may nonetheless exert some influence on the result of the election through their second, third and subsequent preferences. This system is not a form of proportional representation because it does not assist minor parties to gain seats in parliament. Usually, a party can form a government without needing to join in a coalition or an agreement with other parties. Systems of preferential voting that engineer the voting pattern to ensure that one or other candidate receives 50% minimum vote may be efficient, and may come to reflect the wishes of a 'majority', but they do not reflect a pure democratic vote.

Multi-member systems

Mixed member proportional systems   Mixed-member proportional systems allow voters at least two votes, one of which is used to elect the electorate's member, and the other to elect a political party. The legislature would then be composed of some members elected to represent specific electorates, and others elected to represent political parties in the country as a whole. Whether or not a political party obtains seats in the parliament is determined by their obtaining a necessary minimum of votes nationally, for example 5%. The mixed-member proportional system is a form of proportional representation, in which minor parties have an improved chance of having MPs elected. The system will tend to require parties to form coalitions or agreements in order to form the government. Multi-member parliaments having proportional representation include the Indonesian legislature.

Single transferable vote systems   In multi-member systems, the number of MPs in each electorate is determined by the size of population in each. There may, for instance, be advantages to having more members in more densely populated urban electorates, and less in rural electorates. The single transferable vote system, which is a form of proportional representation, allows for the election of minor parties and candidates with strong local support. Coalitions or agreements between parties may be needed before a government can be formed.

Supplementary member systems   A supplementary system adds members to the legislature in addition to those elected under the 'first-past-the-post' requirements. Additional members can be added from political parties, in proportion to the votes obtained by each party. The purpose of adding supplementary members is to recognise the support given by the electorate to the various political parties if this support is not recognised in the return of individual members. It is advantageous to minor parties, which may not have succeeded in placing many members in the legislature, despite receiving a significant number of votes in the electorate as a whole. The system may also be advantageous to the dominant party and give it the opportunity to form a government without the necessity of forming a coalition with other parties. Several constitutions of Asian–Pacific countries include provisions for the appointment of supplementary members to the legislature, although there are few cases in which these provisions have been used.

Functional constituencies   In functional constituencies, a person's eligibility to vote and to stand for candidature comes through being a member of a specific subgroup, in addition to being a citizen in the general sense. The intention of such systems is to ensure the representation of particular groups in the electoral process. Alternately, functional constituencies may be seen as a sophisticated method by which the state controls these particular groups, through controlling their leadership. The political theorist Roberto Bobbio objects to representation of 'citizens' in the state through functional groups, or other (necessarily less fundamental) forms of representation that may exist in a society.[18] But his objections on theoretical grounds are generated in a European rather than an Asian–Pacific perspective. Functional constituencies continue to operate in Indonesia, the Philippines, Malaysia, Hong Kong and Macau, and (depending on definition) in countries with such diverse electoral systems as Vietnam and Papua New Guinea.

In Hong Kong in 1993 Governor Chris Patten introduced changes to the colony's electoral system, broadening the 21 existing functional constituencies (representing industrial, welfare, professional and commercial groups) and creating additional ones (primary production, power and construction; textiles and garments; manufacturing; import and export; wholesale and retail;

hotels and catering; transport and communications; financing, insurance, real estate and business services; and community, social and personal services), ostensibly to increase the participation of these groups in the selection of members of the Legislative Council.

In Indonesia functional groups are organised by the government-sponsored 'Joint Secretariat of Functional Groups', or Golkar (Golongan Karya). Golkar is not officially a political party. Its original purpose was to counter growing Communist influence, but following the turmoil surrounding the departure of President Soekarno, and the rise of Soeharto, Golkar was brought under government control in 1968.[19]

PRESELECTION AND NOMINATION

Preselection and nomination of candidates is a problematic issue in the theory and practice of electoral democracy. In the absence of direct democracy, electoral systems in virtually all Asian–Pacific states limit the numbers of candidates competing for specific electoral seats through systems of preselection and nomination. This restriction on the democratic rights of the electors presumes that the electors are in favour of the range of candidates provided by the system. Political parties frequently 'preselect' the candidates offered to voters on a party ticket. But what if the electors are not satisfied with the qualities of any of the candidates put up by the parties? While the primary motivation for preselection is efficiency (particularly where systems require the winning candidate to obtain 50% or more of the vote), the method nonetheless constrains voters' choices, and all but removes the possibility of voters voting in complete freedom for the candidate they feel is most suited for the office. Furthermore, the system places power in the hands of the political parties, which in theory are the organised expression of the wishes of the masses, but which in practice often express the wishes of well-organised minorities.

In some regional electoral systems intending candidates are subject to scrutiny by the public, as well as by state authorities, before having their nominations accepted. In Indonesia, for instance, political parties' nominees receive public scrutiny before their approval as candidates. Prior to the 1992 general election, for instance, the National Election Committee (LPU) invited public objections to any of the registered candidates. It received 351 letters about the provisional list of 2283 candidates. Of the objections 92% were about personal character and internal party problems, 5% about administrative problems, and 3% about the candidates' past criminal records or involvement in civil lawsuits. The political parties then had two months to defend their candidates, and those who survived this scrutiny became eligible as candidates.[20]

APPOINTED REPRESENTATIVES

Some constitutions acknowledge the existence of leaders whose positions are not attained through democratic election, but whose leadership status is defined by older (pre-constitutional) traditions. In some cases such leaders are allocated positions in the legislature—usually the Upper House (as in Fiji). In other cases leaders sit in constitutionally recognised bodies that have the power to advise the legislature on matters affecting customary issues (as in the Cook Islands).

In the Tongan constitutional system, only nobles vote for noble representatives. Nine parliamentary seats are filled with appointees of the country's 33 noble families, and another twelve are appointed by King Taufa' ahau Tupou IV. Traditional leaders also play a significant role in the constitutional systems of the Federated States of Micronesia, the Cook Islands and Vanuatu.

In Asia, no less than in the Pacific, legislative seats are filled by appointment. In Thailand all 270 members of the Senate were appointed by the military as recently as 1992, although recent changes have transferred the power to appoint to the prime minister. In Indonesia the president appoints members to both the Parliament (Dewan Perwakilan Rakyat) and the Provisional People's Consultative Assembly (Majelis Permusyawaratan Rakyat Sementara or MPRS), the body that selects the subsequent president and sets the guidelines for state policy.

THE ROLE OF INDIVIDUAL REPRESENTATIVES

The activities of individual representatives depend in part on the concepts of accountability that exist in a society. If an electorate views its member of Parliament as its 'delegate', or as its 'mandatory representative', it will expect this member to vote as it determines. If, however, it does in fact 'delegate' the task to the member, then the member is free to consider each issue in good conscience, and answer only to his or her conscience for the decision taken. The question then raised for any system is whether representatives are the mandatories of those who elected them, or elected leaders responsible for making wise decisions from complex choices on the basis of the information that is available to them in their privileged positions.

DEFECTION AND ANTI-DEFECTION

A major issue identified by contributors to this volume is 'floor-crossing', or defection from one party to another. In systems where this is allowed, a political faction able to secure a majority of parliamentary members may then attempt to win control of the executive by defeating the government in a 'vote of no confidence'. The question of whether or not to outlaw 'hopping' between political parties tests competing ideals: should it be banned for the sake of parliamentary stability (and yield to the influence and power of political parties) or should it be allowed in the interests of democracy (and to the detriment of parliamentary stability)? To outlaw 'hopping' strikes at freedom of association (see Chapter 11) but to allow it does not assist the establishment of political stability. As explained in Chapter 12, concerning the situation in India, the Indian Supreme Court has upheld constitutional amendments outlawing defection between political parties, commenting that restricting the freedom of association of members of Parliament was less important than the political stability to be gained. A common practice in Papua New Guinea, to cite a Pacific example, has been for candidates to stand as independent candidates before then aligning themselves with one or other party. 'Horse-trading' following general elections at one stage became so intense that a law was proposed in 1991 to have Parliament meet seven days, rather than 21 days, after elections to minimise the extent of the practice. As well as being destabilised by such bargaining, Papua New Guinea's government was removed through no-confidence motions three times between 1975 and 1988.[21]

VOTE-BUYING AND ELECTORAL CORRUPTION

'Vote-buying' is one of the most troublesome practices in Asian–Pacific electoral systems. In countries such as Japan and Korea, and no less in small Pacific Island states such as Papua New Guinea, the demands of electoral politics have led politicians into corrupt practices. In Japan, electoral reforms in 1993 sought to eradicate the problems of high electoral campaign expenditure and consequent corrupt revenue-raising and revenue-distribution practices. In Thailand, where the Electoral Law allows candidates to spend only 1 million Baht on their campaigns, an incident in elections in 1995 illustrated the scale of the problem of vote-buying. Allegations of vote-buying following the elections abounded, and the Chuan government sought clarification from the Juridical Council as to whether parties had the right to unlimited spending, or whether the total amount spent by both the party and the candidates would count against the rule of 1 million Baht per candidate. In one pre-election raid more than 11 million Baht in Bt100 and Bt200 denominations was seized from a Chart Thai Party candidate in Buri Ram Province, but the police investigation was dropped when the candidate's party won power and he became, in addition, a Cabinet member.[22] It was argued that since the cash had not yet been distributed to voters, those involved had not at that point in time breached the Electoral Code. At about the same time Seritham Party leader Arthit Urairat announced his retirement from politics, saying that politics was 'now too expensive for him as he does not have the money to buy potential candidates for his party'.[23]

In May 1995 Malaysia's UMNO commenced enforcing a 'code of ethics' on its members, which limits the involvement of Cabinet members in business, and requires them to declare the worth of their assets. UMNO recently expelled a party member, Tajuddin Rahman, of the State of Perak, for allegedly using millions of ringgit to buy votes in divisional elections.

In Papua New Guinea an 'Electoral Development Fund' is widely viewed as a source of corruption. In 1991, for instance, all 109 members of Parliament were granted 100 000 Kina each for disbursement on infrastructure (50%), economic activities (25%) and social services (25%) in their electorates; few adhered to existing procedures aimed at monitoring the disbursement of funds in that year, and by no means have all done so in the years since.

One significant institutional response to the proliferation of electoral malpractice has been the articulation of leadership codes and the establishment of leadership tribunals and other anti-corruption agencies, in addition to electoral agencies, to monitor the activities of political parties and their members. For instance, in 1994 the South Korean National Assembly passed three electoral reform Bills aimed at minimising corruption during elections. The new laws reduced the period for national and local elections to a maximum of 26 days, and lowered the limit for spending on presidential election campaigns from Won 36 billion (US$44.6 million) to Won 16 billion. The limit for parliamentary elections was reduced from Won 120 million to Won 53 million, and the number of campaign workers each candidate may employ has been reduced from 200 to twenty. Candidates are now required to pay all campaign-related expenses with officially registered cheques, and to follow a strict accounting system supervised by the Central Election Management Committee.[24]

THE ROLE OF ETHNICITY

Ethnicity has become a significant factor in some Asian–Pacific electoral systems where the idea has taken hold that communally based representation answers the needs of diverse and coexisting ethnic communities. An alternative view is that race-based electoral practices only institutionalise and rigidify divisions that have no substantive purpose other than formalising consciousness of 'difference'.

In Fiji, the politicisation of ethnicity was consolidated by the establishment of communal electoral representation. Prior to independence, Indian and Fijian delegates attended a Constitutional Conference in London, at which the Indian delegates accepted a communal voting system and agreed to postpone their campaign for 'one person, one vote' until a future date. Communal voting included a 'cross-vote' that allowed members of one race to vote for a representative from another, leaving the way open for further cross-voting in the future. But by instituting communal seats, the 1970 Constitution further entrenched a bi-racial Fijian state, and was bound to produce ethnically based political parties. The Alliance Party 'represented' Fijians, while the National Federation Party represented Indians.

In elections in Fiji in 1987 a complex electoral process returned a Labour government that polled 46.2% of all votes cast, but just 9.6% of all ethnic Fijian votes. Subsequent military intervention in the constitutional process demonstrated the depth of ethno-nationalist feeling in what had until then been regarded, whatever the shortcomings of the 1970 Constitution, as a model multi-racial Pacific Island state. Under the 1990 Constitution, the Lower House was composed so as to have at all times a Fijian majority (37 seats), with Indian members allocated 27 seats, Rotumans one, and 'general' representatives five. The racial composition of Parliament is thus defined by the Constitution rather than by the preferences of the electorate. Although all citizens may vote, they are enrolled as voters on a racial basis (Fijian, Indian, Rotuman and general) and can vote only for candidates of their own race. The ability to vote as a Fijian depends on registration in the *Vola ni Kawa Bula* (a register of native land-owning units kept under the Native Lands Act by the Native Lands Commission).

Furthermore, the boundaries of constituencies for the election of Fijian and Indian representatives are established differently. Fijian constituencies are set according to the provisions of the Fijian Affairs Act, and have their basis in fourteen 'traditional' provincial regions, whereas boundaries for the election of 22 Indians, eight Europeans and one member from the island of Rotuma are to be set by the Constituency Boundaries Commission.

In Western Samoa, a referendum prior to independence in 1962, which chose to restrict suffrage to *Matai* (chiefly title holders) only, was reversed by a referendum in October 1990 which extended suffrage to all adults aged 21 and older. Candidature, however, remains limited to adults holding *Matai* titles (who in 1990 numbered 18 000). Of the 47 parliamentary seats 45 are reserved for *Matai* and the remaining two are allocated to citizens of non-Samoan ancestry. Similar qualifications restrict the right to vote in neighbouring American Samoa.

The legislature in Pakistan, in addition to 207 Muslim members, reserves ten seats for minority groups: Christians (four seats), Hindus and the Scheduled Castes (four seats), Sikh, Buddhist and Parsi communities and other non-Muslims (one seat), and members of the Quadiani group or the Lahore group (Ahmadis) (one seat). Allocations are similarly made to ethnic communities in Pakistan's provincial assemblies. There are instances, on the other hand, where communally based seats appear to be a genuine attempt at affirmative action. India's *Constitution (Fifty-Seventh Amendment) Act* of 1987 for example provides for determination of seats reserved for Scheduled Tribes in a number of the Indian states.[25]

In addition to ethnicity, religion plays a role in the operation of electoral systems in the region. While the majority of Asian–Pacific states are officially secular, others identify an official religion in their constitution: Thailand is a Buddhist kingdom; Nepal is a Hindu kingdom; Pakistan and Brunei are 'Islamic' states; and a number of other states, including Bangladesh, Indonesia and Malaysia, while officially secular, face intense pressure from domestic Islamic forces.[26]

ELECTORAL VIOLENCE

The spread of election-related violence is causing concern in a growing number of regional countries, and has prompted a range of legal responses seeking to curb it. The Indian Parliament passed an amendment (Act 1 of 1989) to its *Representation of the People Act* of 1951, providing for adjournment of polls or countermanding of elections in cases of 'booth capturing'—that is, when polling stations are seized, ballot papers are captured, or voters are prevented from voting or threatened about voting—or when there is evidence of 'aiding or conniving at any such activity in furtherance of election prospects of a candidate'. In Indonesia the government banned politics at village and subdistrict level in 1971, a move that restricted the democratic process, but which also reduced the volatility between political rivals: 60 campaign-related deaths were reported during the 1982 elections, and only eight in those of 1987.

Recent electoral reforms in Papua New Guinea were designed to reduce electoral instability. In preparation for elections in Papua New Guinea in 1992 the Organic Law on Provincial Government (Election) law was amended and the Constitutional Amendment (elections) law passed, to promote electoral efficiency, as well as to minimise election-related unrest. National and provincial elections were to be held simultaneously at five-yearly periods, voter identification cards were to be issued, the minimum age for entry to Parliament was increased from 25 to 30 years, a 'first-past-the-post' voting system was introduced, and the use of loud hailers was banned during polling periods. The changes also lifted the nomination fee for candidates from 100 Kina to 1000 Kina, in an effort to ensure that only 'serious' candidates contested the elections.

Placing limits on freedom of speech so as to minimise electoral unrest has been accepted by the Philippines Supreme Court. In a ruling in 1992 banning political advertisements on radio, television and newspapers, the Court said it was 'not unduly repressive or unreasonable', as media was still free to report on the activities of politicians. The ban, which was implemented by the Commission on Elections, aimed to 'equalise, as far as practicable, the situation of rich and poor candidates by preventing the former from enjoying the undue advantage offered by huge campaign chests'.[27]

INSTITUTIONAL DEVELOPMENTS

The significant role of electoral systems in creating effective and efficient systems of governance is becoming increasingly evident, and new institutions are emerging at national and international levels to assist their development. These include the International Institute for Democracy and Electoral Assistance (International IDEA), a Stockholm-based intergovernmental organisation affiliated with the United Nations, devoted to promoting a 'culture of democracy' through strengthening electoral processes. Initiatives are also occurring at the national level. The Australian Parliament, for instance, recognising the role played by the Australian Electoral Commission in facilitating elections in Namibia in 1989 and Cambodia in 1990, amended the Commonwealth Electoral Act in 1992 so as to include international electoral assistance as one of the Commission's functions.

A number of regional countries have established electoral authorities in recent years, providing further evidence of the consolidation of electoral practices. In Thailand, a country subject to numerous military coups since the first in 1932, and in which electoral practices have long been subject to manipulation, Parliament amended Constitutional Article 115 in 1994 to provide for the establishment of an Election Commission to organise general elections. In Bangladesh, a country facing considerable constitutional turmoil, the Representation of the People (Amendment) Bill of 1994 widened the Election Commission's authority to ensure 'fairer and impartial elections of Parliament'. The Commission was given the power to issue identity cards to voters, to refuse to hand a ballot paper to a voter without an identity card, and to stop polling at any station at any stage of the election if it is convinced that it cannot ensure just conduct of the election due to malpractice, which includes coercion, intimidation or other.

FUTURE THINKING

The chapters in this book contribute to an ongoing assessment of electoral practices in countries in the Asia–Pacific region. The issues they raise indicate where traditional approaches to democratic governance are and are not meeting the demands placed on them. These approaches include a developed system of political parties; the acceptance of and adherence to the rules of the political game which limit the struggle for power to a legal struggle; an independent judiciary able to adjudicate on disputed returns; and an honest and impartial administration. But this traditional formula can no longer go unchallenged. The prevalence of electoral instability and scrutiny of the real performance of representatives may in time lead to a review of current assumptions. While the need for independent and impartial administration and settlement of disputes is undoubted, the adversarial nature of current political systems, coupled with the difficulties some of them encounter in meeting the basic social and economic aspirations of their peoples, suggest a need for serious re-evaluation.

For one thing, the theoretical origins of current systems of political parties lie in the notion that there are clear ideological programs of left and right, which are opposed to each other. In practice, a great number of political parties are no more than loose affiliations based on personalities, elite groupings originating in economic and sometimes military associations, or ethnic or regional groupings of other kinds that privilege racial considerations. In the absence of firm party loyalties and clear ideological commitments, prime ministers and presidents may distribute political patronage in order to win—and retain—their majorities, with a proportion of this activity inevitably challenging the boundaries of propriety and legality. The tenuous foundations of political-party systems may eventually lead to questioning of their privileged position. Relegation of talented public leaders to opposition roles is the traditional method of ensuring accountability, and offering an alternative government, but does not necessarily constitute the best method for achieving these ends. 'Party politics' attracts cynicism, but is endured in preference to single-party systems which inevitably restrict democratic freedoms. But to accept that possibilities for the future are exhausted is to evade the challenge to develop an imaginative response. It may well be that familiar leadership structures that provide for the exercise of power no longer meet the demands of contemporary sociocultural conditions, and that complex critical decisions are best made on the basis of group consultation. Increasingly governance may require account to be taken of the considered views of the people directly affected by decisions, as well as the views of technical experts and elected representatives.

The studies in this volume suggests the extent to which countries in the Asia–Pacific region share common goals despite their apparent diversity. They illustrate how electoral systems play a significant role in reducing conflicts in comparatively complex societies and thereby contribute to stable governance and steadily expanding prosperity. These studies demonstrate considerable progress in the definition and operation of regional systems of representation in recent years, and highlight some of the serious challenges that remain.

PART I

The Choosing of Representatives

2

The Cult of *Fatung*: Representational Manipulation and Reconstruction in Taiwan

Jiunn-rong Yeh

According to traditional Chinese wisdom, when in distress, try to be flexible and there should be a way out. Since 1949 the ruling authorities in Taiwan have exhausted this political wisdom, confronting an embarrassing crisis of representation within constitutionally established representative organs, primarily the Legislative Yuan and the National Assembly.[1]

The Nationalists lost the Chinese Civil War and retreated to Taiwan in 1949, but have since continued to claim sovereignty over the Mainland. In order to maintain its legitimacy, the Nationalist government exercised its political philosophy of expediency by holding that national representatives elected in the Mainland who fled to Taiwan in 1949 continued to represent the whole of China, on the basis that the Nationalists would return to the Mainland soon. As the holy mission of national recovery became a 'mission impossible', however, this political flexibility in the manipulation of representation found its limits. Domestic tensions ran high as the demand of citizens in Taiwan for national elections found little outlet. Consequently, the history of political development in Taiwan since 1949 has been one of political manipulation and subsequent deconstruction of the very concept of democratic representation. Constitutional reform in these years has focused on who should be entitled to decide who represents whom and on what grounds.

The Constitution of the Republic of China (ROC) proclaims that 'the sovereignty of the Republic of China shall reside in the whole body of citizens'.[2] Elsewhere, the Constitution[3] provides that 'the Legislative Yuan shall be the highest legislative organ of the State. It shall be composed of members elected by the people and shall exercise legislative power on their behalf'. Accordingly, national legislators represent the whole body of citizens in the Legislative Yuan and are vested with the powers that otherwise belong to the whole body of citizens. Straightforward as these articles may seem to be, questions remain as to which people comprise the whole body of citizens as specified by the Constitution and who are their legitimate representatives—given the reality that two separate authorities have exercised their respective political representation on both sides of the Taiwan Strait[4] and that both sides claim to be the legitimate government of both the Mainland and Taiwan.

Taiwan has been known for its economic success in the international community.[5] This chapter seeks to present the other kind of Taiwan experience, one that has exploited the concept of representation beyond its conceptional limits. It is fair to say that Taiwan is not only a miracle of economic development but also a miracle of the manipulation of representational structure. Moreover, by referring to Taiwan's unique representational status, and to its domestic manipulation coupled with international non-recognition, this essay argues that representational structure determines not only the legitimacy of political control but also national identity in the international arena.

CRISIS, LEGITIMACY AND *FATUNG*

In modern constitutional democracies, representation is a key concept in the analysis of electoral systems and their relation to democratic institutions and processes. Due to Taiwan's unique relationship with China, one must link the issue of representation with political crisis, the struggle for legitimacy and the concept of *fatung*.

POLITICAL CRISIS, NATIONAL MISSION, AND POWER CONSOLIDATION

The Nationalist government has maintained its sovereignty over the Mainland, but acknowledges the impossibility of holding a national election. This position poses dual problems for the government: on the one hand, how to justify its claim over the Mainland when people there are no longer able to vote for their representatives in a government based in Taiwan; on the other, how to convince people in Taiwan that the representative structure in the government can appropriately reflect their interests. In the eyes of many native Taiwanese, the Nationalist government is a foreign regime.[6] For people on the Mainland, the Nationalists are rebels in exile. Accordingly, since withdrawing to Taiwan, the Nationalist government has faced a crisis of legitimacy.

In the years following 1949, the Nationalists responded to this crisis in two ways. Firstly, they maintained that the government would return to the Mainland after the success of their 'holy mission' of national recovery.[7] Accordingly, time would heal all the embarrassing problems. Secondly, they spared no time in consolidating their power by imposing martial law and other means of political control that penetrated into all levels of the government and all sectors of society.[8]

THE QUEST FOR LEGITIMACY

As time passed, the mission of national recovery and power consolidation could not solve the political crisis. To survive the crisis, the authority had to enhance its legitimacy beyond the 'holy' national mission and power consolidation. Max Weber has pinpointed the necessity of legitimacy for such domination: ' . . . Custom, personal advantage, purely effectual or ideal motives of solidarity do not form a sufficiently reliable basis for a given domination. In addition there is normally a further element, the belief in legitimacy.'[9] True, legitimacy is a must for a given governance. But the question of how to define the meaning of legitimacy remains open in the eyes of the Nationalists. Legitimacy requires a level of commitment from various dimensions. As Juan Linz put it: 'Democratic legitimacy . . . requires adherence to the rules of the game by both a majority of the voting citizens and those in positions of authority, as well as trust on the part of the citizenry in the government's commitment to uphold them.[10] Can a regime claim its legitimacy when the representatives are not subject to re-election? The Nationalists claimed yes, and the concept of *fatung*—a traditional Chinese canon for political claim over the authenticity of power succession—served as their theoretical basis.

FATUNG AS LEGITIMACY

Historical and cultural basis of fatung

Fatung, literally translated as the legally authentic succession within a regime, has its origin in Chinese history. In the context of dynastic power struggles, those who successfully claimed *fatung* were in a better position to justify their political power. Before and after the establishment of the Republic in 1911, *fatung* was similarly employed. For example, in the Three Kingdoms period following the end of the Han dynasty in 220 AD, the State of Su claimed a direct succession to the Han *fatung*. In modern China, Chiang Kai-shek claimed his direct link to Dr Sun Yat-sen, founding father of the Republic, against his rivals. Similarly, the recently established New Party, formed by a faction splitting from the Kuomintang (KMT) (which has been denounced by the New Party as being a 'Taiwanese KMT'), has claimed to be the authentic continuation of the Chinese KMT in Taiwan.

The road to representational manipulation

Under the banner of *fatung*, the Nationalist regime after 1949 argued for its legal continuation of the Republic of China founded by Dr Sun Yat-sen and his followers in 1911. According to this reasoning, as long as the symbols of ROC never changed, the government would still represent the whole territory once controlled by the ROC. These symbols might include Chiang Kai-shek himself, the representatives in the Legislative Yuan and National Assembly, or the actual text of the Constitution. Moreover, as the holder of *fatung*, the Nationalist government claimed for itself the legitimacy, not the willingness, of its constituency. It was this political philosophy that led to the road of representational manipulation.

THE POLITICS OF REPRESENTATIONAL MANIPULATION

Strongmen, representatives, the constitution, and the myth of representation

What constitutes the legitimacy of the Nationalist regime's claim to possessing *fatung*? Several arguments have been advanced. One focused on Chiang Kai-shek himself. He and his followers repeatedly sold the image that he was the direct successor to Dr Sun Yat-sen, founding father of the Republic. This is very similar to claims made in dynastic China. However, as a republic had been in place in China for years, the government was supposedly constrained by the ROC Constitution. Accordingly, Chiang's remaining in power for so many terms in Taiwan presented a crisis in constitutional legitimacy. The Constitution vests the National Assembly with the exclusive mandate to elect the president.[11] The president serves a term of six years. If re-elected, he or she may serve one further term.[12] Since the legitimacy of the president is contingent on that of the National Assembly, we turn to the second possible source of *fatung*, the national representatives in the Legislative Yuan and National Assembly.

According to the Constitution, national representatives serve a fixed term and are subject to re-election.[13] As mentioned earlier, owing to the retreat of the Nationalist government to Taiwan, re-election was no longer possible. However, the Nationalists realised the threat this representation crisis posed to their quest for legitimacy. In the name of *fatung*, they had to go so far as to claim that these representatives were themselves *fatung*, and *fatung* was equivalent to legitimacy.

If they wished to act consistently with this logic, the Nationalists should have revised the Constitution. This would have been an expedient solution to the political crisis—but things did not work out in this way because the Nationalists, hoping at some future time to retake the Mainland, intended to return with an unchanged Constitution which they could use as *prima facie* legitimacy for their resumption of control. Accordingly, they continuously insisted that the text of the Constitution should never be changed. In the meantime, unavoidable constitutional change was effected through a separate package called 'Temporary Provisions Effective During the Period of National Mobilisation for the Suppressing of the Communist Rebellion'. Once again, the concept of *fatung* played a significant role. By closing the door of constitutional revision, the authorities pursued a third path to legitimacy—via the judiciary.

Judicial endorsement: Interpretation No. 31

Under the 'no revision' policy, the judiciary was called upon to solve the political crisis. Responding to this political invitation, the Council of Grand Justices—a constitutional organ composed of seventeen Justices, similar to a European constitutional court—rendered a constitutional interpretation endorsing the mainstream position that the representatives elected in Mainland China could remain in power until re-election was possible.[14] The Council did not provide sufficient rationale for the ruling and not a single dissenting opinion was filed.

In light of this interpretation, representatives elected in the Mainland would continue to exercise their political delegation for life as long as re-election remained impossible. The wisdom of this judicial intervention has been disputed. In facing the representational crisis, a decision had to be made so that the government could continue to function. But the issue was highly political in nature and should have been tested by public opinion, through the processes of democratic partisan politics. Knowing the inherent political risk, however, the Nationalist government decided to strengthen its position through the hands of the judiciary. Juan Linz has suggested that '. . . the effort to remove highly conflictive issues from the arena of partisan politics by transforming them into legal or technical questions' has been common to regimes confronting political crisis:

> The aim is to gain time, since legal solutions are notoriously slow. Typically, questions of constitutionality are raised about certain laws and decisions, and issues are referred to constitutional courts. The legitimacy of having judicial bodies make what are essentially political decisions in a democracy is always doubtful, and in countries where judicial bodies have been established only recently, their judgment is even less likely to be considered binding . . . The result is a lessening of the authenticity of democratic institutions, particularly the power and responsibility of parliament.[15]

Linz is not quite right, however, when he describes the practice as an effort to gain time. The Council rendered its decision swiftly in conformity with the political climate. Once again, the fragility of the judiciary in reacting to political invitation was evident. In hindsight, one can draw the conclusion that the Council suffered a serious blow, which did tremendous damage to the reputation of the judiciary and hence to the judiciary's function of channelling constitutional change in a period of political transformation.

Moments of silence in constitutionalism: representation and accountability

The refusal to revise the Constitution coupled with representational manipulation posed a serious threat to constitutionalism in Taiwan and had three major consequences. First, the national representatives of the Legislative Yuan, Control Yuan and National Assembly were not subject to re-election or recall, meaning national representatives enjoyed tenured posts. Second, the president could serve as many terms as he or she desired as long as the National Assembly continued to vote for him or her. Finally, the representation of Taiwanese residents in the national government was diluted by the majority of Mainland representatives.

Indeed, these practices posed a great challenge to the very meaning of democratic representation. True, there is room for variation in definitions of representation, given historical, theoretical and practical complications in democratic institutions and processes. Nelson Polsby observes:

> Only for legislatures in open, specialized regimes is representation a problem . . . For open and specialized regimes, however, there is a problem of finding a formula that adequately related openness to 'specialization' . . . This dilemma is reflected in two complementary strands in theories of representation. One of these defines representation as action by an agent as if the agent were the people represented in all relevant respects. The other proposes a rule of representation which states that a representative acts for those

represented and in their behalf. Under one theory the task of the representatives is solely to ascertain the wishes of the represented; under the other the task is to act in accord with the representative's own view of the best interests of the represented.[16]

Having touched upon these complications in the meaning of representation, Polsby finds accountability to be a good substitute:

> One popular alternative substitute for the idea of representation [is] the idea of subsequent accountability. A legislature is accountable insofar as its members are subject to frequent, fair, contested elections and hence can be turned out of office if they displease the represented.[17]

Accountability is regarded as a key concept of modern constitutionalism, and Polsby suggests that frequent, fair and contested elections are a key element in achieving accountability. The built-in re-election pressure in modern representative democracy is regarded as a driving force for the legislature's responsiveness to its constituency, as David Mayhew elaborates.[18] A system of tenured representatives coupled with an iron policy preventing constitutional revision amounts to the erosion of constitutionalism. It is fair to say that this representational manipulation exceeding any acceptable limit was a major setback to the development of constitutionalism in Taiwan. It reflects a political expediency that has considerably harmed the development of constitutional democracy on the island. The question as to how to improve the system of representation in Taiwan is thus a political issue high on the national agenda.

QUIET REVOLUTION AND REPRESENTATIONAL RECONSTRUCTION

The beginning of representation-reinforcing: supplementary elections

Resolving the political crisis arising from the Nationalists' claim over the Mainland through representational manipulation sacrifices—or at least dilutes—the constitutional representation of people in Taiwan. To lessen this embarrassment, the Nationalists decided to hold partial elections solely for Taiwan representatives in the Legislative Yuan, Control Yuan and National Assembly. In 1969, for example, ten legislators were elected from their Taiwan constituencies into the Legislative Yuan. Furthermore, Taiwan (province) was allowed to choose more representatives than it would have been entitled to had elections been held on both Taiwan and the Mainland. Although this may be seen as a breakthrough, the numbers

of Taiwan delegates remained small when compared with the overwhelming number of tenured representatives.[19]

Power succession and localisation

President Chiang Kai-shek was the force behind the political practices mentioned above. His death in 1975 did not lead to substantial
change, but the 'second generation' did show first signs of reform.
Chiang Ching-kuo, son of Chiang Kai-shek, who was elected president by the National Assembly in 1978, launched in the later years
of his term several significant policies of political liberalisation,
including the lifting of the martial law decree,[20] the liberalisation
of press control,[21] and the green light for the formation of political
parties.[22] Explanations for this succession of changes are still wanting.[23] And yet, in the present context of representation, some
clarification may be in order.

Consider a second generation leader trying to take over the
regime in which the interests of his father and of the ruling elite
(who include the national representatives) are interdependent. His
interests may not be in conflict with his father's, but the national
representatives may be the obstacles to power transition. Faced with
such a situation, Chiang Ching-kuo was smart enough to extend his
legitimacy and seek support outside the ruling club. Localisation
was thus the political philosophy guiding his attempt to establish
greater legitimacy.

In the name of localisation, the president recruited members
of the native Taiwanese elite (including many current political
leaders such as President Lee). This policy seemed innovative in a
period when most important official posts were occupied by members of the small but powerful group of Mainlanders who constitute
just 15% of the population. There is no doubt that the recruitment
of members of the Taiwanese elite into the government helped ease
tensions within Taiwan.

Although recruiting the local elite into the administration
enhanced the legitimacy of the regime, full resolution of the crisis
in democratic representation required larger scale reconstruction
of the national representative bodies. Whether the president was
determined to do so is not known, since his reforms were greatly
resisted by the Nationalists.

THE ROAD TO REPRESENTATIONAL RECONSTRUCTION

Power transformation: the end of the Chiang dynasty

Despite his willingness to face the representational problems, large-
scale reform was not realised during President Chiang Ching-kuo's

terms. On his death in 1988, Vice-President Lee Teng-hui came into office. The power transition was by and large smooth, and for the first time a native Taiwanese became president of the Republic of China. Although the national representative bodies were still in the hands of tenured representatives, social expectations of sweeping political reform rose markedly. As long as the president was willing to respond to popular expectations, competition with the national representative bodies for representative legitimacy seemed inevitable.

Legitimacy and constitutional crisis

President Lee's major appeal for the general public in Taiwan has relied on his identity as a native Taiwanese, and his belonging to the majority group of his constituency. Beyond this he can claim little legitimacy, since he was elected president by the National Assembly, which at the time was largely composed of tenured representatives. He was not chosen by popular vote nor even by indirect vote by representatives elected from Taiwan. This limitation was reflected in the president's ambivalence about the mission of representational reform, and as citizen demands for sweeping reforms were gathering strength—and were now being taken up by the opposition party—a constitutional crisis seemed highly likely.

Political deadlock

As the tenured representatives aged and died, their voices were gradually drowned out by those of the minority Taiwan delegates who could claim better representation and legitimacy than the unproductive 'old thieves'.[24] Even so, the tenured representatives refused to step down, believing they represented the *fatung* of the Republic of China and that their absence from the Legislative Yuan and National Assembly would mark the end of the Republic of China and the birth of the 'Republic of Taiwan'. How could the Republic still survive when they all stepped down? In such a situation, it was quite apparent that the Nationalists could not solve the problem from within. Two forces led to a workable solution: one came from the opposition party, the other from the judiciary.

Judicial intervention: Interpretation No. 261

The passage of time exposed the flaws of the Nationalists' representational manipulation. Even if they were not forced from office, the tenured representatives could not live forever. When the last tenured representatives die, their seats will be taken by persons elected in Taiwan. The issue was therefore not whether the status quo would change, but when. But time was also running against the

Nationalists, who were beginning to find upholding the legitimacy of the tenured representatives an onerous burden. A law was promulgated granting substantial compensation to tenured representatives who took voluntary retirement.[25] To some, *fatung* was not something for sale, and once again the judiciary was called upon.

This time, the judiciary stood firm and—despite tense debate over the wisdom of imposing a deadline in the judicial deliberation—ordered the retirement of the tenured representatives by the end of 1991. A dissenting opinion was filed challenging the wisdom of judicial deadline-setting.[26] Unlike the situation of the previous interpretation, the Council now provided detailed reasons for its decision. After first defending its prior decision by arguing that the extension of authority was necessary for maintenance of the constitutional system, the Council argued that the prior interpretation did not fix the term of national representatives, nor did it intend to make a life-long extension. In addressing the current situation, the Council ruled that representatives were to step down by the end of 1991 and that a national election should be held for the proper operation of the constitutional system.[27] Those who had created the fiction of tenured representatives also destroyed it.

Notice, however, that the Council not only terminated the fiction but also ordered a national election for the proper operation of the Constitution, suggesting that the Council of Grand Justices was responding to the political climate. Did the Council do a good job? It seems the judiciary was forced once again to get involved in a political problem. However, a theory has been advanced that courts should only exercise the power of judicial review at times when normal political processes have in some way failed. John Ely has referred to the operation of courts in such instances, despite the fact that they are not 'majoritarian' institutions, as 'representational reinforcing'.[28] This theory could provide a basis for understanding the court's interpretation No. 261, delivered in the context of political deadlock over Taiwan's representational structure.

CONGRESSIONAL RECONSTRUCTION

Controversies in representational structure of the New Congress

According to the constitutional interpretation a national election was to be held. Citizens' rights to vote and recall were restored and national representatives were subject to re-election. While it was clear that only citizens in Taiwan were entitled to vote, controversy continued over the composition of the national representative bodies. The Nationalists, furthermore, did not give up their claim of sovereignty over the Mainland. It was proposed and seriously considered that there should be delegates representing every province (35 provinces in all[29]) of the Mainland. The underlining rationale of this proposal was the belief that Taiwan would become independent following this congressional reorganisation if there were no representatives from the Mainland—although technically, the selection of delegates who genuinely represented their remote constituencies in the Mainland remained an insurmountable obstacle, regardless of all the theoretical debates.

National proportionate representation as a compromise

The Democratic Progressive Party—the major opposition party, which had already been established for some years—together with bipartisan negotiation, helped in the resolution of this major political issue, and a system of national proportionate representation which would operate in tandem with the regional representational system was agreed upon as a compromise.

The Taiwanese electoral system is similar to the German system in that it offers two routes to the national representative bodies: the constituency and the party list. Unlike the German two-votes structure, however, there is only one ballot showing the names of the candidates. Party lists are not shown in the ballot and voters do not actually vote for the parties. The quota representing a party's proportion of the total votes is assigned to that party according to the sequence of the lists. A 5% threshold is imposed to discourage the proliferation of small parties.[30]

As a result of the reform, there are two types of representatives in the national representative bodies. Regional representatives are elected from various districts in Taiwan to represent regional interests in the national representative bodies; national representatives are elected via party lists to represent national interests. For the Nationalists, the existence of national representatives may be explained as an attempt to avoid the impression that representatives are elected solely to represent the interests of Taiwan. For the reformers, the number of national representatives is acceptable and, more importantly, national representatives are elected according to the total vote of Taiwan residents.

Quiet revolution

By the end of 1991, both the Legislative Yuan and National Assembly were re-elected by popular vote. The new representative bodies are wholly composed of representatives chosen by citizens in Taiwan. Now the major opposition parties, including the DPP and the New

Party, occupied more than one-third of the seats in the Legislative Yuan. Regardless of its partisan structure, these new representative bodies have permitted a greater realisation of democratic representation in Taiwan. From a situation in which nearly 100% of those serving as their representatives were Mainlanders, people in Taiwan now see 100% of representatives of their choice in the Legislative Yuan and National Assembly. Since this revolutionary change occurred through peaceful means, it has been hailed as a 'quiet revolution' in comparison with democratic reforms in other countries.

Constitutional reform and representational reconstruction

In a modern constitutional democracy representation is a core element, and it would be hard to imagine representational reconstruction dissociated from constitutional reform. Recalling the Nationalists' insistence that the text of the Constitution remain unchanged to enable them to claim *fatung*, the electoral reforms of 1991 contradicted the Constitution. To resolve this conflict, the Nationalists separated constitutional revisions from the text. Changes in the representational structure, including the manipulation and reconstruction, were incorporated in successive packages called 'Temporary Provisions Effective During the Period of National Mobilisation for the Suppressing of the Communist Rebellion' and 'Additional Articles of the Constitution of the Republic of China'. The main text of the Constitution, though functionally revised or superseded by the added provisions, remains unchanged.

The National Assembly and constitutional reform

According to the Constitution, the National Assembly is vested with the power to amend the Constitution, to elect the President, and to exercise initiatives and referendum on behalf of the people.[31] Given the historical circumstances described above, with the president and the National Assembly subject to representational crisis, there could be no real constitutional revision. The constitutional invention of the National Assembly was based on the salient features of Mainland China, where territory was widespread and diverse, and where the illiteracy rate was staggeringly high. In Taiwan, where the territory is relatively small and educational standards are among the highest in the world, such a constitutional organ seems odd, and dissolving the National Assembly and returning its mandate to the people has long been proposed. When the National Assembly, the exclusive organ for constitutional revision, is itself the target of constitutional reform, it is hard to expect that it will commit political suicide.

In reality, the reverse has occurred. The National Assembly has been expanding its power, relying on its exclusive mandate to conduct presidential elections and constitutional revision. Like the Legislative Yuan, the National Assembly underwent structural reform, with all members elected from Taiwan following the constitutional interpretation. Surprisingly, as the level of representation increased after the reorganisation, the National Assembly's tendency towards expansion became even more obvious.

Presidential election, accountability, and potential crisis of democratic deadlock

Whereas constitutionally the ROC government is more a cabinet than a presidential system, the office of president has been regarded, since the time of Chiang Kai-shek, as the most significant post. President Lee Teng-hui is no exception to this tradition. Since being sworn into office, he has been able to win general support despite the embarrassing fact that he was elected by the old National Assembly.

In relation to constitutional reform, President Lee has endorsed a Constitution that will allow citizens in Taiwan to vote for their president directly rather than by proxy through the National Assembly. These reforms once divided the Nationalists, but after a 'cooling-off' period they were added to the Additional Articles of the Constitution. No-one knows whether President Lee will run for a second term in office, but a president elected via popular vote will certainly gain more representative legitimacy, and the possible impact of this electoral change on the current constitutional order has been a hot issue for some time.

Rebirth of fatung: *voting rights of overseas Chinese*

The idea of a direct vote for the president has met with resistance from the KMT, who feared the emergence of a president of Taiwan rather than of the ROC. To accommodate this resistance, voting rights have been extended to overseas Chinese. Recalling the myth of *fatung*, overseas Chinese are the second-best alternative to Mainland Chinese, who would not be able to vote for practical reasons.

TOWARDS A GENERAL THEORY OF REPRESENTATION IN LIGHT OF THE TAIWAN EXPERIENCE

Representational manipulation and its limitation

All systems of representation are vulnerable to political manipulation. The Taiwan experience demonstrates manipulation from four dimensions:

1   Person-based manipulation: a translation of representation into the mere existence of political figures.
2   Constitution-based manipulation: a translation of representation into the mere existence of a constitutional text.
3   Time-based manipulation: an extension of representation beyond constitutional time restrictions.
4   Territory-based manipulation: an extension of representation beyond effective territorial boundaries.

In a situation where a constitutional democracy is on the brink of breakdown and legitimacy is lacking, some level of political flexibility in the definition of democratic representation may be justified. Despite this *sine qua non*, the Taiwan experience demonstrates that representational manipulation is not without constraints.

The most obvious constraint on representational manipulation is time, the mere passage of which may unveil the unreasonableness of all the types of manipulation listed above. This is especially true of person-based manipulation because human life, like it or not, is not eternal. Territorial separation, especially when it lasts for a long time, poses structural differences that dilute the very meaning of representation.

The other major constraint on representational manipulation is accountability, according to which, among other things, delegates are subject to election. From the Taiwan experience, the mere fact that delegates hold functionally tenured posts poses a critical challenge to democratic representation.

Representation and national identity

One of the inherent complications behind changes to Taiwan's system of representation has been the issue of national identity. To some, the Republic of China is a foreign regime and the claim over the Mainland is itself at most a fiction. To others, however, residence in Taiwan is just a temporary arrangement in response to national separation since 1949, and national unification is just a matter of time. Indeed, the problem of national identity has polarised the very concept of representation.

From the perspective of a separationist, national representatives should be elected solely by the people of Taiwan. Representatives who were not elected by Taiwanese residents and yet who claim to represent a territory where the government has failed to exercise sovereignty constitute a violation of the concept of democratic representation. From the point of view of a unificationist, as long as the national representatives can only represent the interests of

Taiwan, the Republic of China is functionally overthrown by the 'Republic of Taiwan'.

As the issue of national identity is highly sensitive and controversial, it cannot be examined in detail here. It is apparent, however, that the development of Taiwan's representational structure has been a process of moving towards a *de facto* independent Taiwan. Despite all the official rhetoric, including that about the plain meaning of the constitutional text and governmental proclamations, from the perspective of the existing representational structure Taiwan no longer represents China.

Representation in the international arena

In 1971, the ROC on Taiwan lost its membership in the United Nations, and in the 1990s only slightly more than twenty nations have formal diplomatic ties with the ROC. In the past, when the domestic representational structure served the unrealistic mission of national recovery, gaining international recognition posed great obstacles to the international representational structure. Now, due to efforts in representational reconstruction, democratic representation in Taiwan is more realistic. And yet, when people celebrate their meaningful representation in national government, they also find no representation in international arenas such as the United Nations. Over the last five decades the ROC has not extended its authority over Mainland China, and the People's Republic of China has not extended its control over any part of Taiwan. The unbelievable truth is that there is no representation for the 21 million people of Taiwan in the United Nations. The more representative the national government becomes, the more serious this absence of international representation would seem to be. To what extent changes in the domestic representational structure affect international representation remains to be seen.

CONCLUSION

Political reform in Taiwan over the last ten years has centred on the issue of democratic representation. Against the background of national separation, the Nationalist authorities who faced a legitimacy crisis exercised political flexibility through representational manipulation. This manipulation collapsed in the end mainly because of such built-in limitations as time and accountability. While the people of Taiwan now enjoy full representation in their national government, they feel strongly about the absence of representation in international organisations such as the United Nations.

3

Choosing Representatives: Singapore Does It Her Way

Thio Li-ann

Like that of many other Commonwealth countries, Singapore's system of parliamentary government is a 'branch' off the old British 'vine'. The parliamentary model that germinated and waxed strong in the temperate soils of Westminster[1] has, over the years, assumed a rather different form where transplanted in sunnier climes. Considering the tendency for power to be centralised in the hands of the parliamentary executive in the Westminster political system, the young shoot had a 'propensity to be transformed into a dictatorship when transplanted in societies without political cultures which support its operative conventions'.[2] Government structures do not bear perfect reproductions when introduced into dissimilar cultural soil.

Singapore's erstwhile Prime Minister Lee Kuan Yew is fond of pointing out that a certain 'impulse to democracy',[3] which may be culturally absent, is integral to the functioning of democratic government. Optimal growth conditions for the Westminster transplant were, and perhaps still are, clearly lacking in the Singapore context. These would include a vigorous press, powerful interest groups and an alert public opinion. From 1968 to 1981, the People's Action Party (PAP) enjoyed a monopoly on parliamentary seats. Singapore had a *de facto* one-party state whose paternalistic rulers practised a form of 'soft authoritarianism'.[4] Today, PAP leaders[5] are vocal in retrospectively attributing Singapore's phenomenal economic success to a Confucian value system[6] emphasising discipline, family values, consensus over contention, and the community over the individual. While this itself is a debatable proposition, it is clear that the PAP's brand of authoritarianism has certainly contributed to, if not created, a legal culture based on hierarchy and control.[7] A recurrent PAP theme[8] has been the attempt to socialise or orientate the country towards a belief that a *de facto* one-party state could satisfy the requirements of parliamentary democracy; it has often been reiterated that an opposition presence in Parliament would be dangerous for Singapore as it would bring divisive politics and scare off foreign investors. As recently as the 1992 Marine Parade by-election, it was asserted that 'a two-party system would put us on the dangerous road to contention, when we should play as one team'.[9]

In the past decade, many innovative changes[10] to the legislature and electoral system have sprung forth from the Singapore laboratory of constitutional experiments. Culminating with the introduction of the elected presidency in 1991, Singapore's constitutional framework of powers has, in the words of the Bard, 'undergone a sea change, into something rich and strange'.[11] Two of these changes made in relation to the legislature will be highlighted.

Firstly, two different breeds of parliamentarians were created: in 1984 the post of non-constituency member of Parliament made its debut, followed by the introduction of the nominated member of Parliament in 1990 (see Table 3.1).

Secondly, the introduction in 1988 of the group representative constituencies (GRC) marked the effective demise of the 'one person one vote' or simple plurality electoral system which was a direct British bequest (see Table 3.2). Previously, the basis for representation was spatial: Singapore was divided into single-member constituencies from which one member of Parliament was elected. Under the GRC scheme as it stands at present, Parliament may declare that three former single-member constituencies be merged to form a single mega-constituency or GRC. A voter residing within a GRC casts his or her single vote for a team of three or four members of Parliament, one of whom must belong to a specified racial group. This complicates the spatial basis for representation by introducing novel bases: one alludes to the need to guarantee a fixed multi-racial element in Parliament's composition while another envisages the GRC as a way of enjoying economies of scale in the management of town councils. Indeed, the GRC scheme was originally closely tied up with the town council idea, which was designed to grant residents of public housing estates a measure of local self-determination in the running of their estates;[12] the 1988 Town Councils Act (Cap 329A)[13] provides that the town council itself be chaired by the elected member of Parliament. Rather conveniently, three constituencies making up one GRC

Table 3.1   Provisions for non-elected members of Parliament

	Non-constituency MP	Nominated MP
Purpose	To ensure an opposition element in Parliament in perpetuity	To co-opt alternative, non-partisan views
Powers, privileges, immunities	(a) Same privileges and immunities as per elected MPs (b) Limited voting powers (c) Not town councillors	As per NCMPs
Method of entry into Parliament	Second past the post (a) Top three losers of political parties not forming the government are offered seats (b) Minimally, 15% of the total number of votes must be polled by candidates	Appointed by president (a) Public submits the names of prospective nominees (b) Considered by Special Parliamentary Select Committee (c) Application of Fourth Schedule criteria

Table 3.2   Provisions for elected members of Parliament

Single-member constituencies (SMCs)	Group representative constituencies (GRCs)
One person one vote: for a single candidate	One person one vote: for a team of 3 or 4 MPs: one GRC candidate must belong to the specified minority group
First past the post/simple plurality	Team collectively polling most votes wins

could be grouped together to form one town council as well, thereby minimising the costs of administrative and maintenance services.

This chapter will examine the underlying principles governing the development of the Singaporean manner of choosing its representatives in the light of local conditions. The qualifications and powers of the two different types of parliamentarians will be examined, as will the *raison d'être* for their introduction. It will examine the workings of the mixed single-member and multi-member electoral constituencies in some detail, with particular reference to the constitutional implications of the 1991 general elections. It is interesting to see how election strategies have centred around the GRC concept. Finally, the author will offer her views on the impact these constitutional innovations have had on the state of parliamentary democracy in Singapore as well as her opinion of the latest proposals concerning the legislature and the electoral system that have been mooted but not yet implemented.

ASCERTAINING FIRST PRINCIPLES: THE WEE CHONG JIN CONSTITUTIONAL COMMISSION, 1966

It is important to ascertain the foundational principles concerning the Singapore polity, enunciated by the Wee Chong Jin Constitutional Commission in 1966, to see whether the later evolution of the parliamentary system adhered to or departed from these principles. When Singapore separated from Malaysia on 9 August 1965, the immediate imperatives were the tasks of nation-building and economic development. Hence, at Independence, the pragmatic retention of the existing form of government which had a unicameral Parliament, separate judiciary and ceremonial head of state was favoured over any attempt at brave new experimentation. Continuity prevailed over autochthony.

The Commission was given the task of formulating constitutional safeguards to protect racial and religious minority rights, bearing in mind the needs of a multi-racial, multi-lingual and multi-faith society. In particular, proposals for the legislative representation of minorities were considered in this regard. Two central principles to be gleaned from the Commission's Report were the importance of a commitment towards a non-racial approach to government and, secondly, the attainment of the objective of democracy.

The objective of democracy

Aspiring towards, and instilling the people's faith in, a democratic form of government, which is predicated on the legal equality of individuals, was clearly a central object. The Commission recommended that the principle of equality before the law and equal protection of the law for all persons be categorically laid down, with the proviso that the Constitution could expressly authorise discrimination. This was considered to be a bulwark against racial communalism and religious bigotry as well as the means of establishing a 'firm and lasting foundation' on which to build a 'democratic, equal and just multi-racial society in Singapore'.

The concern for a democratic system of general elections was reflected in the recommendation that a new fundamental right to elect a government of choice, expressed in general elections by universal and equal suffrage held at reasonable periodic intervals by secret vote, be constitutionally entrenched.[14]

The commitment towards a non-racial approach to government

This was considered a precondition to facilitating the growth of a 'united, multi-racial, free and democratic nation in which all its

citizens have equal rights and equal opportunities'.[15] This bias
towards multi-racialism is perhaps best reflected today in Article 53
of the Constitution which provides that all parliamentary debates
shall be conducted in Malay, English, Mandarin or Tamil.

Various proposals for provision for the legislative representation
of minorities were made, for example through proportional representation in the form of a Committee or Second Chamber
consisting of nominated or elected minority leaders. These proposals were rejected on the basis that they would *accentuate* rather than
play down racial differences. The spectre of racial or communal
politicking was raised, as were the perceived difficulties in setting
up separate electoral rolls and having to engage in the complicated
task of defining the various minority groups. The ultimate obstacle
to these proposals was that they would inhibit the achievement of
'a single homogenous community out of the many races that form
the population of the Republic'.[16] Anything that raised the possibility of erecting an invisible but tangible barrier to the creation of a
'tolerant, united, multi-racial society' was to be eschewed; the per-
petuation of both intercommunal and intersectional dissension was
an evil most assiduously to be avoided.

Antipathy towards nominating legislative members

It was envisaged that the 'many and grave responsibilities' that
members of Parliament assume as the people's elected representatives should rest solely on them.[17] As a general principle, it was
asserted that non-elected representation would dilute the elected
chamber and stultify the practice of parliamentary democracy. As
stated:

> In a House where every member is elected on a general franchise and
> by tradition regarded as a representative not only of every member of
> his constituency but also of the whole nation, any participation in its
> debates by persons appointed to represent minorities would not only
> be inappropriate but would also be retrograde.[18]

In 1954, the Rendel Constitutional Commission[19] recommended
that the colony of Singapore undergo a a *transitional* period during
which autonomous institutions could be developed, as a prelude to
full independence. Progress towards self-government was linked with
the transformation of the Legislative Assembly into a primarily
elected body. Granting the governor a discretionary power to nominate members to the Assembly to ensure the voicing of
under-represented interests was considered a strictly interim measure. The Commission observed that:

> as the process of developing a single homogenous community pro-
> gresses, there should be an increasing inclination on the part of

electors to accept without reservation representatives of racial origin other than their own. The need for Nominated Members should therefore decrease as further advance is made in this process.[20]

Between 1969 and 1979 the Singapore Constitution was remarkably flexible, as a simple parliamentary majority sufficed to effect and thereby facilitate many constitutional amendments. In 1979, the pre-Separation rigidity of the Constitution was restored when the constitutional amendment procedure itself was amended to require a special two-thirds parliamentary majority. In the words of then law minister E.W. Barker, 'all consequential amendments that have been necessitated by our constitutional advancement have now been enacted'.[21]

This is ironic because the most significant and major changes to the constitutional landscape were breezily effected between 1984–91, when it was supposed to be harder to amend the Constitution; indeed, this might be termed the era of Singapore's 'Constitutional Renaissance', where fertile minds brought forth the proliferation of innovative constitutional creations. This goes to illustrate the point that in a *de facto* one-party state, the requirement of two-thirds parliamentary majority to pass a constitutional amendment Bill is but a mere formality.

The constitutional experimentation began in earnest in 1984. Significantly that was the year the ruling PAP suffered a major 12.6 percentage point swing of votes against it in the general elections; the opposition polled 35% of the national votes, marking the most impressive performance of the opposition since 1968—though this itself only translated into two opposition parliamentary seats. Pronouncements concerning the 'destabilising tendencies' of the 'one person one vote' system were uttered—a portent of the change to come.

INSTITUTIONALISING POLITICAL PLURALISM: NCMP (non-constituency member of parliament) AND NMP (nominated member of parliament)

The system that produced healthy balance sheets but which lacked effective checks and balances did not seem to fully appease the electorate in 1984. The authoritarian style pursued by the parliamentary executive, which enforced a 'one voice' culture of obedience in Parliament through the 'whip', was unpopular. The self-limitations inherent in PAP backbenchers adopting the 'shadow-boxing' role of playing the opposition were certainly unsatisfactory.

The non-constituency member of Parliament

To remedy this perceived defect, Article 39(1)(b) of the Constitution was introduced[22] to provide for non-constituency MPs[23] in order to 'ensure the representation in Parliament of a minimum number of Members from a political party or parties not forming the Government'. The PAP stated 'we have sensed people want to have a good government, plus a few good people to query the government'.[24] Hence, having NCMPs in Parliament would ensure, in perpetuity, an opposition element in Parliament.

The top three losers of political parties not forming the government who failed to gain a parliamentary seat first past the post would be awarded a seat on a 'second-past-the-post' basis. The sole proviso was that such a candidate must have polled a minimum of 15% of the total number of votes.[25] Furthermore, this provision only operates if no opposition candidate has been directly elected into Parliament. While the Constitution provided for a maximum of six NCMPs, legislation[26] initially provided that three NCMP seats be offered, less the total number of opposition members elected into Parliament.

The reasons proffered by then Prime Minister Lee for institutionalising the opposition in this manner were threefold:[27]

1   to sharpen the debating skills of the younger MPs and ministers, skills that were presumably flabby from lack of exercise;
2   to provide a channel for the venting of allegations of misfeasance and corruption; and
3   to educate the voters as regards the limitation of what a constitutional opposition could do in the local context, that is to afford them a forum in which to display their ineptitude.

The nominated member of Parliament

In 1990, the PAP presented itself as once again assuming the initiative to make provisions for safeguarding parliamentary democracy in the local context by introducing the nominated MPs scheme, primarily to co-opt alternative non-partisan views into Parliament. This would constitute a partial fulfilment of the government's promise to 'systematically *create* more opportunities for Singaporeans to participate actively in shaping their future'.[28] Constructive criticism would be accommodated by a consensus-seeking government.

Whereas NCMPs attained their parliamentary seat by garnering a minimal number of votes from the constituency they contested in, up to six nominated MPs were to be appointed by the president. To placate the scheme's opponents a 'sunset clause' was introduced whereby Parliament had the discretion to resolve whether to have NMPs for that particular term.

The *modus operandi* of the scheme is that the public is invited to submit names of persons to be considered for nomination by a Special Parliamentary Select Committee (comprising the Speaker as chair and seven MPs). The requirements spelt out in the Constitution's Fourth Schedule are indicative of the expectation that NMPs be people of calibre, able to offer the benefit of their special expertise and insights. Being an NMP would be a softer option for such people who 'for good reasons, have no desire to go into politics or look after a constituency'.[29] Candidates must be persons

> . . . who have rendered distinguished public service, or who have brought honour to the Republic, or who have distinguished themselves in the field of arts and letters, culture, the sciences, business, industry, the professions, social or community service or the labour movement; and in making any nomination, the Special Select Committee shall have regard to the need for nominated Members to reflect as wide a range of independent and non-partisan views as possible.[30]

Both NCMPs and NMPs share the same parliamentary privileges and immunities as conventionally elected MPs, but they have limited voting powers. Specifically, both cannot vote on any constitutional amendment Bills, supply Bills, money Bills and votes of no confidence in the government.[31] Unlike normal MPs, NCMPs and NMPs play no role in the running of town councils.[32]

Assessing the new breed of parliamentarians

From the outset, the NCMP scheme has been subject to the criticism that it is merely a ploy to discourage the electorate to vote into Parliament a 'genuine' opposition having both the powerbase and responsibilities that come with representing a constituency. While the scheme guarantees an opposition element in Parliament, NCMPs are second-class parliamentarians compared with elected parliamentarians, given their limited voting powers. It is difficult to see why the scheme could not simply have provided that the top three 'losers' in the general election, regardless of which political party they were members of, should be appointed NCMPs, having the same powers as an ordinary MP.

The legitimacy of the office is also in question: who does the partisan NCMP represent? His or her political party? The lack of provisions concerning the vacation of office leaves the NCMPs' tenure in the hands of a potentially hostile parliamentary majority, a situation that certainly erodes confidence in the efficacy of this office.

In the final analysis, the presence of the NCMPs in Parliament does not seem to go beyond the decorative, NCMPs being nothing more than sparring partners for the untested younger PAP generation. They are watchdogs without teeth, able to bark and *parley* occasionally, but they have no ability to bite and, ultimately, are not a threat to the maintenance of the existing status quo.

After the 1984 general elections, only one NCMP seat was offered, as two parliamentary seats were won outright by opposition candidates: Mr Chiam See Tong in Potong Pasir and J. B. Jeyeretnam in Anson constituency. However, this offer was spurned by the eligible candidates to whom the seat was offered. In 1988 the opposition seemed to undergo a change of heart concerning their initial antipathy to this scheme: Mr Chiam of the Singapore Democratic Party was the only opposition candidate who won a parliamentary seat. NCMP seats were offered to two candidates: veteran opposition politician Dr Lee Siew Choh and former Solicitor General Francis Seow (both of the Worker's Party). Both accepted, although only Dr Lee actually sat as an NCMP, as Mr Seow[33] departed for the United States. In the 1991 general elections, prior to which the number of NCMP seats had been increased from three to four, four parliamentary seats were won outright by opposition candidates and hence no NCMP seats were offered. The disutility of the scheme is obvious when genuine opposition is elected in by the people. It may be observed that an opposition that commands the legitimacy direct elections confer will pose more of a threat than a 'created' opposition in the form of the NCMP.

The legitimacy of the NMP scheme has also been impugned on the basis that appointed members who are exempt from the hustings are apt to be detached from grassroots sentiments. NMPs represent no-one but themselves and their 'ivory-tower'-conceived views. The NMP scheme further dilutes the traditional close links an MP bears with the constituency he or she represents. While an NCMP does at least stand for election, an NMP is just a distinguished Singaporean, who participates in the political process but is himself or herself politically accountable to no-one. This opens the door to potential abuse, whereby an appointed MP might utilise his or her position to pursue a private agenda. Critics, among whom are numbered PAP MPs,[34] derided the notion of armchair critics who could not or would not stomach the politicking process. What *locus standi* had they to address the government as to how it ought to conduct itself?

It was also pointed out that NMPs should not be considered the sole source of alternative views, as such views could be canvassed from such multifarious bodies as the Institute for Policy Studies Feedback Unit, and Government Parliamentary Committees. Since tapping the expertise of the six NMPs would be analogous to tapping the views of the members of an Upper House in a bicameral system, critics wondered whether the NMP role might be better played by an elective chamber or via a modified proportional representation system which set quotas for under-represented interest groups. However, the prospect of factionalism and a weaker government would be anathema to some.

Singapore has had three batches of NMPs since the scheme's inception in 1990; I will assess their contribution to parliamentary democracy in Singapore at a later stage, and show how they have attained a large measure of popular support on the basis of their perceived independence and good performances, particularly in relation to their contribution to parliamentary debate.

A RACIAL APPROACH TO GOVERNMENT? ENTRENCHING MULTI-RACIALISM

The adoption of the group representative constituency scheme in 1988 represents a pessimistic conclusion that having a non-racial society in a 'nation by accident', with its heterogenous[35] composition, was naive and utopian. Making race an overt factor in the electoral process represents a departure from the Wee Commission's espousal of a non-racial approach to politics whereby different racial groups were to be encouraged to disregard their differences and to think in terms of being one collective Singapore entity. The scheme is an implicit acknowledgment that primeval attachments to race and language cannot easily be eradicated.

The Select Committee reviewing the GRC Bill acknowledged that there was no shared culture, no shared historical experience, to bind the nation into a cohesive whole; apart from shared geographical boundaries (and perhaps the love of money which underlies Singapore Incorporated), Singaporeans had nothing in common.

Having an electoral system that entrenched the multi-racial character of Parliament[36] was considered the best way to pre-empt the possibility of disgruntled minority groups engaging in communal politics to protest against the tyranny of the (Chinese) majority. To preserve peace, concessions would be conferred on the minority communities. The government considered as troubling the 'voting trend which showed young voters preferring candidates who were best suited to their own needs without being sufficient [sic] aware of the need to return a racially balanced slate of candidates'.[37]

The original 1982 government proposal sought only to ensure Malay representation in Parliament. Two constituencies would be twinned together, with a Malay MP representing one. The twinning concept was expanded subsequently to incorporate a multi-racial dimension whereby three former single constituencies would merge to form a GRC. The minority member in the three-people GRC would include other minority groups' candidates.

In 1988, the Constitution was amended to provide that the president had the power to declare that an election in a particular constituency be held on the basis of a group of three candidates. By a further amendment in 1991, for not entirely clear reasons, the Constitution was amended to raise the ceiling to permit up to three-quarters of the total number of MPs to be returned via the GRC. The number of MPs contesting a GRC was raised to four and the number of GRCs was increased to fifteen. The total number of GRC MPs was raised to the constitutional limit of 60, a clear parliamentary majority out of an 81-seat Parliament. The PAP won all the GRC seats in the 1991 general elections.

Three-fifths of the GRCs were required to field Malay minority candidates, while the remaining two-fifths were to field teams with an Indian or 'Other' candidate; this was supposed to reflect the relative sizes of the communities.

While this method certainly guarantees ethnic representation in Singapore, it has the unfortunate side effect of institutionalising race ratios. The intractable problem of who should decide who constituted a member of a particular racial group, which the Wee Commission sought assiduously to avoid, was now considered tractable. Pursuant to this, the Constitution provided for the creation of committees to determine whether prospective candidates were Malay or belonged to another racial minority. To satisfy the requirements for candidature, the minority team member needed to acquire a certificate from these committees stating that he or she belonged to the specified race.

The sociological postulate that self-definition was the only valid way to define an ethnic group was accepted; the legislature avoided prescribing criteria and confined itself to providing a mechanism empowering the community to decide the issue for itself. The Malay Committee[38] was to comprise five members of the Malay community nominated by the Presidential Council of Minority Rights. Its decisions, incorporating both subjective and objective considerations, were final. A person belonging 'to the Malay community' would include: 'any person, whether of the Malay race or otherwise, who considers himself to be a member of the Malay community and who is generally accepted as a member of the Malay community by that community'.[39]

By requiring a minority candidate the GRC scheme supposedly had the advantage of compelling leaders of different racial groups who wanted to contest a GRC ward to engage in negotiation and compromise prior to their election in Parliament. Extreme communal politicking, which had alienating effects, would be politically untenable as it would entail losing the support of the candidate whose community's interests were being undermined. The interests of all racial groups would have to be accommodated in election manifestoes and programs.

There is an obvious lack of parity in the weight of a vote cast by a GRC resident *vis-à-vis* an SMC resident, as the latter is able to carry not one but *four* MPs into Parliament by his or her one vote. This might well constitute a breach of the equal protection clause entrenched in Article 12 of the Constitution.

While voted in as a team on a common platform, individual GRC team members are not enjoined to vote in unison in Parliament. It was considered important to preserve the minority MP's prerogative to disagree with his or her team-mates on issues involving his or her community; this is likely to prove inconsequential as the minority MP will be subject to party discipline like all other MPs. The most prized commodity a politician can possess is the party ticket on which he or she is elected; to the party belongs the politician's first loyalty. Voters in general identify more closely with a political party, at least insofar as the PAP is concerned, and its leaders and manifesto, than they do with the individual parliamentary candidates the party puts forward and over whom the whip is exercised.[40]

The team gathering the highest number of votes is collectively voted into Parliament; the presence of an unpopular member is likely to be overshadowed by the outstanding popularity of another, or by the fact that the voter is more concerned with the party label as a whole. The former consideration apparently influenced the PAP's 1991 general elections campaign strategy.

THE USE OF THE GRC AND THE 1991 GENERAL ELECTIONS

In 1988, the number of members to be returned by the GRC scheme was set at a floor of one-quarter and a ceiling of one-half of the total number of MPs to be returned at a general election. Thirteen GRCs were designated in the 1988 elections, all PAP conquests which translated into 39 parliamentary seats. As stated above, the number of GRCs was increased to 15 four-member GRCs in the 1991 general elections, which yielded 60 parliamentary seats for the PAP which repeated its clean GRC sweep.

The GRC scheme has been subjected to a multitude of criticisms, underlying which is the concern that it dilutes the representative link between the government and the electorate. It has also been utilised in unanticipated ways that relegate its original multi-racial representation rationale into a secondary position. These criticisms will now be examined.

The 1991 increase in GRC membership

The rationale offered for this change was that the increase in GRC population necessitated it. The amendment would import flexibility and allow GRCs with increasing populations to remain intact, as they would be adequately served by an additional MP. Furthermore, it would have the salutary effect of according some permanence to the areas falling under the charge of town councils—so argued Mr Goh Chok Tong.[41] This rationale is completely unrelated to the original rationale as a means of entrenching multi-racialism in Parliament. Stretching this to its logical conclusion, one could keep increasing the number of candidates a GRC team is to field as populations expand; eventually, we could end up with one mega-Singapore GRC staffed by 81 members.

The link with town councils

When the idea of team MPs was first mooted, the idea was to merge three constituencies and then have three elected MPs serve as local government councillors. However, when the GRC Bill was tabled, Mr Goh Chok Tong insisted that the town council idea, conceived to devolve more power to citizens over the running of their housing estates, was conceptually distinct from the GRC idea, which was to institutionalise multi-racial politics. Nevertheless, both concepts were considered compatible: 'After an election, three MPs, although they are voted in separately, can get together to form a town council. Also, a group of [three] MPs in a GRC can also form a town council.'[42]

Obviously, as the size of the GRC population expanded, the town council's jurisdiction would similarly increase. It was argued that a town council that collectively managed three former SMCs would enjoy economies of scale and reduction in administrative and service costs. This is unconvincing, as Section 3(1) of the Town Councils Act allows a number of SMCs to informally group to form a single town council. No loss of economies of scale or efficiency need be sustained, nor does the number of GRC members have to be increased as a town expands. Bearing in mind that the PAP employ professional managers to run their town councils, it is hard to see the link between the number of MPs and the efficient running of the town councils. If indeed this increase from three to four members per GRC was the imperative that it was said to be, one would have thought that by-elections ought to have been called when 2 four-member GRCs were deprived of one of their non-minority members.[43]

Section 2A of the Parliamentary Elections Act provides that there is no need to call elections to fill any vacancy 'unless the

Members for that constituency have vacated their seats in Parliament'. Effectively, this means that through death or resignation we could theoretically have a situation where one GRC is represented by a single original member—minority or otherwise—of the four-member team. This certainly does not seem to gel with the rationales either of multi-racial representation or of the efficient running of town councils through garnering economies of scale! If the rationale for increasing the GRC membership from three to four in 1991 was so compelling, it follows that a GRC should always be fully manned by four MPs. However, an additional MP would not seem to affect the performance of a competent professional manager running an enlarged ward. Tagging on the town council concept to the GRC concept, linking estate management with political representation, presents itself as a haphazard attempt to conflate two separate issues in one constitutional institution, which can only cause confusion.

Influence on election strategy

Political reshuffling: party crossovers The GRC concept influenced election strategy in the 1991 general elections. The opposition parties, in a co-operative spirit, allowed their members to switch teams in order to contest a GRC ward. For example, the Worker's Party was hard-pressed to find a Malay candidate to stand with its team to contest the marginal Eunos GRC. It managed to persuade veteran opposition politician Jufrie Mahmood to switch from the Singapore Democratic Party to the Worker's Party in order to field a GRC team. This illustrates a straining of the opposition's limited membership resources.

Political manoeuvring There was a great deal of political reshuffling on the part of the PAP, whereby stronger candidates were paired with a weaker or unknown candidate or sent to marginal GRC wards to bolster the PAP's chance of optimising electoral success. For example, the PAP had polled a disconcerting 50.9% in Eunos GRC in the 1988 elections. To bolster the 1991 team, the PAP put on its slate a popular Malay candidate, Minister of State Sidek Saniff. While campaigning in Eunos the prime minister even dangled the carrot that if the PAP were voted into Eunos, Saniff would then have the clout to push for the promotion of Malay interests.

However, the net effect of uprooting MPs from constituencies where they may have developed strong grassroots links over the years is that MPs may become increasingly remote and detached from the concerns of constituency members. After all, a displaced MP not only loses the close ties he or she worked at establishing, but he or she has also to do the legwork to cultivate the new ground. Team

MPs would also face the formidable task of reconciling the interests of more than one ward. The PAP tactic of allocating its candidates on the strategic basis of ensuring sufficient heavyweight vote-pullers per GRC ward has further diluted the representative link between representor and the represented.

Greenhorns and smooth initiation rites It is interesting to note that of the eleven[44] new PAP candidates fielded, ten entered Parliament as GRC members, with only two newcomers standing in contested GRCs. Paired with seasoned campaigners, they simply could not lose. That these newcomers only began to cultivate ties with the residents on an *ex post facto* basis after being elected to Parliament decries the idea of an MP representing people whose concerns he or she has invested time and effort getting to know. Where is the relationship of trust between MP and voter when the voter does not know the newcomer?

Perpetuating PAP hegemony

Exacerbating the uneven playing ground The GRC concept has been attacked as being no more than a ploy by which the PAP can perpetuate its rule. The racial precondition greatly exacerbates the unevenness of the electoral playing field from the opposition's point of view. It is hard enough for the opposition to attract candidates of any degree of calibre into its fold, let alone compile the right racial mix with its limited membership resources. This scheme makes it even more difficult for the opposition to contest the elections. Resolution of this imbalance is crucial to the maturing of democracy in Singapore and the development of a genuine two-party system which better safeguards limited government.

It is noteworthy that the present four opposition politicians all contested in SMCs. Of course, implementing a GRC system has necessarily entailed the death of many SMCs; it also precludes the individual independent candidate from running in a GRC constituency, though four independents could decide to do so. It could be argued that in future the theoretically neutral concept of the GRC could be empirically demonstrated if an opposition team captures a GRC ward—at one fell swoop, four opposition politicians could enter Parliament; the double-edged sword that is the GRC might turn against its creators.

Foreclosing on opposition wards: the Anson experience There is also the fear that the scheme could be abused through gerrymandering which could effectively extinguish an opposition-oriented ward. In 1988, Anson constituency, notorious for supporting opposition politicians, was swallowed up by its neighbouring constituencies.

An inequitable system   One can easily sympathise with the desire to ensure that the minority groups always have a voice in policy making in lieu of a 'tyranny of the (Chinese) majority' scenario. However, it is not clear that the GRC best achieves this object. Logically, multi-racialism could easily be entrenched by modifying the GRC concept and providing for a two-member GRC with one member belonging to the requisite minority group. This would help the GRC to escape the criticism that there is something clearly inequitable about a system that allows a political party successfully contesting all GRC wards to win about 75% of the seats in Parliament by capturing only about 42% of the national vote.[46]

Finally, the very premise of the GRC, pre-empting the negative effects of racial polarisation, has been attacked by opposition politician J. B. Jeyeretnam.[47] He has argued that the problem of racial representation existed only in the minds of the PAP. In the 1984 elections contested on the basis of SMCs, all the PAP minority candidates had won while the two defeated PAP MPs were Chinese; and one of them was defeated by Jeyeretnam, member of a minority himself.

CONCLUSION

The state of parliamentary democracy post-1991

The modest toehold attained in 1981 when the PAP's parliamentary monopoly was breached by the loss of Anson constituency was translated into a modest foothold when a grand total of four opposition MPs were voted into Parliament in the mildly ground-breaking 1991 elections.[48] The presence of the opposition MPs has denuded the rationale underlying the window-dressing that is the NCMP, revealing the deficiency of this system in the light of opposition MPs who are wrapped in the cloak of legitimacy that being voted into Parliament confers. The return of competitive politics in Singapore might well signal the *quietus est* of the NCMP scheme. Conversely, the NMP scheme was activated for the first time in 1991. Propelled by the sterling performances of certain NMPs, it appears to be an institution growing from strength to strength.

Although the PAP won a clear 61.9% of the national vote, this outcome was almost construed to constitute a defeat. Prime Minister Goh at the post-election press conference gloomily stated that he had not received the mandate to pursue his consultative style of government; to his mind, Singaporean politics had irrevocably become contentious rather than consensually based. Premature statements were made to the effect that Singapore now had an adversarial, bipartisan system. Consequently, PAP MPs no longer needed to play the constructive opposition role. Dissenting voices could be channelled through the opposition with Mr Chiam See Tong as its unofficial leader.[49]

However, it cannot be overemphasised that while Singapore at present formally has the structure of an inchoate bipartisan system, it is a very long way off having a substantive bipartisan system after the Westminster model, replete with an alternative viable government which could assume power at the next elections. Of course, a parliamentary minority that may become the parliamentary majority at the next election is the predicate for the effective operation of the Westminster system; hence a parliamentary 'gap' still exists in Singapore.

Bolstered by their electoral success, the four opposition MPs, might well have borrowed a motto from Shakespeare: 'There's a tide in the affairs of men which, when taken at its flood, leads on to victory.' But the 'turning tide' became a dismal trickle as the opposition—particularly the Singapore Democratic Party to which the unofficial leader of the opposition and two other opposition MPs belonged—squandered their chance to consolidate their positions and public standing. Much-publicised internal party struggles have marred the cause of the already disjointed opposition movement and revealed their internal lack of cohesion.

The notoriously pro-establishment press has closely scrutinised the performance of the opposition MPs in Parliament and has been quick to point out the superior performance of the NMP, particularly with respect to parliamentary censure and scrutiny. Unlike the NCMP scheme, which seems to have gone the way of the dinosaur, the NMP is an institution which has attracted a lot of interest in its practical outworking. The English-language *Straits Times* has been astute in pointing out the success of the NMP scheme in terms of the quality of detailed and coherent arguments NMPs have been able to offer, thereby raising the level of debate in Parliament. Gone is the initial reservation that NMPs might be pro-government stooges, part of a scheme whereby the PAP might put its own supporters in by the back door, as the selection of MPs is by a panel led by the Speaker. The second slate of NMPs erased such fears by displaying considerable independence of mind.[50]

The criterion by which to assess the NMP scheme seems to have shifted from concerns with principles of legitimacy to more pragmatic considerations of ability. No longer do concerns that unelected NMPs lack legitimacy or that NMPs, who are unwilling to go through the thicket of personal electioneering and hence do not deserve to sit in Parliament, seem so important. It should also be noted that many PAP MPs, particularly first-timers, often come into Parliament through standing in uncontested GRCs, without so much as a political baptism of fire. Getting talented citizens into Parliament has trumped other considerations. In reporting on the Budget Debate, the *Straits Times*[51] singled out NMP Kanwaljit Soin, an orthopaedic surgeon, as topping the list of MPs actively partici-pating in question times, with fourteen questions on ministries such as law, education, finance, health and labour. Lately, NMP Walter Woon, a law academic, has made constitutional history by tabling a private members Bill, the *Maintenance of Parents Bill*, which has been passed. This shows that even backbenchers, when they take the time and effort, can contribute in an initiatory way to the legislative agenda, rather than confining themselves to behind-the-scenes lobbying and debate.

The scheme seems to be emanating signals that in Singapore there are acceptable and less acceptable forms of dissent. As such, it would be in one's self-interest to direct dissent via institutionalised channels rather than to adopt an overtly adversarial stance of dissent, for example by joining an opposition party. Being impartial and non-partisan, NMPs lack the incentive to play up to the gallery to win political Brownie points, or to humiliate the government gratuitously. Unencumbered by the dual role of legislator/town councillor that elected MPs are expected to juggle, a neutral NMP can focus on offering objective, constructive views. An NMP is unlikely to introduce an overtly adversarial spirit into Parliament and hence constitutes a less threatening source of ideas or criti-cisms.

The institution appears to be evolving into an outlet for interest representation. Dr Soin in particular is concerned with raising women's issues and heightening public consciousness of women's role as full citizens, with a part to play in the political process.[52] In this respect, NMPs are fulfilling an important educative function. The present slate of third generation NMPs[53] represent such diverse interests as those of labour, economic policy, and Malay and legal concerns.

If one is willing to forgo principle for pragmatism, the NMP scheme perhaps deserves a reappraisal. The success of the scheme in raising the level of debate in Parliament will of course vary with the quality of candidates it attracts. But recognising the utility of the scheme in strengthening the political system by offering more opportunities for political participation must concomitantly entail a recognition that no true democratic ethos has developed in a society where people are singularly reluctant to enter the political fray. Nevertheless, the scheme has served as a means to familiarise distinguished members of the public with the internal workings of Parliament, perhaps encouraging them to consider a career in public office in the future. Their exposure to the public and particularly the favourable light in which the press depicts them would stand NMPs in good stead in this regard. Effectively, they could start the ball rolling through showing that constructive dissent can be accommodated, with the dissenters being able to dissent with impunity. The criticism of this is that the government is grooming a pool of approved critics. But as NMP Woon has recently stated, it is better to speak through government-established channels than not to speak at all. It may be that the NMP scheme may serve as a temporary expedient as Singapore awaits the development of a more mature democracy. Though theoretically and institutionally imperfect, it could serve a useful function, but with the overriding proviso that it be viewed as an interim measure.

The darker side of the scheme is that it may conceivably serve as a safe buffer that would help contain or stultify the growth of a genuine grassroots opposition, as preference would be accorded an articulate, intelligent NMP who outshines an ineffectual, if earnest, opposition politician. Indeed, the poor performance of the opposition MPs *vis-à-vis* the NMPs is in part due to the fact that the opposition parties have largely failed to attract good candidates. In time, the NMP may be thought of as the real alternative in Singaporean politics, to the detriment of opposition politics. Insofar as this scenario is concerned, its effects might be to raise the threshold of political apathy, to dull the hitherto latent but now budding democratic instinct for political choice and pluralism. The electorate may be lulled into a slough of complacency by the thought that there will always be an 'opposition' voice in the form of NCMPs or NMPs in Parliament.

GRC-related issues

With much speculation afoot as to the setting of the next general elections date, it is interesting to note that the prime minister has asked the Electoral Boundaries Review Committee to consider the feasibility of detaching McPherson ward from his own Marine Parade GRC to accommodate the desire of his team-mate, Mattias Yao, to have a one-on-one contest with the Singapore Democratic Party's Chee Soon Juan. Both have been engaged in a 'war of words' via letters published in the press. Chee had challenged Yao to a debate on policy and on whether he dared to come out from behind the prime minister and contest a ward singly. If this request is approved, it will set an unusual precedent. It also seems to show that the GRC concept is not so crucial, if a part of the GRC can be detached simply to satisfy the egos of two politicians.[54]

Distrusting the electorate: the 'some persons two votes' proposal

The 'one person one vote' system is no longer sacrosanct in Singapore. Senior Minister Lee began to speak against its appropriateness in the context of an Asian democracy as early as 1984. Then, he criticised the electorate's abuse of votes by using them to protest against incumbent politicians rather than to positively choose a representative. How a voter utilises his or her vote is surely a matter of his or her personal prerogative.

To guard against the irresponsible use of votes, Senior Minister Lee has stated[55] that the Singaporean political system would be better off if every man above 40 who had a family be given two votes (one vote, double weightage) as such a man would be more likely to use his votes carefully, because he would be voting for his children as well. However, Lee also proposes that at age 65 such a person should return to one vote, the fear being that he will hold the state hostage to unsustainable welfare demands. Besides posing practical problems in providing for the beyond-age-65 reversion to one vote, this proposal would certainly violate the Article 12 equal protection clause. Its premise is open to a battery of criticisms.[56] Voters between the ages of 40 and 60 with families are supposed to vote more responsibly, but they could also easily pursue their own sectoral concerns. Indeed, with aged parents to support, they might well clamour for increased health care benefits! Theoretically, any government can stay in power in perpetuity so long as it can take care of the interests of a group to which it gives double weightage votes.

The upshot is that this paternalistic scheme envisages a clear distrust of the electorate, perhaps heightened by the fact that the PAP's share of the votes is steadily diminishing with every general election. The culturally relativistic argument that Asian or Singaporean 'democracy' can exist in the context of a one-party state with an 'economics first' policy, and that the legislature should eschew the route of the Western prototype which experiences political turnover, might well be a mask behind which its wearer seeks to extend hegemonic rule for as long as possible.

FUTURE DEVELOPMENTS: A FINAL WORD

The days of what Samuel Huntington calls 'democracy without turnover', in which opposition parties legally exist but hold no parliamentary seats, are over. It is certain that the growth of an opposition movement, while slow, is ineluctably taking place. As Lee Kuan Yew noted in 1972:

> Opposition in this Chamber will and must inevitably return. But the
> Opposition will not be individuals claiming to act as the conscience

of the people or offering themselves as necessary accoutrements of parliamentary democracy on the spurious ground that because there is no Opposition, there is no parliamentary democracy. Singapore is not that gullible and credulous.[57]

Parliament in Singapore is today a site for national and municipal concerns, a place where some special interests can be articulated and where there is some ethnic representation. It will be interesting to see whether the proposal for a Women's GRC will ever be adopted; one might speculate on the impact upon the political scene of the loss of a PAP-held GRC ward to a team of opposition or independent politicians in the next elections. One wonders whether the era of constitutional experimentation has finally come to a halt. The effects of the latter-day modifications to the electoral and legislative system will continue to be made a little clearer come the next general elections.

4

Choosing a New System of
Representation for New Zealand

David Bradshaw

At the bottom of all the tributes paid to democracy is the little man walking into the little booth with a little pencil making a little cross on a little bit of paper. No amount of rhetoric or voluminous discussion can possibly diminish the overwhelming importance of this point.

(Winston Churchill, House of Representatives 1944)

INTRODUCTION

New Zealand's view on democracy is encapsulated in that oft-quoted description of democracy: 'Government of the people, by the people, for the people.'

The practical question is how to translate the wishes of the people into an effective government. The variations adopted to achieve this are many but they all have in common, as an essential ingredient of a democratic system of government, the regular election of governments by the free choice of the people choosing between competing parties or individuals. The electoral system stands at the very heart of our democratic system of government, for it is through its procedures that the electors determine who shall govern the country. General elections held every three years are the means by which the electors of New Zealand give their consent to the exercise by Parliament and by the government of the considerable powers vested in each of those bodies. The preservation of the integrity of the electoral system is fundamental to the process of democratic government.

New Zealand has recently voted to change its electoral system as from the next general election. New Zealand will no longer have a 'first-past-the-post' (FPP) electoral system but instead has chosen a form of proportional representation. In reforming the system the government sought the views of the voters of New Zealand. To paraphrase, the little person making his or her little cross on a little bit of paper decided the nature of the electoral system for New Zealand for the future. This was a true case of democracy in action.

This chapter will examine the procedures and events, occurring over a number of years, that culminated in the decision of electors to change to a system of proportional representation. It will explore the factors existing within New Zealand that influenced electors to vote in favour of the change, as well as the processes that were followed, and some of the expected outcomes of the new electoral system.

The New Zealand experience in reviewing its electoral system has demonstrated some of the difficulties of having a relatively complex constitutional issue determined through a series of referenda. One can never be certain about the reasons individuals vote in any particular way, if indeed they vote at all. No matter how extensive the campaigning, or how logical or persuasive the arguments may appear to be, ultimately our democratic process comes down to the very personal and mostly private reasons that dictate how the individual electors exercise their right to vote.

HISTORY OF NEW ZEALAND'S POLITICAL SYSTEM

New Zealand has had a system of representative government since the New Zealand Constitution Act 1852. In 1856 the British government agreed to 'responsible government' for New Zealand. Ministers of the Crown became responsible to the members of Parliament as the representatives of the electors, rather than to the governor. Franchise was given to males over 21 years of age with interests in land, although this property qualification was dropped in 1879. In 1893 New Zealand became the first country in the world to grant universal suffrage to women—although they were not permitted to stand for Parliament until 1919.

From 1852 until 1950 New Zealand had both an Upper House and a Lower House of Representatives. The Upper House or Legislative Council was a nominated body, while the Lower House or House of Representatives was an elected body of representatives. Elections were held every three years except between 1852 and 1879, when elections were held every five years. The Legislative Council was abolished in 1950, leaving the House of Representatives as the supreme body governing the country.

New Zealand since 1852 has elected its members of Parliament on the basis of a 'first-past-the-post' (FPP) electoral system (although there were some minor variations to a true FPP electoral system between 1852 and 1914). The candidate with the most votes in a constituency was elected, and the party that won a majority of seats in Parliament was invited by the governor-general to form a government.

New Zealand does not have a written Constitution, but has a number of Acts that prescribe certain constitutional matters. Matters pertaining directly to the electoral system are contained in the Electoral Act.

THE ROYAL COMMISSION ON ELECTORAL REFORM

In February 1985 the government established a Royal Commission, chaired by a judge of the High Court, to undertake a far-reaching examination of New Zealand's electoral system. Foremost among the matters to be considered was whether the existing FPP electoral system should continue, and, if not, whether there should be a form of proportional representation or some other voting system. After extensive consultation and consideration of the issues, the Royal Commission reported in December 1986. It recommended that a mixed-member proportional (MMP) electoral system replace the FPP system, if such a proposed change were to be agreed to by the electorate through a referendum.

The Royal Commission adopted ten criteria against which to test the different possible electoral systems, and although no voting system would be able to meet all of these, the challenge was to find the electoral system that provided the most satisfactory balance between the different criteria, taking into account the particular circumstances of the country. The criteria used by the Royal Commission were:

1 *Fairness between political parties* Voters at an election are primarily choosing between alternative party governments. In the interests of fairness and equality the number of seats gained by a political party should be proportional to the number of voters who support that party.

2 *Effective representation of minority and special interest groups* Members of Parliament are elected to represent their electorates. It is therefore appropriate that membership of Parliament should reflect the significant characteristics of the electorate such as gender, ethnicity, socioeconomic class, locality and age.

3 *Effective Maori representation* In New Zealand, Maori occupy a

special position constitutionally and should be fairly and effectively represented in Parliament.

4 *Political integration* All political groups should be encouraged to respect other points of view and to take into account the good of the community as a whole. The electoral system should unite the country behind the final result.

5 *Effective representation of constituents* There must be close links maintained between individual members and their constituents to ensure effective representation of the concerns of constituents.

6 *Effective voter participation* Voters must be able to easily understand the procedures that they are to use in determining who is to govern the country. All votes should be of equal weight.

7 *Effective government* Once appointed the government must be able to act decisively and have reasonable continuity and stability.

8 *Effective parliament* Parliament occupies a central role in the governing of New Zealand. It is important that the voting system should provide an effective Parliament.

9 *Effective parties* Political parties today play an essential role in modern politics. This should be recognised in any electoral system.

10 *Legitimacy* Voters must have confidence in the fairness of the electoral system so that they can accept its decisions even when many may have preferred an alternative government. (That is, do people on the losing side accept the results?)

CHRONOLOGY OF SIGNIFICANT EVENTS IN THE PROCESS

The report of the Royal Commission was subject to considerable discussion and consideration, including a quite lengthy evaluation by a Select Committee. Seven significant steps towards the current changes, outlined below, followed general elections in 1990.

The Electoral Referendum Act 1991

This legislation was introduced in Parliament in August 1991 as the Electoral Poll Bill. It provided for a two-tiered approach to any change. In September 1992 an indicative referendum was to be held to determine whether or not electors wanted a change to the electoral system, and, if so, to indicate which was the preferred alternative voting system out of four options presented in the ballot paper.[1] Depending upon the outcome of that referendum a further referendum would be held at the time of the 1993 general election to determine finally whether there would be any changes to the electoral system. At this final referendum electors would choose between the present system and the alternative voting system selected by the indicative referendum.

Electoral referendum panel

From the outset the government recognised that managing the necessary public education programs for the referendums was going to present political difficulties. A change to a proportional representation system of government was not necessarily in the interests of the two main parties. How then was the government to ensure that the public were well informed in an unbiased manner about the options, prior to the referendums? The approach decided upon was to establish an Electoral Referendum Panel headed by the chief ombudsman (who in New Zealand is an officer of Parliament and not a part of the executive). The key task of the Electoral Referendum Panel was to provide a publicity campaign to explain to voters in an impartial and unbiased manner how each of the various reform options would operate. MMP at this stage had a considerable advantage over any of the other options in terms of public recognition, primarily as a result of the Report of the Royal Commission.

The indicative referendum

At the indicative referendum 84.7% of the votes cast favoured a change to the electoral system. The MMP alternative was the preferred alternative, attracting 70% of the vote. The turn-out at the referendum was however low in comparison with the turn-out for general elections in New Zealand, with only 55.2% of electors participating.

Electoral Referendum Act 1993

This Act passed by Parliament in August 1993 provided for a binding referendum on the proposals for the electoral system to be held at the time of the general election in 1993.

Electoral Act 1993

Parliament passed the Electoral Act 1993 in August 1993. This Act detailed how MMP would be implemented if it was to be the preferred alternative at the referendum held at the time of the 1993 general election. Full details, such as the size of Parliament under MMP, and the future of the Maori seats, were debated by Parliament and finally determined in the Electoral Act 1993.[2]

Second Electoral Referendum Panel

Following the experience with the indicative referendum in 1992 the government decided to conduct a publicity campaign before the 1993 electoral referendum, to explain to voters how the two different voting systems would work. Another independent Electoral Referendum Panel was established, again chaired by the chief ombudsman. Its task was to present impartial information to the public about the two options. Its public information campaign was to be independent of the government's political parties and the supporters of the two options. The aim of the Panel was to communicate to every registered voter sufficient factual information on the two referendum options to enable an informed choice to be made.

Final referendum

The final referendum was held at the same time as the general election in 1993. In that referendum electors were asked to indicate whether they wanted to retain the FPP system of voting or move to MMP for future general elections. The final vote saw 53.9% of the voters favour a change to an MMP electoral system. In the final referendum 83.3% of electors voted—a figure slightly below that for the 1990 and 1993 general elections where the figure was approximately 85%, but well above the turn-out for the indicative referendum.

MOTIVES FOR RECONSIDERATION OF THE ELECTORAL SYSTEM

No single event led the New Zealand electorate to change the way it elected its governments. Nor was its reconsideration a rapid occurrence. Rather, the environment for electoral change had developed gradually over a number of years and at a time of considerable social and economic change within New Zealand's society. It is also important to note that this was not a situation where there was a total rejection of the present electoral system—the final vote saw 46% of electors favour the existing FPP system. The FPP system was widely understood among electors; had achieved a high level of involvement by voters at the time of elections; and had produced governments that were effective in terms of providing security, continuity and stability. Local members of Parliament provided an important link between local constituents and Parliament—even where the local member came from a different political party to the one that the constituent supported at the election. Under the FPP electoral system successive New Zealand governments had governed effectively for many years. But by the 1980s questions were being asked as to whether what had served New Zealand well in the past was now the right electoral system for the future. One of the issues facing the electors was whether it was the electoral system that needed changing, or the way that governments governed and the nature of the economic and social policies that had been introduced.

Two factors at the time appear to have had a large influence on the final outcome: the perception of fairness in terms of Parliament representing the wishes of the voters; and the feeling that there were inadequate constraints constitutionally on the government of the day. These factors need to be set in the context of the changes that had been occurring in New Zealand over the previous decade.

Fairness of the electoral system in reflecting the wishes of voters

The FPP system meant that in many instances both individual members of Parliament and the government itself were appointed with less than a majority of the votes. This outcome was perceived as being unfair and undemocratic—the aggregate of the views of the majority of the population may not be represented in Parliament. The FPP electoral system does not give political parties a number of seats in Parliament proportional to the votes that they receive. In this regard New Zealand has had governments that have had a minority of the total votes since 1951. Where there are minor parties the disadvantages of this system can at times appear significant, although the extent to which this electoral system has promoted 'protest' votes in the New Zealand environment needs to be kept in mind in making any judgments from the figures. Previous elections had, however, made it quite apparent that a third party in New Zealand could get a sizeable share of the votes under the FPP system—but few if any seats.

New Zealand does not have a lengthy history of two-party politics. From 1938 to 1951 there were just two main political parties—National and Labour. During this period, with the exception of the 1943 election, the party in government had not only a majority of seats in Parliament but also a majority of the votes cast. At each election since 1951, however, there has been at least one other party of some significance involved in the contest, and the government has received a minority of the votes cast.

In several elections the results were regarded as a 'landslide' in terms of the seats that the new government obtained in Parliament, despite the fact that the government had not received a majority of the total votes cast. From 1954 to the present a third party received more than 10% of the votes on six occasions. (The highest counts

Table 4.1   Percentage of votes received by the government since 1951, and seats held by the government as against the total number of seats in Parliament

Year	Govt vote (%)	Govt seats	Seats in Parliament
1954	43.8	45	80
1957	48.3	41	80
1960	47.6	46	80
1963	47.1	45	80
1966	43.8	44	80
1969	45.2	45	84
1972	48.4	55	87
1975	47.6	55	87
1978	39.8	51	92
1981	38.8	47	92
1984	43.0	56	95
1987	48.0	57	97
1990	47.8	67	97
1993	35.0	50	99

being 16.1% of the vote in 1978, 20.7% of the vote in 1981, 12.3% of the vote in 1984, and 18.2% of the vote in 1993.) In 1981 the third party, Social Credit, won 20.7% of the vote, but obtained only two seats (2.2% of the seats). Whereas the National Party won one seat on average for every 14 900 votes, and Labour one seat for every 16 300 votes, it took 186 000 votes to elect each Social Credit member of Parliament. The situation was even more pronounced in 1984 when the New Zealand Party—a party with substantial but evenly based electoral support—obtained 12.3% of the votes (236 000 votes) without winning a single parliamentary seat.

By the mid 1980s the succession of governments having only a minority of the votes caused New Zealanders to begin to seriously question whether their electoral system was entirely adequate. This questioning arose not simply in respect of the electoral system itself but rather as part of a growing dissatisfaction with a number of aspects about the political system in New Zealand. The main third party from 1954 to 1984—Social Credit—had advocated a system of proportional representation for some time, but its call went unheeded during the 1960s and early 1970s, a period of relative prosperity and stable government in New Zealand. Social Credit did get one or two members elected in 1966 and 1978–84, and in 1981 came close to holding the balance of power. In that year the two main parties held 47 and 43 seats respectively, and Social Credit held two seats (remembering that the government party provided the Speaker, reducing its effective majority during this period to one).

Associated with this element of fairness was the concept of equality of votes. As the majority of electorates were strongholds for one or other of the two main parties, the outcome of an election held according to the FPP system was generally decided by the outcome of a small number of 'marginal' seats. The perceived effect of this was to place a much higher value in practical terms on the votes of the electors in the marginal seats. Many electors, in other words, felt their vote was unlikely to have any real impact upon the ultimate decision, and 'the system' was such that certain results were almost inevitable no matter what candidate might be fielded by the party.

Constraints on executive government

Another major factor was a growing concern about the potential for abuse of power by the executive. There was a feeling that the electoral system had got away from the people, with a resultant loss of confidence in the political process. While the FPP system provided for strong governments capable of responding quickly to events as they occurred, there was growing disquiet over the lack of checks and balances during a government's term of office. For example, the government introduced large-scale changes in the public sector in 1985–87 without a clear mandate and without any meaningful consultation with either the people directly affected or the general public.

At the apex of New Zealand's constitutional system is the cabinet. The overlap of membership between the Cabinet and Parliament (all ministers being members of Parliament), and the absence of any other constitutional checks, results in what has been described as 'a dangerously centralised concentration of power in the Cabinet'.[3] The cabinet, reflecting its links to the Westminster style of government, operates a system of collective responsibility which requires all ministers to be unanimous in their public support of the cabinet's decisions and to vote accordingly when legislation implementing those decisions is put through Parliament. Tight party discipline ensures that backbench members—concerned with their prospects of re-election, which depend heavily on remaining within one of the two main parties—will generally be unwilling to go against policies once decided by the cabinet. The system in New Zealand has been such that, once elected, a government that had a reasonable majority of seats was unlikely to lose a confidence vote in the House. With no Upper House to review its actions, the executive had virtually an unfettered ability to implement its policies for the three-year term of office. That is not to say that there is any significant evidence of governments acting improperly or corruptly abusing the power that came from having effective control both of the executive and of the House of Representatives. It has meant, however, that minority groups believed their concerns were not getting the degree of consideration that they felt was warranted. The difference between a strong government and a dictatorial government in these circumstances may often be in the eye of the beholder.

The National Party was in government from 1975 to 1984. During the latter part of this period it faced some difficult decisions on both economic and social issues that had virtually divided the country. On the economic front unemployment was rising significantly and overseas borrowing was increasing. The government, through a policy of tight fiscal and monetary controls and government interventions, had created a heavily regulated economy. As well as experiencing these major economic problems New Zealand was going through a period of intense internal dissension on social issues such as the government's policy towards South Africa and its decision to allow a South African rugby team to tour New Zealand. A combination of events led to the government calling an early election in 1984—which it lost in a landslide defeat to the Labour Party.

What followed was a fundamental restructuring of the economy. The economic policies changed radically to address a financial crisis. The emphasis was on deregulation and significantly reduced government involvement in the economy. The restructuring did not, however, stop the increase in the unemployment figures. Many voters felt that they had exchanged one extreme party for another— the detailed economic considerations behind many of the changes would be unlikely to have been fully understood by many voters, although the need for some change of direction seems to have been recognised by the fact that the Labour government was returned for a further term of office in 1987. The welfare state that New Zealanders had known in the prosperous times was changing, with the government being forced to make many hard political decisions which were often unpopular. Many people experienced a drop in the standard of living that they had come to take for granted in New Zealand, reflecting a previous period of low productivity, low growth and living beyond our means. The 1987 world stockmarket crash was particularly severe in New Zealand. Greed, the narrow base of our economy and our small size all came together to ensure that New Zealand was affected more severely than most other countries.

Parliament had seemed to become impotent in the face of a strong executive. There were perceived abuses of Parliament both before and after the change of government in 1984. However, there was a growing feeling, particularly after 1984, that matters were not adequately debated in Parliament; changes were made by the executive government without adequate consultation with the people affected; and perhaps the most significant factor was a growing distrust in the commitment of political parties to adhere to the promises made during the lead-up to the election.

There can be little doubt that New Zealand needed a very strong executive to bring about the changes in the 1980s that are now assisting with the country's economic recovery. The cost of that strong government, however, was a growing public disillusionment with the political system as a result of the harsh economic realities confronted by the government. While there were local circumstances that fed into the New Zealand situation, we were part of an international trend of disaffection with politicians.

Not surprisingly, attention focused on the role of Parliament itself at this time. The processes for examining legislation and for evaluating government policies and government spending had been improved by strengthening the Select Committee processes, but despite these changes the government retained a majority in all of the main Committees. There was still no effective control in Parliament to prevent successive governments pushing through legislation at great speed and occasionally with a minimum of consultation. The cabinet in this respect had powers akin to an elective dictatorship. New Zealand was described by one prominent commentator as being 'the fastest law-maker in the West'.[4]

Looking back on the events that occurred it can be seen that electors were influenced by at least two quite different motivations for change to the electoral process. On the one hand there was a group of people who strongly believed philosophically that proportional representation was the fairest way for any government to be fully representative of what the people wanted. New Zealanders have a strong sense of fairness and equity—a proportional representation system was seen to better reflect these values. On the other hand there were many people in New Zealand by the end of the 1980s who were questioning the way that governments were governing and were beginning to feel that the executive had too much power. Any system that was seen to remove some of the power from the executive and place it back in the hands of all of the elected representatives (that is, Parliament) was seen to be an advantage. One needs to be careful, however, about attributing too many motives to the voters, as recent surveys have suggested that despite the intensive education campaign there is a relatively low level of understanding of the proportional representation system that has been endorsed. For many voters it could have been a case of simply wanting to show politicians that they were fed up with the existing style of politics and that they wanted a more consensual and less combative style of government, which was more concerned for individuals and less market dominated.

COMMENTS ON THE PROCESS FOLLOWED

Democracy in New Zealand presented a series of apparent contradictions when it came to a consideration of a change to the electoral process. For the two major parties in New Zealand any change to the FPP system would almost inevitably mean a reduction in their power to govern. How then was change to be brought about when the very people who have to pass it into law were those who may well be the least likely to support it? Members of Parliament are there to represent the will of the people but, ultimately, it is for each individual member to determine how he or she will vote on any issue (although for the Members of the two main political parties there will be a party policy that is required to be followed on most issues). Electoral law in New Zealand is entrenched in that certain specified provisions in the Electoral Act, which include the method of voting, may only be repealed or amended where the proposal is passed by a majority of 75% of all the members of the House of Representatives, or has been carried by a majority of the valid votes cast at a poll of electors. (Section 268 of the Electoral Act 1993 repeated Section 189 of the Electoral Act 1956 which was the current provision at the time of the referendums.) Whatever their reasons may have been, both major political parties supported the approach that the public be invited to have its say through the process of two referendums.

In theory the process that was followed ought to have ensured that electors had ample time to become familiar with the different systems. The final voting figures at the indicative referendum showed that only 55.2% of electors voted, whereas between 80% and 90% vote at general elections. It is ironic given the criticisms that were being made of the FPP system that in the indicative referendum, which was the first step towards MMP becoming the new electoral system, MMP received only a 'minority vote' of the total number of electors.

The Electoral Referendum Panel in reporting to Parliament after the indicative referendum commented on two major difficulties that it encountered with the running of its public education campaign. The first difficulty related to its task of providing impartial and unbiased information. The Panel was not to advocate any one system ahead of the others, but to put all the information to voters in an unbiased manner, leaving the voters to decide which option was to be preferred. In the political setting in New Zealand this was an unusual approach in relation to an issue going to a vote by the general public—but it was a necessary one nevertheless. New-Zealand-style politics has tended to see different parties advocating their respective party proposals and pointing out the defects, real or imagined, in the policies of other parties, the ultimate aim being to sell their policies to the voters. It is undoubtedly easier to make out a positive case for an option that your party strongly believes in than it is to impart information in a neutral manner in respect of all options. This difficulty was compounded in the indicative referendum, as there were no strong advocates for each of the four alternatives being put forward.

The second difficulty arose from the complexity of the indicative referendum itself. The process was quite different from anything that voters in New Zealand had previously been asked to participate in. If a voter rejected the FPP system then there were four alternative electoral processes to choose from, one being MMP. Each alternative electoral process required a careful consideration of a number of difficult and complex issues about how it would apply— factors that did not lend themselves to an easy presentation to the public. Furthermore, the differences between some of the options were not altogether clear. The complexity of the alternatives was compounded by the fact that there were no precise details available before the indicative referendum as to exactly how each of the options would be implemented. Two issues in particular assumed significance in the debate leading up to the indicative referendum, and later at the time of the general election. They were the proposed increase in the size of Parliament (99 seats to 120 seats) to accommodate the balance between constituency and list seats (MMP was reinterpreted to stand for 'Many More Politicians'); and the future of the Maori seats in Parliament.

Parliament was probably the only body that could have given an authoritative statement on the detail of the various options. It did address these matters before the second referendum—but only in respect of the MMP option. In the period leading up to the final referendum an extremely active interest group supporting the retention of the FPP electoral system (but with reforms being made within that system) emerged. After details of the MMP system were established in the Electoral Act 1993 there was a much higher level of meaningful public debate on all of the issues. Parliamentarians did not enter the debate in any substantive manner—possibly because their attention was focused on the issues of the general election itself rather than on the referendum.

Whether the public education campaign conducted by the Electoral Referendum Panel before the final referendum was successful will remain a moot point. It will always be extremely hard to educate a whole nation on a complex issue such as the details of alternative electoral systems. Whether electors will act logically rather than emotively when casting their vote lies beyond the determination of any education campaign.

Two 'hidden' factors may well have played an important role in the final outcome of the referendums which saw MMP predominate: the traditional respect that New Zealanders have for the outcomes of Royal Commissions—the fact that the Royal Commission after detailed study preferred MMP gave that alternative a clear head start in the polls; and the fact that in New Zealand as in other democratic systems electors tend to vote against something rather than in favour of a particular issue—governments fail, oppositions do not win.

It is interesting to contrast the two referendums that were held to see what lessons might be learned from them. The first referendum was held as a separate exercise and involved a complex set of considerations for voters. The result was to be indicative only and would not of itself result in a change to the electoral system (although it would determine which option was to go forward to the final referendum). The turn-out at this referendum was low—at only 55.2% of voters. The final referendum, which was held at the time of the general election, had a clearer focus and was going to be binding. A total of 83.3% of the voters participated in this decision. Only time will tell whether it was advantageous to hold this final referendum at the time of the general election, rather than allow voters to consider it separately. The experience with the electoral reform may also be significant for the holding of future referendums, particularly since New Zealand has recently passed a Citizens Initiated Referenda Act giving greater opportunity for issues to be put to a public referendum.

EXPECTED OUTCOMES OF THE CHANGES

The New Zealand political scene is in a state of transition. The incumbent national government was returned to office in the 1993 general election with 50 seats out of 99 seats, a majority of just one. The Speaker was chosen from the Labour opposition, thereby ensuring that the government maintained a majority in the House. The government faced the prospect of governing the country on that small majority while at the same time making the changes that will be required to implement an MMP system of government. The closeness of the 1993 election result has added a further complication to the current situation. In order for there to be an election held under MMP there are a number of prerequisites that must be fulfilled in terms of the Electoral Act 1993, for example the redrawing of the boundaries for the electorates. Should a general election be called before all of the prerequisites have been completed, that election would be conducted under the FPP system notwithstanding the results of the 1993 referendum. That could see a government returned under the old electoral system for a further three years of office, thereby delaying the introduction of MMP.

There are two major outcomes that most New Zealanders expect will flow from the change to MMP. These reflect the environment that led to the change in the first place.

Fairer representation of the people in Parliament

Under a proportional system of representation the constitution of Parliament will reflect the proportion of votes given to each party. One of the most likely consequences of this, based on past election results in New Zealand, will be an end to one-party government, and the formation of coalition governments. Already several new parties are being formed—each looking to find its own place in the political spectrum. For a party to be certain of obtaining seats in Parliament it must achieve a threshold of 5% of the party list votes, or win at least one electorate seat.

The change to proportional representation has meant a funda- mental change to the electorate boundaries within New Zealand. The Representation Commission has redrawn the boundaries to reduce the number of electorates from 99 (including the four Maori seats) to 65 (including five Maori seats, which number was deter- mined according to the number of Maori electors who were registered on the Maori Roll). The balance of the seats in the Parliament will be list seats determined from the party lists. Parties are now in the process of determining which of their current members of Parliament will continue to represent electorates and which ones will be placed on the party list. There was an expectation that the senior members of the major parties would be placed high up on the party list, thereby offering the best chances of being returned to Parliament. The current discussions would suggest, however, that the change from representing an electorate to being a list member may take some time to occur. Members of Parliament who have spent many years representing electorates clearly have an affinity with their electorates and electorate work.

Achieving fairer representation in Parliament may have a cost for the access that New Zealanders currently have to their repre- sentative in Parliament. With 99 electorates being reduced to 65 there is a corresponding increase in the size of each electorate. New Zealand has only a small population. The local member of Parlia- ment has traditionally played an important role in his or her community. Even ministers, notwithstanding their heavy workload, have generally made a point of keeping in touch with their elector- ates and representing the interests of their constituents. Recent provisional boundaries have indicated that the average number of constituents in an electorate will increase from 33 500 to 55 000.

This is still not a large number when compared with overseas jurisdictions but it does represent a significant cultural change for New Zealanders, particularly when it is put alongside the greater geographical area that each electorate will have to cover. The uncertainty is how list members will interact with the constituency members in representing electors. It is too soon to predict whether or not list members will feel an obligation to any particular group of electors or whether they will see their re-election being dependent upon how well the policies of the party that they represent are being received. One possible outcome is that list members will assume a presence in electorates—possibly even in those electorates where the party member was defeated. This would then, arguably, enhance local representation and provide electors with the opportunity to have their concerns represented by a person from the party of their choosing—an option that is not currently available. We may also see list members chosen to liaise with particular groups, for example Pacific Islanders or farmers.

Effective Parliament

The change to proportional representation is expected to contribute to a more effective Parliament. The executive will continue to govern the country on a day-to-day basis but it is unlikely to dominate Parliament and its proceedings in the way that has occurred in the past. With more members of Parliament there should be a greater opportunity for scrutiny of the actions of the executive. The accountability of the executive to Parliament should be greatly enhanced. Parties may be more likely to be held to account for keeping their election promises once they get into power.

There is the prospect that a new group of people, who prefer to concentrate on policy formulation and the more consensual and less adversarial style of politics expected under proportional representation, might be attracted to stand for Parliament in list seats rather than as electorate candidates. Other members of Parliament will also be able to be protected from the vagaries of plurality elections through the greater certainty that can be provided by being included on a party list rather than having to obtain the support of an electorate—particularly in a marginal seat. These members could contribute to Parliament's ability to make sound laws and to its scrutiny of executive actions.

The combination of coalition governments, different groups of people standing for Parliament, and a lessening of party discipline, may encourage members to examine proposed policies more rigorously and to debate their merits more openly than has occurred in the past. Whether such a change would extend to a lessening of the concept of collective responsibility that currently applies to the cabinet is hard to predict, but I feel it is unlikely to occur. Even under a coalition government there will be incentives for the coalition parties to ensure that the government continues to have the confidence of the House. It could be expected, however, that cabinet will adopt a more consensual approach to major issues.

Other expected outcomes

Among the many other possible outcomes of New Zealand's adoption of the MMP electoral system are included a removal of emphasis on the two-party system, better representation in Parliament, and changes in the Public Service.

Removal of emphasis on two major parties   Under the previous system two major parties dominated the political scene, and in all but one or two instances members who left those parties to stand as independent candidates failed to get re-elected. Party discipline ensured that members of the party supported it on critical issues in Parliament. The expectation is that the two main parties will become less dominant under MMP, opening the way for a wider range of views to be considered—views coming both from within the main parties and from other parties. Consensus and consultation are expected to be key words for the future as New Zealand moves into a new political environment.

Better representation in Parliament   The introduction of list seats is expected to see some movement towards improving the representation in Parliament of women, and of Maori. Although members are more likely to be elected on their individual appeal than on their gender or race, parties will most likely seek to present a balanced choice of list members in order to appeal to the widest cross-section of the community. There is also now the potential for small parties to form and to seek to represent the views of specific groups within society. Under the new electoral system each party requires a minimum of 5% of the votes to obtain list seats. Whether or not the smaller parties will be able to achieve this threshold is difficult to judge, since New Zealand voters have not previously had two separate votes—one for the constituency member of their choice, and the other for the party of their choice—and the extent to which they will vote for the smaller parties is unknown.

Changes for the Public Service   The fundamental premises on which our Public Service is based are likely to remain—an apolitical Public Service, with appointments based on merit, with senior public servants providing free and frank advice to ministers, and implementing the policies of the government of the day in an efficient and effective manner. But the relationships between the Public Service, the executive and Parliament will almost inevitably change, and the Public Service will need new rules and procedures to ensure that it retains its apolitical character. The challenge facing the New Zealand Public Service is to ensure that it maintains its present high standards of performance, impartiality and integrity. Political advisers are likely to become much more important, taking responsibility for the political dimensions of putting together the coalition and for determining how the various political views of the coalition partners can be accommodated. The traditional role of the Public Service in New Zealand has been to remain apart from such political decisions in order that it can serve any government with equal dedication and commitment, and the interface between the new political advisers and the traditional public servants is an area currently being carefully considered. The prevailing view is that procedures and protocols need to be put into place to ensure that the Public Service does not lose its apolitical role—if anything that role will become even more important in ensuring continuity and stability of central government under MMP.

CONCLUSION

New Zealand has demonstrated that it is possible to make significant changes to an established electoral system through a carefully constructed democratic process. Such a change does not occur, however, without significant commitment on the part of those in government, and considerable effort by those given the task of implementing the changes. Above all, the environment for change needs to be there—the electors must perceive that there are some benefits from making the change.

I would expect to see a redistribution of power in New Zealand's constitutional system. Parliament, minor parties and the public are likely to have a greater say in government in New Zealand in the future under MMP. These parts of the Constitution will be better able to provide checks against the powers of the cabinet. New strategies will need to be developed by the different participants to ensure that the changed system of government is fully effective. The extent of changes that may be needed in other parts of our system of government may also shape the behaviour of both voters and candidates. Whether or not the expectations of the 'little person' in selecting MMP ahead of the existing FPP electoral system will be met will not be known for quite a few years to come. What is important is that a change of this dimension was able to be made in a truly democratic manner.

5

The Choosing of Representatives in Korea

Dai-Kwon Choi

The Republic of Korea is governed through representative democracy. The National Assembly is the single-chamber parliamentary institution of Korea, constitutionally co-equal to the popularly elected president (the head of the executive), and to the judiciary. The Korean form of government[1] is essentially a presidential one with some features of a parliamentary form of government, such as prime ministership instead of vice-presidentship and the National Assembly's power to vote for the removal of prime minister and ministers—a version of the vote of no confidence. The president owes nothing to the National Assembly for his or her existence, and is not politically responsible to it for actions he or she takes during the single five-year presidential term of office.

Whereas the National Assembly has the legislative power, the president has the power to veto National-Assembly-made legislation; although the National Assembly can in turn override such a veto by a two-thirds vote.

Since the establishment of the Kim Yong-Sam administration in February 1993, it has undertaken unprecedented and wide-ranging reforms, including reforms to the election system, and to laws regulating political parties—in particular the financing of political parties. *The Election of Public Officials and the Prevention of Corruption in Elections Act* (1994) exemplifies the changes brought about by reform. This chapter explains how Korea's election system is organised, and examines the influences political parties exert on the operation of the government and on elections, the conducting of election campaigns, the regulation of political parties, and how each of these matters are affected by the reformist legislation. Finally, it discusses problems that exist in the theory and practice of Korea's program of electoral reform.

THE ELECTORAL SYSTEM IN KOREA

Constitutional Article 77 provides:

> (1) The National Assembly shall be composed of members elected by universal, equal, direct and secret ballot by the citizens. (2) The number of members of the National Assembly shall be determined by law, but the number shall be more than 200. (3) The constituencies of members of the National Assembly, proportional representation and other matters pertaining to the National Assembly election shall be determined by law.

Constitutional Article 78 provides: 'The term of office of members of the National Assembly shall be four years.' Consequently, the methods of choosing members of the National Assembly (including proportional representation) and the exact number of members of the National Assembly are statutory matters for the National Assembly to determine. According to the *National Assembly Members Election Act* (1991) or the recently legislated *Election of Public Officials and the Prevention of Corruption in Elections Act* (1994), the National Assembly is composed of two groups of members totalling 299 representatives, who are selected by different methods but who otherwise have the same rights, privileges and obligations.

The first group of 237 members is elected from the 237 single-member local electoral districts; and the second group of 62 members is selected from the national political party lists, according to the performance of their respective parties at the general election which chooses the first group of 237 members. In each of the 237 electoral districts, the candidate who obtains the largest number of votes cast wins a National Assembly seat. A single candidate in a particular local district has to obtain votes equal in number to at least a third of the total number of voters in the district in order to win the National Assembly seat unopposed. The current 62 seats from 'the national district' were allocated among the political parties according to provisions of the *National Assembly Members Election Act* (1991), in proportion to the seats they respectively attained from local districts in the general election of 1992. Under the *Election of Public Officials and the Prevention of Corruption in Elections Act* (1994) (the so-called *Combined Election Act*), national district seats are allocated on the basis of the ratio of the votes that the political parties gained in the general election for the local district seats. Under the old law (1991) a seat from 'the national district' was to be assigned to a minor party that had not been allocated a national district seat, in accordance with the rule that applied when a party won no seat at all or won less than five seats from local districts if it had got 3% of the total valid votes cast in the general election. Political parties are thus very important to a candidate, but are not decisive in a candidate's success in running for a local seat. One can run as an independent without a party nomination. The political parties are, however, integral elements of the national district system.

The second group of 62 members is called the National Assembly 'members from the national district'. The term 'members from the national district' is a misnomer in the sense that the voters do not have any say over their selection. Only exceptionally is a 'national district' seat allocated to a minor party that obtained no seat or won less than five seats from the general election for local district seats if it got 3% of the total votes cast at the election; that is, according to the ratio of the votes acquired under the old rule, and if it got 3% to 5% of the total votes cast under the new rule. The apportionment of local electoral districts is also a statutory matter for the National Assembly to determine in consideration of population sizes, local administrative divisions, physical features of the units, traffic and other conditions. The population size of each local electoral district in fact varies from 80 000 to 340 000, with the average size being about 200 000.

A Korean national who is twenty years old or older is entitled to vote, unless he or she (1) is declared by the court to be incompetent or to have a limited capacity on the ground of insanity, and so on; (2) is sentenced to imprisonment or to a heavier penalty whose execution has not yet been terminated or suspended; (3) is sentenced to a fine of more than 1 million Won (about US$1250) for an election-related offence and five years have not elapsed, is sentenced to probation for an election-related offence and ten years have not elapsed, or is sentenced to imprisonment or to a heavier penalty for an election-related offence and ten years have not elapsed since its termination or suspension; (4) is suspended or deprived of his or her right to vote by a decision of the court.

A Korean national who is 25 years old or older is entitled to run for the National Assembly, unless he or she (1) lacks the right to vote according to rules 1, 3 and 4 mentioned above; (2) is sentenced to imprisonment or to a heavier penalty which has not been declared elapsed; (3) is suspended or deprived of his or her right to vote by a decision of the court or by any other statutory provision.

Intending candidates must register at an appropriate election management committee during the two-day period sixteen days prior to the election day (within three days of an election announcement, under the law of 1991). Under the new law a determinate day—the first Thursday 50 days after the day when the term of office of the former National Assembly members expires—is statutorily set as the election day. Prior to this new law, any day could be announced as election day. Intending candidates for local district seats must file with the proper local election management committee a recommendation (nomination as a candidate) letter from the political party of which he or she is a member—or, if he or she has no party affiliation, a recommendation signed by 300 to 500 voters (700 or more voters under the law of 1991).

Formerly, intending candidates for national district seats were required to file with the National Election Management Committee their party list of names for the national district and a letter of their consent within five days of the announcement of the impending election. Under the new law the nominating party must file the registration form, nomination certificate, party list of names for the national district, and each candidate's letter of consent. The party determines the order of the names in the national party.

A person who intends to run for a local district seat is also required to deposit at the proper local election management committee a sum of 10 million Won (about US$12 500). This deposit requirement is in fact designed to discourage one from making a hasty, unconsidered decision to run, in order to avoid the emergence of extreme pluralism with multiple irresponsible splinter groups on the political horizon. The deposit requirement remains unchanged under the new law. Initially an independent candidate without party affiliation had to deposit double the amount, that is, 20 million Won, but this discriminatory requirement was struck out as repugnant to the equal protection of law clause of the Constitution (Article 11) by the Constitutional Court.[2] In the event that a candidate who wins the election, dies, or acquires more than half of the number of votes calculated when the total valid votes are divided by the number of the total candidates in each district, his or her deposited money is returned minus expenses for removal of illegal posters and so on and/or minus the cost of fines incurred. A candidate who quits, wins less than half of the number of votes calculated when the total votes are divided by the number of candidates, or whose registration is found to be invalid has his or her deposit forfeited to the national treasury. If none of a party's candidates win the national constituencies in which they contested, that party also forfeits its deposit. Under the 1991 law deductions were made for legitimately incurred campaign expenses.

Statutorily a party member may not register as an independent. This rule applies for the particular election even if he or she leaves his or her party, changes his or her party affiliation, or is expelled from his or her party during the registration period (during a period falling between the day when the election day is officially announced and the day when the registration is closed for candidacy, under the old law). This particular provision is to discourage a party member from changing his or her party affiliation or from running as an independent after he or she has failed to get his or her party's endorsement (nomination) as a candidate. The constitutionality of the provision is, however, doubtful, in the sense that it interferes with one's freedom to run as a candidate with unnecessary severity.

Once a candidate has been elected to the National Assembly, there is no rule preventing a member from changing party affiliation or quitting party membership; and in 1992 about 35 members either changed their party affiliation or quit their party membership (thus becoming 'independents') following their swearing-in as National Assembly members. The change of party affiliation by three national district National Assembly members provoked particular controversy because they were originally selected on the grounds of party affiliation and party strength in the National Assembly (or in the popular vote at the general election).[3] No action was taken against them, but the National Assembly adopted a statutory rule as a provision of *The Election of Public Officials and the Prevention of Corruption in Elections Act* (1994) against members retaining their status as National Assembly members should national district representatives change party affiliation (Article 192 Section 4). As a corollary of the rule (*expressio unius exclusio alterius*) members representing local districts will not lose their National Assembly membership status even if they have party affiliation.

THE POLITICAL PARTIES IN THE ELECTORAL SYSTEM

One can run for a local National Assembly seat as a candidate without party endorsement or nomination, but the influence and power of the major parties are such that in many electoral districts party endorsement practically guarantees electoral success. Those whose names appear on the major parties' list for the national district, moreover, can even become members of the National Assembly with a small campaign effort. The chance to become a member for the national district is particularly guaranteed if the candidate's name tops the party list, and this leads to competition among political aspirants to acquire a major party's endorsement or nomination for a local electoral district or for the national district.

This keen competition may have helped to create the highly centralised party nomination process. In the lead-up to elections the leadership of each of the major parties form committees to select from among many aspirants the most suitable nominees for particular local districts and for the national district.

Control over the nomination process by centralised party organisations is under criticism, and 'in-party' democracy is being advocated.[4] Accordingly, the major parties have introduced some measures giving a voice to district-level party members when nominating candidates for their electoral districts and also when choosing chairpersons for their district party organisations. But the influence of the practically self-appointed bosses in party organisations is such that it will take time for full-scale in-party democracy to be realised.

Another aspect of the nomination process facing criticism concerns the favouritism that is shown to the aspirants who donate the most to their party's coffers. In the financially less-endowed opposition party the nomination process for the national district is almost openly utilised as a tool to raise party funds. Thus critics of the practice liken it to a modern form of sale of official positions. Money involved in the nomination process is, however, only part of the bigger problem of 'big money politics' closely associated with corruption and illegal electoral practices.

The existence of National Assembly seats for the national district is presently justified on the basis that it allows for the recruitment— for the good of the party and of the nation—of nationally recognised talented persons, including professionals, who are locally not well known or popular. This method can be used as a substitute functional representation institution in addition to political representation based on local electoral districts. Professionals, business executives, labour leaders and others have indeed been recruited for the national district seats. Overall, however, it is doubtful how they can be 'representatives' of the people or of their professions or of their walks of life without the existence of any election process by which the voters or the candidates' professional colleagues can have a say over their selection as National Assembly members in more than just an indirect way. Their selection as candidates for the national district is more likely to be determined through their personal ties with party bosses or party influentials, or on the basis of their monetary donations to their party's treasury.

One proposal is that voters have two votes, one for a particular political party, and another for candidates from their particular local district. This idea of a second vote has not been adopted in the new law, however, although the change in the method of selecting the national members from a system based on the party strength of local members to a system based on the ratio of the popular votes cast in the general election for local seats is partly designed to meet the criticisms mentioned above. This aspect of the recent electoral reform makes a return to the institution of the National Assembly members for the national district provided for in *The National Assembly Members Election Act* of 1963. Before the law of 1963 Korea did not know any other election methods other than that of one representative from each of the local electoral districts.

The political parties clause of the Constitution (Article 8) provides for the principle of pluralism (plural party system), the right of freedom to form a political party, state subsidies to political parties and the dissolution of political parties found to be unconstitutional. According to the *Political Parties Act* implementing the clause, a political party must meet several requirements in order to be qualified for all the privileges and rights its party status provides. Parties must situate their central organisation in the capital, and local district party organisations must be located in a certain number of the local electoral districts scattered across the nation. District party organisations are furthermore required to have certain numbers of party members. Although this statutory requirement favours big parties above minor parties, it also contributes to political stability by preventing extreme pluralism (that is, very small parties with limited public support) from emerging. The requirement has also led to a considerable number of new, imaginative, parties—particularly progressive parties—seeking to enter the political arena. The current government party (the Democratic Liberal Party) and the major opposition party (the Democratic Party) are both conservative parties, and no liberal, progressive party is represented in the National Assembly.

Nationally based political parties are top-heavy organisations internally, and many important party decisions, including decisions concerning endorsement of candidates for the local electoral districts and for the national district, are *de facto* determined by party bosses and various party committees and offices. In many cases a political party is a confederation of the party bosses whose power lies in their ability to lead their followers and to raise funds to support their followers and their party. It is only natural that party decisions are made on the basis of consensus reached among these bosses rather than by a simple majority rule. When a strong or charismatic leader emerges, however, they dominate in the party.

These statements have implications for the classic presidential form of government: in a presidential government—whose classic characteristic is supposed to be a strict separation of power, with an independent parliament *vis-à-vis* the president—an integration of power is brought about through the party link between the parliament and the president when the party that produces the president occupies the majority of the parliamentary seats.

Consequently the National Assembly, rather than being a co-equal
constitutional institution, has now been rendered a secondary institution in its power relations with the president. It has in fact become
merely an important forum in which interactions (including con-
frontations, concessions and compromises) between the government
and the government party on the one hand and the opposition
parties on the other are taking place as part of the policy-making
process.

CAMPAIGN FUNDS AND ACTIVITIES

Perhaps the most drastic changes brought by the reform drive have
occurred in political financing matters.[5]

A Presidential Emergency Decree announced on 13 August
1993[6] a system in which all bank accounts must be held under one's
real name. Previously one could open accounts under a false name
or somebody else's name, and such accounts were widely used for
various illegal and immoral purposes, including bribery, storing
illegally obtained donations, money laundering, tax evasion, and so
on, all entailing little fear of the perpetrator being caught. This
'underground economy' is said to have accounted for some 30% of
the national economy. Consequent to the Presidential Emergency
Decree all illegal, publicly unaccounted for donations used by
politicians and the political parties have been virtually foreclosed.
Culturally, the idea of an 'open political donation' has never been
favourably perceived by the citizenry; from now on it will not be
easy for politicians to raise sufficient funds to meet their former
expectations, and future electoral campaigns will have to exercise
uncharacteristic economy.

The *Political Financing Act* provides for four ways by which
political funds can legitimately be raised by the political parties and
politicians, including the present National Assembly members and
future aspirants: (1) party membership dues; (2) private monetary
donations; (3) financial support from organisations specifically
organised by particular political parties or politicians (a version of
North American political action committees); and (4) state subsidies to the political parties. The problem with membership dues is
that funds from this source constitute only a small portion of the
total income of a party: few parties have sufficient members willing
to pay their dues. Regarding methods 2 and 3 the opposition parties
complain of poor results, because typical middle-class people are
reluctant to provide open financial support to them.

The newly amended law of 1994 provides for the sale of 'cou-
pons' (anonymous receipts for money contributed to political
parties) which can be bought without the purchaser's name being

revealed. The problem with the fourth source of political finance, state subsidies, is that it derives from taxpayers' money at the rate of 800 Won (US$1) for every voter, annually. Under the new law state subsidies are allocated annually and in election years to political parties having members in the National Assembly. This allocation is made on the basis of party strength and popular votes at the previous general or local election. Thus, the independent candidates do not get any comparable subsidies from the state treasury for running in the general election. In principle, moreover, state subsidies do not conform with the idea of political parties as voluntary organisations which people freely form, dissolve, join or quit. In 1993, state subsidies formed roughly a quarter of the total budget for the government party (DLP) and three-quarters of the total for the opposition party (DP).

The Election of Public Officials and the Prevention of Corruption in Elections Act (1994) has roughly halved the sum candidates were statutorily allowed to disburse for campaigning expenses in each local electoral district, from approximately 120 million Won (US$150 000) to approximately 65 million Won (US$81 250). The amount of money statutorily allowed for election campaign expenses—to be determined by district election management committees—varies between districts, depending upon such local conditions as population size and the number of administrative units. (Under the old law, rents, hiring expenses for campaign workers, and so on were included for the calculation of the permitted amounts of campaign money.)

What has changed concerns not only the total amounts of the allowed campaign expenses but also the enforcement of the statutory provision limiting the amounts of campaign expenses allowed in each electoral district. Previously the provision was not vigorously enforced and candidates were only required to report total campaign expenditure to the local election management committee after the election.

In reality no-one was bound by the statutory limitation and it was said that in most cases the real levels of expenses incurred were several times larger than the reported amounts. Now all the money for campaign uses must be deposited in bank accounts and drawn out of them, and all the details of what amounts of money for campaign purposes were disbursed to whom—of what address and identification number—when, and where have to be reported to the local election management committee after the election. All reported campaign expenses have to be reported and an election management committee is empowered to request necessary papers from banks for investigation purposes when there is a doubt about the accuracy of reported campaign expenses. Moreover, the penal measures to be taken against violators of the election law are much strengthened: a person who is sentenced to a fine of 1 million Won (US $1250) or more is deprived of his or her right to run for public office for five years, and someone who is sentenced to imprisonment combined with an immediate release on probation or to heavier punishment is barred from running for public office for ten years. A seat becomes vacant when a member, his or her spouse, campaign manager, parent or child commits an election-related offence.

CONCLUSION

The idea of elections in which an able person, even without a fortune, can successfully run for a seat in the National Assembly has been entertained by the citizens of South Korea for a long time. It was the motivation behind reforms to the law concerning elections, political parties and political financing and marks an important step in the recent reform drive.

Yet the new law does not mean that such desirable features as in-party democracy, cleaner politics, and other ideas of political reform in relation to political parties, elections and financing, will take root quickly. Mass society has emerged concurrently with industrialisation in Korea, and so mass-based political parties will have to emerge. There is always the chance that representatives will emerge who are prepared to yield to the caprice of the mass mood, rather than leading the nation with determination towards democracy and prosperity, navigating the turbulent sea of world politics and the world economy. There is no doubt that there will be numerous politicians, especially given the present system of political parties, financing, and elections; but there is no guarantee that Korea will have the statesmen and stateswomen whom it so badly needs at this historical juncture.

6

Back to the Future: Panchayats and Governance in India

Rajeev Dhavan and Ruchi Pant

DESIGN FAULTS AND FAILURE TO DESIGN

Few Indians witness democracy as part of their daily lives. India's relative success as a political democracy founded on the rule of law conceals more than it reveals. If general elections in India portray the maturity of the ordinary voter in making difficult choices for complex reasons, they also show that democracy is losing rather than gaining ground. Elections are fought with money and muscle power. Intimations of the public interest have given rise to self-seeking politicians and public servants, mindful only of their own future and determined to make the most of their stint in public life to garner the spoils of development. The greater and more expansive have been the government's plans to redistribute resources and opportunity, the greater has been the corruption of its own processes. This is not because honest politicians have been diverted into wrongful greed in order to win the next election. The enormity of caprice is much greater than the necessities that are claimed to inspire it. High on rhetoric and pregnant with enormous programmatic resources, the system itself has failed to make its rulers accountable. Vigilant activism, a persistent press and activist law courts have threatened, exposed and reversed whatever they can; but within limits. By and large, India's rulers—who include all those who exercise public power in petty and powerful positions alike—have been relatively free to do what they like; and they have chosen to exercise this responsible discretion in their own favour! Public power has, willy-nilly, become the fiefdom of private interests. The various measures taken to engage this corruption—through special vigilance commissions, ombudspersons (called lokpals and lokayuktas), parliamentary investigations and commissions of inquiry—have failed to stem the tide. The abandonment of the regulatory system of permissions (pejoratively referred to as licence raj) may transfer some of the arbitrariness of irresponsible power from public fora to private interests in civil society, but without any enhancement of participation or control by ordinary people, who will remain victims rather than beneficiaries of India's system of democracy.

Without entering into a wider examination of the failures of Indian democracy, we are concerned here with an inherent design fault in the Indian Constitution, which the Constitution-makers were aware of but brushed aside. The essential feature of this design fault was the creation of a social and political distance between those who exercise power at civil, political and state levels and those against or in respect of whom power is exercised. This distance is not founded on geography, but rather is based on the extent to which ordinary people subjectively and objectively feel that they can approach decision-makers to obtain favourable outcomes. We are concerned not just with consequential outcomes but also with the manner and extent to which people feel part of the system of social and political governance. By focusing on both social and political governance, we emphasise that the feeling and factum of dis-empowerment exists at all levels in society. Exclusive concern about improving access to governmental processes fails to acknowledge that 'civil' and 'political' are only theoretically separable entities, which in reality feed on each other.

What the Indian political system has witnessed is the creation of highly personalised, idiosyncratic and wholly unaccountable mediators of social and political distance who have either usurped power or become power brokers who pimp decision making and state patronage. If the system of governance has a very loose system of accountability, the parallel and, often, alternative power system has virtually none. Deriving strength from their own excesses, both civil and public governance have become irrepressibly irresponsible. But the 'design faults' are much too extensive for these powerful forces in private and public society to suffer continual and ongoing discipline. The Constitution made too many unwarranted assump-tions about the manner in which power would be appropriated. It left the people with no control over their representatives; and the representatives with no control over the rulers. Based on a system of delegation of authority, Indian society has ceased to be people oriented. Instead of making room for the greater participation of people, the Constitution encouraged those in power to do no more than simply manage a minimal consent on the basis of a rock-bottom legitimacy that played on the people's habitual respect for authority, and on their inherent lack of choice in a system that was simultaneously superconductive to its own abuse and ruthless towards those who questioned civil and public authority. Essentially systems of minimal legitimacy/maximum delegation, private and public governance have neither inspired respect nor succeeded in delivering the goods. Most of the plans of government suffer from entropic disease, so that they fritter away as people hijack the benefits of the state's welfare programs from the intended beneficiaries and into corrupt pockets.

Against this, there are only a few checks and balances: public opinion, activist protest, elections and the rule of law. All of these are insufficient monitors if the constantly shifting boundaries of abuse are substantial so that they cannot be breached. But the design fault in formulating the system of governance was not that an inherently good system was vulnerable to abuse. The design fault was that given the enormity of the social and political distance between the governors and a viable democracy, the system was as unworkable as its abuse was inevitable. None of the methods of bridging this distance were bona fide. Even though the press and activists were vigilant and the law courts enunciated a great deal of public interest and due process doctrine to stimulate sensitivity, participation and results, these successes were engulfed in the sea of unaccountable power over which there was little control and which yielded little compassion. This major design fault, which had both practical and normative implications, was lost sight of during the making of India's Constitution. The framers of the Constitution assumed that the same parliamentary model that had succeeded elsewhere in the world would succeed in India.

Yet despite the existence of schemes of local government in some of these other countries, the problem of social, political and public distance remains crucial in determining the widespread disempowerment of people. Uninformed consent based on limited or distorted information remains the norm. People easily become the by-product of governance rather than its central concern.

THE CONSTITUTION AND AFTER

The Indian Constituent Assembly was elected in mid-1946 and the Constitution for the new Indian Union was debated in the Assembly between 1947 and 1949. The Assembly itself operated as a provisional parliament for India until the first general elections were held in 1952. In the Constituent Assembly of India there was some focused concern about this design fault in the constitutional scheme. This concern centred around the Gandhian alternative to India's overcentralised Constitution, which, though high on goals, made the government remote from the people. Gandhi had not actually spelt out any constitutional alternatives, even though a blueprint attributed to him was doing the rounds[1] and was referred to in the Constituent Assembly.[2] Apart from the general dispute as to whether the Constitution fulfilled Gandhi's 'great mission'[3] or whether 'Gandhiji's socialism was not represented',[4] there was major concern about the overcentralisation of the Constitution, which had created a very powerful Union. This, it was repeated again and again, was necessary. A weak Centre was an invitation to real and illusory enemies. Planning imperatives dictated that the Centre be given definitive control over revenue raising and resource distribution. Even in the crucial areas of trade, commerce, mining and industry—which were exclusive State subjects—Union regulation was permitted, and has since ruled the roost.[5] The argument over centralisation was generally lost and did not resurface until the Sarkaria Commission showed that the Union had undermined Indian federalism in a number of political, administrative and financial respects[6]. With centralisation in place over the unsystematic protest of some members, the Assembly voiced pointed concern over what the Constitution would mean to ordinary citizens if Gandhi's struggle and *ashirvad* (blessing) gave power to the peasants and to labour.[7] A proper transfer of power should have been from the British to the villagers.[8] The Assembly maintained that without local government there would be 'sovietization and totalitarianism'.[9] But given the design of the Constitution, which knowingly transferred power to political elites and administration with little restraint, the case of the people could not be rewritten into the Constitution. It could only be added on as an 'extra'—almost as a sop. And this little extra consisted of making a case for village panchayats (councils) and local administration. Panchayats were created at village level as part of an effort to recreate traditional forms of government.

It is fashionable to recall Ambedkar's famous statement that the

> love of intellectual Indians for the village community is . . . infinite but pathetic . . . What is the village but a sink of localism, a den of ignorance, narrow mindedness and communalism. I am glad that the Draft Constitution has discarded the village and adopted the individual as its unit.[10]

This created a storm of protest, even if some people, indulgently explained that his 'strong remarks . . . were apparently based on his own experience'.[11] Ambedkar had seen and experienced the prejudice and power of village communities in meting out inequity and injustice without remorse. Even if Ambedkar's remarks had caused 'great pain',[12] they reflected a truth that could not be left unstated. The panchayat system was used by 'local influential classes . . . for their selfish motives (to enable) village zamindars, village talukdars [landowners and educated groups], the Mahajans and the money lending class to exploit the less cultured, the less educated poor classes of the villages'.[13] This is not to accept the argument that villages had to be 'freed from the shackles of ignorance and superstition [before they became] . . . the backbone of the Constitution',[14] but rather is to emphasise that given the extent to which local/social power would reproduce itself as tyrannical public and political power, 'the Assembly would have very carefully to consider whether by throwing the village panchayats into the whirlpool of party politics, [it] . . . would not be destroying once and for all their usefulness as agencies of Administration'.[15] Yet, this no more than posed the problem. The solution lay not in rejecting local democracy, but in ensuring that the Constitution 'should provide for the establishment of village republics'[16] to ensure that the new Constitution gave 'villagers real power to rule and get money and expend it in the hands of the villagers' so that, even if 'the individual is the soul of the Constitution, the village should be made the basis of the machinery of administration'[17] and a fabric of governance that simply had to be rebuilt.[18]

The response of the Constitution-makers seemed stage-managed. If there was a demand for village republics, the way out was to introduce a Directive Principle involving a constitutional commitment to 'organise village panchayats and endow them with such powers and authority as may be necessary to enable them to exist as units of self government'. Proposed by Santhanam, it was immediately accepted by Ambedkar.[19] This was greeted as an act of grace that would be an antidote to Chinese Communism[20] and which would provide Indians with 'something they can call their country's Constitution'[21] because '. . . if there was any living cell in the Constitution, it will be this panchayat amendment'.[22] Doubts about villages being self-sufficient economic and administrative units were rejected on the ground that they would be viable 'if properly worked and organised on the basis of self sufficiency'[23] and through mutual exchange with other villages.[24] Yet what was abundantly clear was that the Constitution-makers had, in fact, made no commitment to creating self-sufficient social and economic units. Villages were seen very much as part of the mainstream economy and vulnerable to its extravagances. The Directive Principle (Article 40) simply stated: 'The State shall take steps to organise village panchayats and endow them with such powers and authority as may be necessary to enable them to function as units of self government.'

In order to effect this, the State legislatures (Seventh Schedule, List II E.5) were given powers over: 'Local government, that is to say, the constitution and powers of municipal corporations, improvement trusts, district boards, mining settlement authorities and other local authorities for the purpose of local self government or village administration.'

The Constitution prescribed a weak and general duty and a discretionary legislative power to fulfil the demands of local democracy. Everything else in the Constitution militated against providing any kind of local resources or empowerment for these units of local administration. Even where State legislatures had powers to raise revenue by imposing a tax on professions, trades, callings or employments, the constitutional limit for such an imposition was Rs 250 (Article 276), later raised to Rs 2500 (Constitution (Sixtieth Amendment Act 1988)).

Within the constitutional scheme local government was incidental, something that existed and operated as a matter of course and which would fit into the overall system of centralised planning. It was not a foundation stone on which the Constitution rested. It was a concessionary playground in which Gandhians could go and play until the planning process found better use for local administration as an outlet for planned change.

Panchayats were set up immediately in all States.[25] But, once they were there, what was to be done with them? Even if the Soviet collectivisation models had commended themselves, India's agrarian reform legislation had been formulated in such a way that vested interests in individual holdings had been too deeply entrenched in the new agrarian economy. Proposals for collectives and co-operatives came well after property rights were individuated. Village administration would have virtually no 'common property' or 'common resources'. They would also have no control over 'common programs'. If village identities were founded on a commonality of culture, there was a decreasing commonality of interests as the economy of the village was powerfully recast so that the new emerging interests were ready to appropriate any power vacuum and transcend any traditional authority that stood in their way. The principal problems with the new panchayats established immediately after independence were that they were powerless. Common property notions were limited (as in the case of Uttar Pradesh) to gram sabha land (land belonging to the assembly of the panchayat), which was very limited in its extent and which could be resumed by the State.

The great uncertainty about finding an appropriate role for panchayats arose from the certainty about centralised planning—and the power structure needed to give effect to it. The parallel district administration and new programmatic bureaucracies monopolised power and resources. Under the earlier dispensation, if panchayats had any place, it was as adjuncts to the planning process. This finds strong reflection in the Balwantrai Mehta Committee's deliberations in 1957. Including—in addition to Mehta—Shankar Dayal Sharma, B. G. Rao, Phool Singh and G. Ramachandran (with D. P. Singh as secretary), the group was a 'Team for the Study of Community Projects and National Extension Service' constituted as a 'Committee on Plan Projects'. Its brief focused on the extent of success in 'utilizing local initiative and in creating institutions to ensure continuity in the process of improving economic and social conditions in rural areas'. The Committee's Report had many tentative elements and reflected uncertainties about what should be allocated where and for what reason. There was, however, little difficulty in assigning to women the care of the cow, kitchen garden and poultry, as well as the use of needle and thread and conducting of cookery classes. But, if parts of the Report represented co–ordinated decentralisation, panchayat power remained a democratic 'extra' to be fitted into the existing structure of planning. The process of planning was not adjusted to respond to the imperatives of people's power. The creation of the middle 'block' or tier was a requirement of co-ordinated planning and not a mechanism to assimilate the power of the people into a position of strength. The Balwantrai compromise which, taken at its most cynical, represents the rock-bottom concession that something is better than nothing, came to be reflected in other reports[26], and the Planning Commission perspective on panchayats as adjuncts never totally disappeared. It remains with us. The Ashok Mehta Committee[27] was aware of the parsimonious release of genuine power to the panchayats. This was reflected in two distinct ways. The first was that the people who came together as the village assembly or gram sabha were not to be given power. Thus, even at village level people were not to be empowered. It was their delegates who were to be empowered. The position of the gram sabha has always been regarded with little confidence by the designers of panchayat institutions. Even when the Joint Committee on the Constitution (72nd Amendment) Bill 1991 considered the position of panchayats, it made the telling determination: 'The Committee feel that the Gram Sabha cannot exercise any powers and that at best it can perform certain functions—the details of such functions can be best laid down by the legislature of the State.'[28]

Although the Constitution (73rd Amendment) 1992 does not reflect a denial of power to the gram sabha, the idea that gram sabhas are really electoral bodies and no more defeats the whole purpose behind empowering communities in their local presence.

The second problem from the perspective of effective people's empowerment was that real decision making eluded panchayat structures. The Ashok Mehta Committee recognised that the then existing legislation did not delineate clearly defined functions for panchayats but used shifting and vague categories such as 'optional', 'agency', and 'obligatory' to define empowerment. What was essential was that ' . . . all the Panchayati Raj Institutions are vested with the authority to take their own decisions and plan according to their own requirements'.[29] But where was this genuine empowerment to come from, if the panchayats did not use a wider concept of 'common property', did not have powers of land-use planning, and were not given real and effective powers and functions over the things that really affected people's lives such as food, health, education, work and programmatic support? These welfare benefits have been called the 'new property'.[30] Understandably, the custodian of the 'new property' possesses real power. And, if State and planning authorities were not willing to share this custodianship with local persons and institutions, the latter would be marginalised into redundancy.

If the panchayat movement came into being despite government opposition, it was because certain State governments took steps to breathe life into relatively moribund institutions. This was generously but accurately admitted by Rajiv Gandhi when he moved the Constitution (64th Amendment) Bill 1989.[31] The experiments referred to were the Andhra, Karnataka and West Bengal experiments. The Andhra Pradesh Mandal Praja Parishads, Zila Praja Parishads and Zila Pranalika Abhivrudhi Mandals Act 1986 ('Mandal' Act) sought to break down the power barrier by providing effective reservation for women and Scheduled Castes and Scheduled Tribes (SC & ST) and shifting financial and programmatic responsibility further down the line. The Karnataka Zila Parishads, Taluk Panchiyat Samities, Mandal Panchayats and Nyaya Panchayats Act 1983 enlarged representation, responsibilities, functions and powers within severe limitations of finance and with only a partial readjustment of planning perspectives.[32] Like the Bengal experiment[33] the experiments in Andhra and Karnataka must be treated as significant but transitional in nature. They are significant because they made a dent in the top-heavy planning framework within which all government discourse had hitherto been located. They were transitional because they were in the nature of experiments, which succeeded to the extent they did because the barrier of distrust against empowering people (other than as voters) was lifted. They proved to be important catalysts which immediately flung the slogan of 'the empowerment of people through panchayats' to echo down the labyrinthine corridors of party politics.

THE PANCHAYAT AMENDMENTS

The idea that an amendment of the Constitution was needed to secure a place for panchayati democracy was proposed by the Ashok Mehta Committee.[34] It was presumably to this that Rajiv Gandhi made reference when he defended State government's power to dissolve panchayats as an idea originating from the Bharatiya Janata Party.[35] The Mehta proposals were skeletal, suggesting a two-tier structure: financial responsibility in the matter of fund-raising, and legislative responsibility, devolving upon State legislature in the assignment of executive and administrative functions; and responsibility devolving upon nyaya [equity or justice] panchayats for civil justice. The basic framework was accommodating, and hoped that the 'State Government shall . . . endeavour to devolve progressively greater powers and responsibilities on the councils to enable them to function effectively as institutions of self-government'.[36] This was really an oversimplified scheme of administrative devolution, leaving something to the State legislatures but a great deal to State governments.

It is because matters lay fallow for over a decade that surprise greeted the Constitution (64th Amendment) Bill 1989, which was personally piloted by Rajiv Gandhi, and which subsequently became an electoral issue when it was defeated by one vote in the Rajya Sabha (upper house or Council of States).[37]

The opposition could not have taken the line that the amendments creating panchayat democracy were misplaced. The Janata Dal Party approved of such devolution, and the lead had been taken by opposition governments. In July 1989, the Janata Dal strongly approved of such devolutionary initiatives.[38] In the actual debates themselves, opposition members took the somewhat technical line that the amendments would threaten the basic federal structure of the Constitution. This was a political ploy, because very little of the argument has been heard of since.

The proposal plunged into controversy in advance of revelation. The *Indian Express* revealed that what was brewing involved all kinds of top-down control destined to make the proposed rural and urban bodies candidates for a puppet show.[39] Not surprisingly, when the 64th and 65th Constitution Amendments reached Parliament one of the members acidly remarked, 'Prime Minister Gandhi is a great lover of super computers and electronics. Probably he wants to control panchayats and nagarpalikas sitting here in Delhi . . . It is a kind of madness to bring these amendments'.[40] When Mr Gandhi was confronted in Parliament with the indictment that governors could suspend panchayats at will (just as President's Rule was arbitrarily imposed on States), he claimed that all that had been 'thrown in the dustbin . . . (a)nd those that grovel in the dustbin only find what is in the dustbin'. But, adding insult to intrigue, he insisted that it was the Janata government who had suggested this clause in 1978.[41]

But, why did the Congress propose to include it? And was it sent to the dustbin only because of advance adverse publicity? Was the entire induction of these panchayats 'thoughtless, with little application of mind?'[42] The 64th and 65th Amendment Bills surfaced, after a period of considerable embarrassment, in mid May 1989. The charge of thoughtlessness was brilliantly expressed by L. C. Jain:

> We appear to have suddenly discovered a magic wand to solve the problems of the country overnight: in instant law for panchayats (64th Amendment), for municipalities (65th Amendment), for Cooperatives, (66th Amendment), for land reforms (67th Amendment). But all these pale into insignificance compared to the likely 68th Amendment—to ban the practice of carrying night soil on the head.[43]

But the Local Government Amendments (for Rural Panchayats and Urban/Nagarpalikas) had acquired an important place in the electoral agenda, replacing earlier economic promises to remove poverty and redistribute wealth with new political agendas ostensibly suggestive of people's empowerment. This had become crucially important at this critical juncture because the opposition ministries in Bengal, Karnataka and Andhra had, as Mr Gandhi confessed, successfully advanced beyond the Congress States in carrying out effective statutory schemes of local political empowerment.[44] And since the States had already done their bit,[45] what was the point of this exercise? The newspaper response to this was as mixed[46] as popular reaction was dormant. Nobody could oppose decentralisation of power. But there was something unconvincing about the Congress's claims that there had been a national discussion[47] or that the Special Committee which had written a 'Concept Paper on the Revitalization of Panchayati Raj institutions for Democracy and Development' had vetted the proposal properly.[48] The Concept Paper was not otherwise available for public scrutiny. Given the newspaper leaks that a Draconian proposal was in the pipeline, it is hardly surprising that the panchayat proposals were greeted with a denigrating suspicion.

The second attempt to formulate a constitutional amendment in 1991–92 was discussed in a much more politically relaxed atmosphere. Much had happened since 1989. The easy way out of the controversy was to refer the Constitution (72nd Amendment) Bill of 1991 to a Joint Committee. It is difficult to state with confidence that the Joint Committee displayed much incisiveness in its deliberations. Public response to it was significant but not far-flung. The

Committee emerged with an overall consensus except on a few specific issues such as nyaya panchayats,[49] the non-extension of the provisions to the hilly regions of the Darjeelini Gorkha Council,[50] and the election of the panchayat chairperson.[51] More generally, a view was expressed that the basic structure of the amendment should be to do no more than ensure regularity of election, reservations for women and SC & ST and constitutional sanction of devolution of powers.[52] What the Joint Committee did discover was the gram sabha. An effort was made to make it a constitutional collectivity rather than just an electoral body. But as we have already shown there was a reluctance to empower it on the basis that 'the Gram Sabha cannot exercise any powers and that at best it can perform certain functions'.[53] The distinction between powers and functions is a fine one and is not reflected in the text of the amendment. There are a number of other changes in the manner of elections; and, more especially, in the matter of entrusting the electoral process to the hands of a specially appointed autonomous State Election Commission.[54] In terms of basic design, it was more complex than the Ashok Mehta Draft and built on the structure of Rajiv Gandhi's original proposal of 1989. Even the controversy over the power of the government to dissolve panchayats (akin to the Union's power to impose President's Rule on States) impliedly remained, even though such a fuss had been made about it in 1989. Now, the Joint Committee simply left it in the hands of the State legislatures to determine how, and in what way and by whom, a panchayat could be dissolved 'sooner' than its constitutional term of five years (see Article 243 E). The debate on the Bill was more historic than plenary.[55] There was a feeling that too much deliberation had already taken place, and that it was now time to discharge pledges and face the local politics of contemporary history.

The Panchayat Amendments of 1992 do not, in fact, alter the basic pattern of devolution that pre-existed in the Constitution. The positive features are compulsion (the devolution must take place—Article 243 A), and a reservation of seats for Scheduled Castes and Scheduled Tribes and women. The negative features are a clumsy and incomplete devolution with a delimitation of subjects (in the 11th Schedule) leaving important aspects of the devolution to the State legislatures. The amendment revels in ambiguity. At the root of the problem is the superimposition of a new system on an already settled structure which has been appropriated by highly individual, often greedy, vested interests who simultaneously, will not surrender devolved power to the panchayats and will corrupt what exists so that the third layer of governance may well become a layer of corruption.

It is academic to provide an intellectual critique of the problems.

Certainly, where the political economy of the village, taluk (intermediate) and district levels is divisive and acquisitive, the extent to which commonality, cohesiveness and consensus will develop can only be left to people's struggle, in the hope that through their activism they will be able to render local authorities more accountable bodies, and more able to deliver just governance. It is precisely because this cannot be vouchsafed that the structure and other aspects of the implementation require considered attention.

But there are several aspects of the amendment. The first of these pertains to the very existence of the panchayats, namely, the guarantee of institutional existence. The issue has been fudged. Article 243 E reads: 'Every panchayat unless sooner dissolved under any law for the time being in force, shall continue for five years from the date appointed for its first meeting and no longer'.

The words 'unless sooner dissolved' reveal underlying mischief. Who will make the dissolution? One set of circumstances under which a panchayat may be dissolved is that of internal dissolution, namely where the panchayat itself decides that it cannot carry on. But, if this possibility is permitted panchayats will be subject to all kinds of *aya-ram-gaya-ram* politics, which has not been stopped at the State and Union levels even by the Anti-Defection Law. There is a great danger in allowing party politics to cause political fissures in these bodies, which need to find their strength in the popular— and not the party political—community. The other circumstance of dissolution is external, where the State or some other functionary dissolves the panchayat because they feel that it is not functioning properly. External dissolution can require ratification by the legislature (at least for some classes of panchayats) or may simply be left to the legislature. At one level, it is possible to argue that such a power is a normal default power which exists in all local government legislation.

At another level, it is a power similar to President's Rule and is likely to be exercised with a total lack of responsibility. There is very serious doubt whether such a power should exist. If included, it must be both procedurally and substantively safeguarded to ensure that it is used in a narrow range of circumstances subject to legislative approval. If a blanket power is retained, Indian governance will be littered with the corpses of prematurely terminated panchayats, and the whole experiment will have floundered.

If the institutional existence of panchayats is not assured, questions relating to the 'institutional capacity' and powers of panchayats have also been left up in the air. Section 243 G of the amendment states:

Subject to the provisions of the Constitution, the Legislature of a State may, by law, endow the Panchayats with such powers and authority as may be necessary to enable them to function as institutions of self-government and such law may contain provisions for the devolution of powers and responsibilities upon Panchayats at the appropriate level, subject to such conditions as may be specified therein, with respect to

(a) the preparation of plans for economic development and social justice;

(b) the implementation of schemes for economic development and social justice as may be entrusted to them including those in relation to the matters listed in the Eleventh Schedule.

This is the only place where the 11th Schedule of the Constitution is mentioned. The schedule delineates those areas where the panchayats are to be entrusted with the implementation of 'schemes for economic development and social justice'. These include:

1 Agriculture, including agricultural extension
2 Land improvement, implementation of land reforms, land consolidation and soil conservation
3 Minor irrigation, water management and watershed development
4 Animal husbandry, dairying and poultry
5 Fisheries
6 Social forestry and farm forestry
7 Minor forest produce
8 Small-scale industries, including food-processing industries
9 Khadi (handmade cloth industries inspired by Ghandian ideals), village and cottage industries
10 Rural housing
11 Drinking water
12 Fuel and fodder
13 Roads, culverts, bridges, ferries, waterways and other means of communication
14 Rural electrification, including distribution of electricity
15 Non-conventional energy sources
16 Poverty alleviation program
17 Education, including primary and secondary schools
18 Technical training and vocational education
19 Adult and non-formal education
20 Libraries
21 Cultural activities
22 Markets and fairs
23 Health and sanitation, including hospitals, primary health centres and dispensaries
24 Family welfare
25 Women's and children's development
26 Social welfare, including welfare of the handicapped in the Scheduled Castes and Scheduled Tribes

27 Welfare of the weaker sections, and in particular of Scheduled
    Castes and Scheduled Tribes
28 Public distribution system
29 Maintenance of community assets

/ The Article is somewhat unhappily worded. While the concept
of the 11th Schedule leaves open the possibility of an innovative
three-tier federalism, Article 243 G leaves it to the States to effect
such devolution as they wish in respect of the preparation of plans
for economic development and social justice (which are not linked
to the 11th Schedule) and the implementation of such plans (on
matters listed in the 11th Schedule). An unimaginative 'planning
commission' view of this article may well reduce panchayats to being
mere consultative bodies which also play some kind of role in
implementing programs. But certain important aspects of this devolution must be borne in mind. The devolution is entrusted to the
State legislature. The legislature enact laws that effect the devolution. The same purpose is not achieved through State laws simply
stating that the 'executive' is authorised to devolve such powers as
it thinks fit. If that had been the intention of the amendment,
devolution would have been left to the State executive and not the
legislature. What must not be overlooked is that the amendment is
infected with the constitutional purpose of the Directive Principle
of establishing functioning 'units of self-government' (Article 40).
This is reiterated in the amendment, which articulates panchayats
as 'institutions of self government' (Article 243 G). In order that
this constitutional objective is achieved, the panchayats must have
well-defined areas of empowerment which are not left to the whims
of the State government, clearly defined executive agencies which
are answerable to the panchayats, independent rule-making powers,
predictable financial discretion, extended notions of common property, and real functions in respect of the everyday life of people in
the matter of food, health, work, welfare, land use, water and
environment.

What is to be properly understood is that unless institutional
existence and institutional capacity are guaranteed to panchayats as
incidences of institutional viability, these new creatures of local
government will not be any different from their previous counterparts. The amendment has been careful in trying to ensure a
separate and independent electoral machinery (Article 243 K) and
to ensure due deliberation in the allocation of finances (Articles
243 H, I; 243 J). What the amendment cannot, and should not, be
read as authorising, is a blanket power in the legislatures to surrender Draconian powers to the State executive and its officers to grant
such powers as they wish to panchayats, to interfere with their
everyday functioning and working and—to top it all—to dissolve

them out of existence at will. The experiment will fall on its face if the spirit behind these amendments is effaced by legislative lethargy and greedy politics, which will convert a fresh layer of governance into the third tier of corruption.

THE QUEST FOR A MODEL ANSWER

Centralisation of power has also led to a centralisation of the policy-making mind. There are not necessarily all-India answers to all questions. The spirit of post-independence governance is infected with the oversimplified prescription that plans for every-thing are made in Delhi; and that the rest is really no more than a matter of local implementation. Legislatively, initiative is left to the State legislature. But the discretion of State legislatures is invariably blunted by magnum schemes which each legislature is expected to adopt faithfully. We have got so used to the idea of all-India models that we tend to overlook their suitability for the object to be achieved. Panchayat Amendments are no exception. Certainly, a political charge made against the 1989 initiative was that it was designed to do no more than liquidate the existing opposition experiments in local government by trying to place local self-government on a higher Congress pedestal. The amendment of 1992 allows the existing schemes simply to peter out (Article 243 E). All inconsistencies between the amendment and legislation would stand repealed within one year (Article 243 N). One possi-bility is to allow each legislature to evolve its own answers to the extent of the inconsistency. The inconsistency will be self-evident in respect of the machinery of elections (which must, under Article 243 K, be entrusted to a State Election commission), the reservation for women and SC & ST (Article 243 D), the introduction of a three-tier structure except in States not having a population exceeding 20 lakhs (lakh is an Indian unit of measure for 100 000) (Article 243 B), and making financial arrangements (Article 243 H, I and J). In some States it would be necessary to start afresh; in others, changes can be made piecemeal. The other possibility is that all States must start afresh and follow the example of model legislation.

The idea of model legislation has been mooted strongly. The National Institute of Rural Development (NIRD) has produced a Model Bill. To some extent that Bill understates its 'model' inten-tions, for it is incomplete. The more strongly politically mooted model is the Karnataka Panchayat Act 1993. Passed in an atmos-phere of acrimony, it was accepted unanimously on the specific understanding that unanimity must accompany the rites of passage. However, there is an understanding that certain opposition amend-ments will also be passed. Form and politics seem to have triumphed over content. There is little point in passing imperfect Bills in order to give the impression of political support. Little is achieved. An effective scrutiny of the legislation is obviated.

Yet despite all this, the Karnataka Bill is increasingly being presented as the 'Model' Bill. That is why it is necessary to examine the ingredients that compose it. On close reading, the Karnataka Bill turns out to be a massive subversion of the Panchayat Amendments and will undermine its purposes. In order to test the Karnataka Act, it would be useful to apply the tests of institutional existence, capacity and viability which have been articulated earlier.

We have already noticed the disquieting provision in the Constitution that permits premature dissolution before the mandatory five years is over. While the Model Bill of the NIRD simply reiterates that the power exists, the Karnataka Act reposes an extensive power of dissolution:

1 in the case of gram panchayats, in the commissioner (Section 268);
2 in the case of the taluk and zilla (administrative districts), in the State government (Section 268).

Such a dissolution can be brought about where there is an excess or abuse of power or persistent default in the discharge of duties. The fact that there is natural justice and a right to be heard (Section 268 (3)) neither provides a safeguard nor redeems the situation. Even if some default power should exist, it must be much more strongly monitored. To place the very existence of a gram panchayat in the hands of a commissioner is to secure the bureaucratic defeat of democracy. The dissolution power also exists where the government feels like altering the panchayat area (Section 302)—and this can be at any time. But the pinpricks go deeper. The government has taken upon itself a vast investigative power: '. . . for any reason to be recorded . . . on matters concerning it, or on any matters with respect to which the sanction, approval, consent or orders of the Government is required under the Act 11, (Section 236 (1)). The malady goes further. There is a power to suspend the execution of any order or resolution

> . . . or any order of any authority of officer of a Gram Panchayat or the doing or anything which is about to be done or is being done by or on behalf of a Gram Panchayat (which is) unjust, unlawful or improper or is causing or is likely to cause injury or annoyance to the public or to lead to a breach of peace (Section 237).

Similar powers exist for the panchayat at other levels (Section 237 (3), (4)).

If these are Draconian powers, there is also a power to remove taluk and zilla members for misconduct in the discharge of their duties or in the case of any disgraceful conduct or if they have become incapable of performing their duties as a member (Sections 136; 175). Chairpersons in their incarnation as adhyakshas and upaadhyakshas (minister in charge of cities) can also be removed for 'misconduct' or for being 'persistently remiss' in the discharge of their duties, by the assistant commissioner in the case of gram panchayats (Section 48 (4)), and by the government in the case of taluk and zilla members (Sections 140 (4), (5); 179 (4), (5)). All this is in addition to removal for no confidence by the panchayat in question (Sections 48 (3); 140 (3); 179 (3)). Thus, the members are subjected to accountability from their peers—but to summary removal (after being heard) by the State government or its officers.

During the functioning of panchayats, the government retains an overall supervisory power of immeasurable proportions. Consider Section 240:

> Government's power to specify the role of Panchayats—The Government may, by general or special order, specify from time to time, the role of Grama Panchayat, Taluk Panchayat and Zilla Panchayat in respect of the programs, schemes and activities related to the functions specified in schedule I, II and III, in order to ensure properly coordinated and effective implementation of such programs, schemes and activities.

This is in addition to the general or specific powers of governments in various areas (for example, Section 191 on various kinds of expenditure).

The real joker in the pack emerges when we examine the manner in which devolution is effected. There is no clear delineation of the devolved power; it is left to the government to assign such powers as it thinks fit to the panchayat, and to keep changing the brief as it wants (Sections 58–9; 145–61; 185–6). Even the schedules in the Karnataka Act that define respective powers at gram, taluk and zilla levels can themselves be amended by the government by simply placing the amendments before the legislature without requiring an affirmative or negative resolution (Section 312; see also Section 319).

With such precariousness marking both the term and sweep of powers of the panchayat, the sanctity and integrity of its decisions remain flawed and hopelessly impaired. There is an appeal structure from the decisions of the panchayats which is nothing short of remarkable. Appeals from decisions of the panchayats and its officers are subject to the State bureaucracy in all the areas that matter—building and planning (Section 64(5), (6)), the granting and renewal of licences (Section 70 (3), (4)), appointment and control of employees (Section 113 (2), (4), (5)), the levy and assessment of taxes (Section 201), decisions on property questions

(Sections 211 (2); 217 (2); 224 (2)) and various other matters (Section 269). Now, if all the major decisions of the panchayat are subject to appeal to bureaucracy, who will take the decision making of panchayats seriously? The gram and taluk panchayats have already been undermined to the extent that the zilla panchayat can simply 'annul, revise or modify' any of their decisions (Section 270). But the surrender to bureaucracy by way of appeal is to make their decision making meaningless. All this is quite independent of the fact that the rule-making power of the panchayats is totally under the control of the government (Sections 313–17), in addition to the massive overriding power of the government to make any kinds of rules under the Act itself (Section 311). We are here talking of the basic and crucial decision-making capacity of the panchayats and witnessing its denunciation.

The powers of the government over panchayat decision making are consistent with its stranglehold over such bureaucracy and officers that would be placed at the disposal of the panchayats. Gram panchayats will submit their requirement for approval to the chief executive officer whose approval will be required for appointments and who will sit in appeal over disciplinary decisions of the panchayat over its employees (Sections 111–13). At taluk and zilla level, the government can make transfers (Sections 155 (2); 199 (4)). It is the government that will constitute zilla panchayat services (Section 196 (5)). There is every reason to believe that the panchayats will have no control over their employees, who will look to the chief executive officer and beyond for instructions and orders. This uneasy relationship between panchayats and their own staff can only swing the balance of equations in favour of the latter against the former for whom they work.

This curious situation extends further, because although the Act rightly creates a State Election Commission (Section 308), it is the government and its officers who not only exercise powers of delimitation (Sections 124; 163), but also perform decision-making functions about the conduct and holding of elections that truly belong to the Election Commission (Sections 5 (1), (5), (6), (7), (8); 8 (1), (3); 10 (3); 12; 13 (2); 14 (2); 33; 36; 40; 45; 128; 129). Thus bureaucratic domination and control extends not just to the elected bodies but to the electoral process also.

What the Karnataka Act still lacks is a genuine respect for democratic processes. Even in planning matters, the planning co-ordinating committee shall eclipse democracy (Section 310), the grants will be arbitrary (Sections 206–8), the financial levies will be appealable (Section 201) and the community property notions will be skewed and subject to government regulation. What will emerge is elected panchayat members who do not know when they will be removed or dissolved, whose decisions will have a transient sanctity and whose overall powers shall be in doubt.

If the NIRD model seems incomplete, the Karnataka Act of 1993 is by contrast dense in content. With all its schedules, its word length is equal to that of the Constitution of India. But its wordiness has a purpose that subverts the purpose of local self-government. It is a gift to government and bureaucrats. The usual dilemmas of devising local government legislation remain. Based on foreign models, the Karnataka Act does not strike a just balance between local democracy and meaningful monitoring. It goes further and exhausts democratic processes, entrapping them with schemes of over-regulation. It endows the State with powers to humiliate panchayats and their members with a merciless ease.

Model solutions often produce perverse answers. Instead of reaching for the highest common denominators, they sink to the level of the lowest denominator. The result is that rock-bottom solutions to control, restrict and stifle find their way into the remedial configuration. We have to be careful lest such solutions destroy the very purpose for which these amendments were devised. One cannot resist the thought that such prescriptions are not legacies of accident, but products of design.

A PLEA AGAINST ALL-INDIA SOLUTIONS

What would have happened if there had been no Panchayat Amendments? One cynical answer could be that panchayat legislation exists in all States; and that imposed willy-nilly the new legislation will not make too much of a difference. If the object of the Panchayat Amendments was to create a new kind of three-tier federalism, this has not been achieved by the amendments. The 11th Schedule does not assign powers to the third tier. It leaves the sanctity and integrity of the third tier to the good sense of the legislatures. Nothing will come out of this exercise if the legislatures, like the Karnataka Panchayat 1993, extend such abdication further by leaving everything to the good sense of the governments in assigning such powers as they want and controlling them in such ways as they please.

But this does not make the amendments pointless. The very fact that panchayats must exist is significant, although the provisions allowing dissolution breach this mandate. The creation of compulsory reservations for women and SC & ST will bring fresh forces to the political fore. All this has been built into the structure. But the structure itself becomes malleable because the institutions that are created can be moulded by the executive. The answer does not lie in all-India solutions but in drawing out certain principles that will honour the purpose and spirit of the amendments. In the quest for principles, there must be a guarantee of continued existence. If that is not assured, the panchayats will not survive the mischief of politics. The powers of the panchayats must be clear and known. Panchayats must have clear legislative and executive authority, working with employees who answer to them and not to the State government. The panchayats must be subject to accountability from below and not to arbitrary threats and investigation from above. Given the panchayats' financial viability, the true test will lie in the capacity of various State governments to trust panchayats with real power to manage common property, effect land use, undertake planning and take decisions that affect the life, health, education and environment of ordinary people. In order to manage this, there is a very heavy baggage of planning, bureaucratic control and political corruption that has to be shed. Such an experiment can only work if people are truly empowered to confront their rulers and each other.

7

The Electoral System of Chinese People's Deputies

Li Qixin and Xie Manhua

The Constitution of the People's Republic of China ('the Constitution') expressly provides that: 'All power in the People's Republic of China belongs to the people. The National People's Congress and the local people's congresses at various levels are the organs through which the people exercise state power.'[1] 'The State organs of the People's Republic of China apply the principle of democratic centralism.'[2] So the people's congress system, which is constituted in accordance with the principle of democratic centralism, is the organic form of state power of the people in China; that is, it is China's essential political system.[3] The electoral system of the people's deputies is an important part of the people's congress system in China.[4]

Presently the laws regarding the electoral system include the following, besides the provisions of the Constitution:

1   Electoral Law of the National People's Congress and Local People's Congresses of the People's Republic of China ('the Electoral Law', adopted on 1 July 1979; first amended on 10 December 1982; then amended on 21 December 1986);

2   Organic Law of Local People's Congress and Local People's Government of the People's Republic of China ('the Local Organic Law', adopted on 1 July 1979; first amended on 10 December 1982, and again on 2 December 1986);

3   Decisions of the Standing Committee of the National People's Congress Regarding Direct Election at the County Level (adopted on 3 March 1983);

4   Representative Law of the National People's Congress and Local
     People's Congresses of the People's Republic of China ('the
     Representative Law', adopted on 3 April 1992).

The implementation of these laws gives great play to improving
electoral work, developing socialist democracy, and strengthening
local power. This chapter discusses the basic principles of the
electoral system in China, its electoral organisation, and its electoral
procedure.

THE PRINCIPLES OF THE ELECTORAL SYSTEM IN CHINA

The generality of the right to vote

All citizens of the People's Republic of China who have reached the
age of eighteen have the right to vote and stand for election,
regardless of ethnic status, race, sex, occupation, family background, religious belief, education, property status or length of
residence.[5] Thus, the electoral qualifications of Chinese citizens are
not limited.

The equality of the right to vote

Each voter has the right to vote only once in an election.[6] The
equality of the right to vote in China emphasises substantive equality, not the formal decision. According to the Electoral Law, the
number of deputies to the local people's congresses at various levels
shall be defined in accordance with the principle of facilitating the
convening of meetings and discussion and solution of problems as
well as ensuring appropriate representation of all nationalities, all
localities and people of all walks of life. The number of and method
of selection of deputies to the local people's congresses at various
levels are established on the basis of the fixed number of people
in electoral districts or units. The Electoral Law, according to the
actual situation in China, determines the distribution of deputies
among the people in rural areas, cities and those of Han nationality.
The Law is not absolutely equal as regards the proportion of
selecting deputies; for example, even though the population of
some minority nationalities is small, they still have appropriate
representation. However, in view of the fact that each nationality
has appropriate representation and takes part in the management
of the state, regardless of the size of their population, we in China
believe that representation of each nationality is substantially equal.
Therefore, we also believe that the application of the Electoral Law
is substantially equal.[7]

Direct and indirect elections

Deputies to the National People's Congress and to the people's congresses of provinces, autonomous regions, municipalities directly under the central government, cities divided into districts, and autonomous prefectures are elected by the people's congresses at the previous, lower, level. Deputies to the people's congresses of cities not divided into districts, municipal districts, counties, autonomous counties, townships, nationality townships, and towns shall be elected directly by their constituencies.[8] On the basis of the actual situation in China, the Electoral Law expands the scope of direct election from the 'lower' town level to county level. At the same time, deputies to the people's congresses above the county level (not including the county level) are elected indirectly. It shows that China applies the principle of direct election and indirect election conjointly in the election of the deputies to the people's congresses at various levels.

Why doesn't the Electoral Law simply provide 'direct election'? China is a multinational state with vast territories, abundant resources and a very large population. Politics, the economy and culture have not developed in a uniform manner across China. The situation differs between the cities and the countryside, and there is a world of difference between autonomous regions. In many regions, the means of communication, for instance, are not well developed. Because voters are not familiar with the candidates for deputies, and because deputies are not closely connected to voters, direct election of deputies to the National People's Congress would not assist deputies to exercise their functions and powers and fulfil their duties. Therefore, it is appropriate in the Chinese situation, and assures people of better administration of state affairs, that deputies to the people's congresses at and above the county level are elected indirectly.

Secret voting

Deputies are elected to the national and local people's congresses by secret ballot.[9] A voter may vote for or against a candidate for deputy, or may vote instead for any other voter, or abstain.[10] This principle offers an important safeguard for democratic election. It ensures that voters' privacy will not be affected or disturbed by 'outside' influence or interference, and that they will elect persons whom they trust to be the people's deputies, according to their will and having freely exercised their right to vote.

Voters' supervision and recall of deputies

The right to vote and stand for election and the right of supervision and recall make up the inseparable whole of the socialist election system in China. All deputies to the national and local people's congresses are subject to supervision by the voters and the electoral units that elect them. Both the voters and the electoral units have the right to recall the deputies they elect.[11] Voters exercise the right of supervision and recall of deputies in order to prevent them from going against the people's will, and to ensure that they perform their duties faithfully. This is an important measure to compel deputies to perform their duties conscientiously, to prevent them from transforming the role of public 'servant' into that of 'owner', and to guarantee that the people are in control.

The material safeguard and legal safeguard of the right to vote

Election funds for the National People's Congress and the local people's congresses at various levels are disbursed by the state treasury.[12] Therefore, each voter and each candidate for deputy can participate in the election free from any restrictions that could arise from any great disparity in their possession of property. It safeguards the citizen's ability to fully exercise his or her right to vote in the material sense. The Electoral Law and other statutes regarding elections provide electoral principles, organisation and procedures. This legally affirms the substantial rights of voters and procedurally ensures the achievement of these rights. At the same time, the Constitution and the Electoral Law stipulate the legal consequences of violating the citizen's right to vote. The standing committees of the people's congresses of provinces, autonomous regions, and municipalities directly under the central government may formulate the detailed rules and regulations regarding elections, according to the Electoral Law, in order to guarantee the legitimacy of elections to be held under specific local conditions. The laws concerning elections also provide legal sanctions against acts that interfere with electoral processes.

ELECTORAL ORGANISATION AND PROCEDURES

Electoral organisation

The Constitution stipulates that the Standing Committee of the National People's Congress conducts the election of deputies to the National People's Congress, and that the standing committees of the people's congresses of provinces, autonomous regions, municipalities directly under the central government, cities divided into districts, and autonomous prefectures conduct the elections of deputies to the people's congresses at the corresponding levels. In cities that are not divided in these ways, election committees are established to conduct the election of deputies to the people's congresses at the corresponding levels. The election committees of cities not divided into districts, municipal districts, counties, and autonomous counties are under the leadership of the standing committees of the people's congresses at the corresponding levels. The election committees of townships, nationality townships, and towns are under the leadership of the city election committees. The standing committees of the people's congresses of provinces, autonomous regions, and municipalities directly under the central govern- ment give instructions concerning the election of deputies to the people's congresses below the county level within the corresponding administrative division.[13]

Electoral procedures

Zoning of electoral districts   The number of deputies to the people's congresses in cities are allocated according to the electoral districts, the zones for which are decided on the basis of production units, institutions, work units, and the number of voter's residences.[14]

Registration of voters   Voter registration is conducted on the basis of electoral districts. Once registration has been completed it is valid permanently. Prior to each election voters who have reached the age of eighteen in the period since the last registration of voters, and whose political rights have not been expropriated, are registered. Voters who move between electoral districts after the registration are not included in the roll of voters of the electoral district into which they move. The names of voters who have died, or whose political rights have been expropriated in accordance with the law, are removed from the roll of voters. Citizens suffering from mental illness and incapable of exercising the right to vote or standing for election are not to be included in the roll of voters, upon the affirmation of the relevant election committee.[15] The roll of voters is made public 30 days prior to the date of election, and voter registration cards are issued.[16] Anyone who has an objection to the roll of voters may appeal to the election committee, which must make a decision on the appeal within three days. If the appellant is not satisfied with this decision, he or she may bring a suit in the People's Court five days prior to the date of election, and the Court must make a decision—which is final—prior to the date of election.[17]

Nomination of candidates for deputies

Candidates for deputies to the national and local people's con-gresses are nominated on the basis of electoral districts or electoral units. The Communist Party of China, the democratic parties and various people's organisations may either jointly or separately recommend

candidates for deputies. Any voter or deputy may also, with ten or
more people supporting his or her proposal, recommend a candidate.
The recommender must give details of the candidate's background to
the election committee or the presidium of the people's congress.[18]
The number of candidates for deputies to the national and local
people's congresses must by law be greater than the number of
deputies to be elected.[19] Candidates for deputies to be directly elected
by the voters are nominated by the voters in the various electoral
districts and by the Communist Party of China, the democratic parties
and various people's organisations. The election committee is required
to collect and publish, twenty days prior to the date of election, the list
of nominees for deputies, and after a period of public debate and
consultation it decides on a formal list of candidates. This formal list
must be made public five days prior to the date of election. A similar
process takes place for elections by local people's congresses to
positions in the people's congress at the next, higher, level.[20]

Political parties, people's organisations, voters and deputies who
have nominated candidates for deputies may brief voters or deputies
on their candidates at group meetings of voters or deputies. However, such briefings must stop on the day of election.[21]

Balloting and affirming the results of elections

Balloting is the decisive stage in the course of elections. Where the
deputies to a people's congress are to be elected directly by the
voters, the election is conducted at polling centres in the various
electoral districts or in election meetings, which are presided over
by the election committee.[22] Where a local people's congress at or
above the county level is to elect deputies to the people's congress
at the next, higher, level, the election shall be presided over by the
presidium of the lower-level people's congress.[23]

Where the deputies to a people's congress are to be elected
directly by the voters, the election is valid only if they have obtained
more than half of the votes cast by all the voters in the electoral
districts. When the number of candidates for deputies who have
obtained more than half of the votes exceeds the number of
deputies to be elected, those who have obtained the most votes shall
be elected. If the number of votes for some candidates is tied,
making it impossible to determine who is to be elected, another
ballot shall be conducted between those candidates to solve the tie.
If the number of elected deputies who have obtained more than
half of the votes is less than the number of deputies to be elected
another election shall be held, among the candidates for deputies
who failed to be elected, to make up the difference. Those who
obtain the most votes shall be elected; however, to be elected they
must obtain no less than one-third of the votes cast.[24] The election

committee or the presidium of the people's congress shall determine, in accordance with the Electoral Law, whether or not the
result of an election is valid, and shall announce the result accordingly.[25]

Termination of delegates' credentials

The delegates' credentials committees passed by the first session of
each people's congress of townships, nationality townships, and
towns exercise their functions and powers until the expiration of
the terms of office of the present people's congress. The terms of
office of deputies to the local people's congresses at various levels
last from the first session of each people's congress at the corresponding level to the first session of the next people's congress at
the corresponding level.[26] Delegates' credentials committees shall
be established by the standing committees of the local people's
congresses at or above the county levels.[27]

According to the provisions of Article 41 of the Representative
Law, delegates' credentials shall be terminated on the following
conditions: (1) Deputies to the local people's congresses at various
levels move or transfer from their respective administrative areas;
(2) Deputies have their resignation accepted; (3) Deputies do not
attend sessions of the people's congresses at the corresponding
levels twice, and without approval; (4) Deputies are recalled; (5)
Deputies forfeit citizenship of the People's Republic of China; or
(6) Deputies are deprived of political rights in accordance with the
law.

The termination of the credentials of delegates of the people's
congresses at or above the county level is reported to the standing
committees of the people's congresses at the corresponding levels
by the delegates' credentials committee, and is announced by the
standing committees of the people's congresses at the corresponding levels. The termination of the credentials of delegates of the
people's congresses of townships, nationality townships, and towns
is reported to the people's congresses at the corresponding levels
by the delegates' credentials committee, and is announced by the
people's congresses at the corresponding levels.

THE INFLUENCE OF DEPUTIES ON THE OPERATION OF GOVERNMENT

Deputies to the National People's Congress and to the local people's
congresses at various levels are elected in accordance with the law.
Deputies in the National People's Congress are component members of the highest organs of state power, while deputies to the local

people's congresses are component members of local organs of state power at various levels.[28]

Deputies have the right to examine and approve the Bills and reports submitted to the people's congresses by governments, and the right to address inquiries to the relevant state organs. They are required to attend the plenary session of the people's congress, the plenary session of the deputation, and group meetings, and they have the task of examining and approving all Bills and reports that are included in the agenda of the people's congress. Deputies may be elected or invited to attend the session of the presidiums and the session of the special committees as non-voting delegates, and to express an opinion.[29] Deputies may address inquiries to the relevant state organs at the corresponding levels while they examine and approve the Bills and reports. The relevant state organs in charge must answer the inquiries.[30] For example, during the people's congress, governments entrust the leading cadre of the planning and financial department for the people's congress to make the required economic plans, budgets and financial reports; governments then convene a conference of all the deputies and pass the economic plans, budgets and financial decisions.

Deputies also have the right to address inquiries to the State Council and its departments or committees, and to local governments at various levels and their departments, in accordance with the legal procedure.[31]

Deputies to the people's congress at or above the county level shall make an inspection of the work of the state organs at the corresponding levels or at the previous, lower, level, and of the relevant units according to the unified arrangement of the standing committees of the people's congresses at the corresponding levels. Deputies may put forward proposals, criticisms and opinions to the inspected units, but cannot directly decide on solutions to the problems while they make an inspection.[32] For example, the standing committees of the people's congresses may organise the relevant deputies to make an inspection of systems for the implementation of the economic plans and budgets, and to put forward proposals and opinions.

Deputies should constantly heed the opinions of the people. They should, for example, answer inquiries from the units that elected them or from their constituencies into the work and actions of deputies, relay the opinions and demands of the masses, and assist the people's governments at the corresponding levels.[33]

Deputies to the people's congresses at various levels who are elected in accordance with the Electoral Law represent the interests and will of the people, participate in exercising state power in accordance with the functions and powers that the Constitution and the laws vest with the people's congresses at the corresponding levels, and play an assisting and supervisory role in the work of the people's governments.

In short, the existing election system of people's representatives is appropriate to the situation in China, and meets the requirements of the level of democracy that it has been possible to reach at the present stage.[34] No doubt the Chinese election system of people's representatives will be made even more democratic as Chinese society develops and progresses.

PART II
The Role of
Representatives

8

Representative Democracy and the Role of the Member of Parliament: The Sri Lankan Experience

Rohan Edrisinha

Constitutional developments in Sri Lanka in recent years have highlighted the question of the role of the member of Parliament in a liberal democracy. The relevant constitutional provisions, and the manner in which the judiciary has interpreted them in a series of decisions, have demonstrated convincingly the importance of the freedom of conscience of members of Parliament and the indispensable nexus between this fundamental principle and a truly representative liberal democracy.

The Second Republican Constitution, which was promulgated in 1978, introduced a particular variety of proportional representation[1] which replaced the 'first-past-the-post' or simple plurality system that had existed in the country since independence in 1948. The system introduced in Sri Lanka contained several distinctive features: a bonus seat for the party/group that came first in a particular district, and a high cut-off point, both designed to give an advantage to larger parties and prevent smaller parties from entering Parliament; and preferential voting permitting the voter not only to choose the party of her or his choice, but also the individual candidates on the party lists. These details were contained in a relatively rambling constitutional provision with the marginal note, *Proportional Representation*, and which contained thirteen paragraphs: Article 99 (1) to (13).

Article 99 (13a) provides for the principle of expulsion of members of Parliament from Parliament if they cease to be members of the party to which they belonged at the time they were elected to Parliament. The paragraph reads as follows:

> Where a Member of Parliament ceases by resignation, expulsion or otherwise, to be a member of a recognised political party or independent group on whose nomination paper (hereinafter referred to as the 'relevant nomination paper') his name appeared at the time of his becoming such Member of Parliament, his seat shall become vacant upon the expiration of a period of one month from the date of his ceasing to be such member:
>
> Provided that in the case of the expulsion of a Member of Parliament his seat shall not become vacant if prior to the expiration of one month he applies to the Supreme Court in writing, and the Supreme Court upon such application determines that such expulsion was invalid. Such petition shall be inquired into by three judges of the Supreme Court who shall make their determination within two months of the failing of such petition. Where the Supreme Court determines that the expulsion was valid, the vacancy shall occur from the date of such determination.

Due to the fact that the expulsion provisions were spelt out in the same article that described the details of the proportional representation system—but due also perhaps to the fact that generally in the liberal democratic world it has become unfashionable to stress the importance of the freedom of conscience of MPs—the myth that proportional representation necessarily entails the supremacy of the political party over MPs elected to Parliament on that party's ticket was perpetuated in Sri Lanka. The Supreme Court of Sri Lanka, in a series of decisions, seems to have grounded its judgments on this assumption, and has therefore not thought it fit to attempt to whittle down the scope of this obnoxious constitutional provision through a process of constitutional interpretation consistent with the values of constitutionalism.

A TALE OF THREE CASES

Case 1: Gunawardena and Abeywardena v. Fernando S.C. (Spl.) 50–51/87 Decided on 18 January 1989.
In the first case dealing with the so-called expulsion provisions,[2] two MPs belonging to the ruling United National Party defied the party whip and abstained from voting in favour of the controversial Thirteenth Amendment to the Constitution and the Provincial Council Bill[3] at the stage of the second reading of the Bills, but voted in favour of the Bills at their third reading. At the disciplinary inquiry initiated thereafter by the party Working Committee, Mr Abeywardena explained his abstention on the ground that the various party organisations within his electorate were 'unequivocally

opposed' to the Thirteenth Amendment. The Working Committee, nevertheless, decided to expel the two MPs from the party. In terms of the Constitution, if the expulsion from the party was *valid*, the seats of the MPs would thereafter automatically become vacant. The two MPs, as provided for by the Constitution, applied to the Supreme Court for a determination that their expulsion was not valid.

In a decision that revealed little if any sensitivity to the basic principles of representative democracy, the Supreme Court held that the expulsions were valid, enabling the UNP to expel the MPs from Parliament.

Case 2: *Dissanayake et al. v. Kaleel S.C. (Spl.) 4–11/91. Decided on 3 December 1991.*

Gamini Dissanayake and Lalith Athulathmudali, two senior leaders in the ruling United National Party, masterminded a plot, with the co-operation of the opposition, to impeach President Ranasinghe Premadasa. They also launched an island-wide campaign against the executive presidential system and its incumbent. The Disciplinary Committee and Working Committee of the party recommended that the eight UNP MPs involved in the abortive attempt be expelled from the party. The Working Committee Resolution calling for their expulsion stated that President Premadasa was the leader of the party and that the dissidents' action amounted to 'a betrayal of the party membership and confidence placed by the people in the Party and leadership'. It also condemned the dissidents for failing to raise their concerns within the party.[4] The Resolution went on to say:

> And whereas the said eight members had at the General Election of 1989 sought and obtained nomination on the lists of the UNP and the voters had elected them to Parliament on the basis and understanding that they are members and candidates of the UNP who accept the leadership of the party and the Executive Presidential system of Government and are therefore bound to adhere to the party manifesto and the party constitution and policies *whilst being representatives of the party in Parliament* . . . [original emphasis][5]

Justices Kulatunga and Wadugodapiitiya held that the expulsion of all eight MPs was valid. Justice Fernando, in his dissenting judgment, held that the expulsion of six MPs was invalid on the grounds of breach of natural justice. The expulsion of the other two MPs who, unlike their colleagues, were cabinet ministers at the time the impeachment motion was signed and who appeared to have participated at a cabinet meeting after signing the motion, was held to be valid. Fernando J found their conduct to be abhorrent and the facts undisputable, so that an antecedent hearing would have in His Lordship's opinion made no difference to the decision to expel them.

Case 3: *Tilak Karunaratne v. Sirimavo Bandaranaike et al. S.C. (Spl) 3/93.*

The petitioner was a member of Parliament belonging to the opposition Sri Lanka Freedom Party, and an advocate of party reform to reverse the trend of electoral defeats since 1977. He was publicly critical both of the party leader, Ms Sirimavo Bandaranaike who, he argued, had been at the helm of the party for too long, and of the lack of internal party democracy, as elections to various important committees of the party had not been held as scheduled under the party constitution.

A Disciplinary Committee was appointed to inquire into the conduct of the MP. The petitioner refused to participate in the inquiry on the grounds that no useful purpose would be served by doing so as the committee was constituted by persons who were not duly elected. The petitioner who was, thereafter, expelled from the party, applied to the Supreme Court for a declaration that his expulsion from the party was invalid.

A majority of the Court took the view that since Mr Karunaratne had repeatedly tried to raise his concerns within the party at various fora, and since the party constitution required that elections for party organisations and the party leadership be held annually, the public statements that were critical of the party were a legitimate exercise of his freedom of speech guaranteed by the Constitution. Mr Karunaratne's expulsion from the party was therefore held to be invalid, and the party was prevented from causing Mr Karunaratne to be expelled from Parliament and appointing someone else as an MP in his place.

The constitutional implications of the cases

The facts of the three cases illustrate the fundamental problem: the undesirability of the constitutional provision, Article 99 (13), and in particular the principle contained therein that expulsion from the party *automatically* results in expulsion from Parliament as well. Due to the defects in the provision itself, a court that may want to prevent an MP from being expelled from Parliament is compelled to declare that that MP cannot be expelled from a party. The implications or consequences in terms of constitutional principle cannot be compared. Expulsion from a voluntary association, consisting of persons committed to a similar political ideology, is different from an elected representative of the people in the supreme legislature being expelled from that institution without any consultation of the electors. Therefore, though it must be conceded that the fault lies in the constitutional provision, it is submitted that the Supreme Court failed to recognise the fundamental constitutional issues involved, and indeed often developed constitutional 'doctrines' which lacked validity and legitimacy. Instead of using constitutionalism and creative interpretation as a basis for rendering the obnoxious constitutional provision innocuous, the Supreme Court often extracted 'doctrines' which enlarged its ambit and in effect undermined the very essence of representative democracy and constitutionalism.

This was particularly unfortunate given the fact that several other features of the Constitution—including the unprecedented powers vested in the executive president who is immune from any legal proceedings, the absence of judicial review of legislation, the entrenchment of a Public Service controlled by the cabinet of ministers, and a chapter of fundamental rights which permits the executive to curtail such rights for a host of reasons almost at will—have prompted commentators to condemn the Constitution as one that promotes authoritarianism. The combination of an 'over-mighty executive'[6], and a relatively weak legislature lacking independence and vitality—and further devalued by the decisions of the Supreme Court in the cases discussed in this article—have done little to promote liberal democracy in Sri Lanka in recent years.[7]

The worst judgment in this respect was that of Sharvananda CJ in *Gunawardena and Abeywardena v. Fernando*,[8] where His Lordship developed a bizarre theory of representative democracy with the aid of factual inaccuracies. Sharvananda CJ somewhat cavalierly declared that:

> But today thanks to the evolution of the party system, democracy has assigned to the individual member the role of a cog in the party wheel and it is the party that has become the spokesman of the country's interests. The party system has reached the stage where the individuality of the average party member has scarcely an opportunity of finding independent expression. The party caucus tends to override all opposition and once the party line is decided, the member becomes little more than a rubber stamp for its decisions. The party gives a mandate to the member; he gets his directions or instructions from them and he carries them out; even the speeches he may make and other activities in Parliament are settled by the party, ultimately on behalf of the constituencies, but immediately on behalf of the party itself.[9]

He went on to suggest that this novel interpretation of representative democracy existed even in Britain: 'The British system of government is government by party; the Conservative and Labour parties there, are no less democratic parties, because they discipline their members by threat of expulsion.'[10]

Sharvananda CJ did not cite any examples of the discipline and threats he referred to. He must also have been unaware of the numerous occasions on which the so-called 'wets' within the Tory Party, including former Premier, Edward Heath, savaged their own party leader Margaret Thatcher both in Parliament and outside it. There have also been countless instances of dissidents within parties speaking and voting contrary to the official party line. For example, 63 Conservative MPs voted against the Conservative government on the adoption of the Treaty of Maastricht. Political parties in Britain or in other liberal democracies are not monolithic units. As Paul Silk observes,

> Political parties are broadly based. Inside each there are disagreements about most individual aspects of policy, though there may be broad agreement about the broad direction of economic and social thinking. Analysis of voting records in the House of Commons has shown that MPs have increasingly shown their disagreement with party policy by voting against their party's line.[11]

It is significant that Sharvananda CJ did not deal with the argument put forward by one of the MPs that his constituents and local party organisations did not want him to support the legislation. It is submitted that the judgment totally ignored the fundamental principles of representative democracy.

In *Dissanayake et al. v. Kaleel*, both Justices Kulatunga and Fernando distanced themselves somewhat from the 'cog in the party wheel' reference of Sharvananda CJ. Nevertheless they both, it is submitted, failed to pay sufficient attention to the constitutional cornerstone involved in the case, preferring instead to base their decisions on issues of natural justice and the relationship between the Working Committee and the Executive Committee of the party.

Kulatunga J[12] took the view that the party constitution imposed obligations on all members of the party. These obligations included being bound by the directions of the leader of the party regarding matters in Parliament, the duty to harmonise with the policy and code of conduct of the party, and the duty to vote in Parliament according to the mandate of the parliamentary party as conveyed through the party whip. He stressed the fact that under the Sri Lankan Constitution, 'the party is pre-eminent and carries the mandate of the electors'.[13] He expressed the view that this was essential for stability, order and the smooth functioning of the party system.

His Lordship's failure to appreciate the core constitutional issues involved is demonstrated by the fact that he thought that an important constitutional provision which describes how the sovereignty of the people is exercised, and which some judges and commentators have considered an entrenched provision,[14] was subordinate to the provisions in the Constitution spelling out the details of proportional representation:

It is true that Article 4(a) refers to 'elected representatives of the people' but this is subject to Article 99 which provides for proportional representation which gives pre-eminence to the party.[15]

While Justice Fernando's judgment was more cautious and sensitive to the need for an MP to exercise his or her discretion free from party dictates in certain situations, he too, it is submitted, attached too much importance to the role of the party. Fernando J therefore placed considerable importance on the implied obligation on the part of the dissidents to have raised their concerns within the party first, before participating in the abortive attempt to impeach the president. He also rejected the argument that Article 99 (13) should be interpreted restrictively so as to give as much freedom of conscience as possible to the MP. Quite surprisingly, Fernando J considered it inappropriate to deal exhaustively with theories of representation, and preferred instead to focus more than 50% of his judgment on the more familiar issue of natural justice:

> The word representative in Article 4(a) is by no means conclusive in favour of the 'free mandate theory' and the position of the Member has to be determined by examining the relevant provisions of the Constitution as a whole. It is neither possible nor necessary in this case to attempt a comprehensive definition of that position and it is sufficient to ascertain whether he retains a power of independent action, in any significant respect.[16]

In the third case, *Tilak Karunaratne v. Sirimavo Bandaranaike et al.*, Dheeraratne J, for the majority,[17] seemed to adopt a similar approach to that of Fernando J in the previous case. Since Mr Karunaratne had, however, raised his concerns within the party and was in fact raising matters that were designed to promote intraparty democracy and ensure that the values and principles enshrined in the party constitution were adhered to, Dheeraratne J held that Mr Karunaratne's impugned statements were justified as an exercise of his freedom of speech guaranteed by the Constitution of Sri Lanka.

Dheeraratne J rejected the argument put forward by counsel for Ms Bandaranaike and the party, that with respect to 'nonconstitutional functions of a member' the cog in the wheel theory remained applicable.

> I am unable to agree with that proposition. If, for instance, the party gives a direction to a member in direct violation of a fundamental policy of the party, is that member meekly bound to obey such a direction? . . . I am unable to subscribe to a proposition which tends to devalue the nature of the contractual bond of a political party vis-à-vis a member (and particularly a Member of Parliament) to a relationship perhaps that of master and servant.[18]

It is submitted that it is not possible to categorise the various functions of a member of Parliament into those that are constitutional and non-constitutional. Justice Dheeraratne's judgment is welcome as it went further than that of Fernando J in stressing the importance of the freedom of conscience of MPs and the nexus between freedom of speech and the role of an MP.

The right to dissent is an essential prerequisite for a free society. This right, however, should be exercised not only by the ordinary citizen or political organisations, but by members of Parliament as well. Unfortunately—with the possible exception of the majority judgment in *Tilak Karunaratne v. Sirimavo Bandaranaike et al.*—the Sri Lankan Supreme Court in the decisions discussed has taken a constitutional position that might have been considered ambiguous, and interpreted it as unambiguously opposed to the exercise of dissent and independence by members of Parliament.

The main justification for the stifling of the freedom of conscience of MPs was the widely held view that seemed to have been shared by most of the judges of the Supreme Court: that the system of proportional representation necessarily entails diminution in the freedom of MPs. It was implied in the cases that under proportional representation it is the *party/group* that receives the votes rather than the individual candidate, and that *ipso facto* the mandate theory demands that MPs are bound by the dictates of the party. The apparent logic of this thesis is, however, not borne out in practice. In over 34 liberal democracies in the world, including Germany, Denmark, Belgium, the Netherlands, Spain, Sweden, Iceland and Norway, which use different varieties of proportional representation, members of Parliament are permitted to dissent from their parties and even to leave the political parties from which they were elected. In *none* of these countries can such members of Parliament be expelled from Parliament.

This is because the fundamental importance of free, independent members of Parliament for the effective functioning of representative democracy has been recognised by the constitutions of these nations. Its paramount importance outweighs even the apparent logical consequence of the principle of proportional representation. The *free mandate theory* of representative democracy as opposed to the *imperative mandate theory* of representative democracy is, therefore, applicable in nearly all liberal democracies, whether they have the simple plurality (first-past-the-post) system or a system of proportional representation.

The basis of modern representative democracy is that governmental power should be exercised not arbitrarily but on behalf of the citizens of the country. The legislature, therefore, should consist of representatives of the *people* whose primary responsibility is to the people, rather than to a party or a party leader. Indeed the notion that a member of Parliament is primarily loyal to his or her party is unknown in the liberal democratic world.

THEORIES OF REPRESENTATION

There are two main theories of representation in modern democratic theory: the free mandate theory and the imperative mandate theory. The free mandate theory states that, once elected, members of Parliament exercise a free mandate in the national interest. The people elect a representative because they approve broadly of that person's party, policies and credentials, and they place their confidence in the representative to exercise his or her discretion and judgment on their behalf for the duration of the parliamentary term. As stated earlier, this theory of representation is widely accepted in most liberal democracies because it is recognised that in the modern welfare state, where the executive wields so much power, a vibrant, independent legislature is a *sine qua non* for an effective system of checks and balances.

For example, the free mandate theory is recognised in Germany, which has a proportional representation system. Article 38 of the Basic Law provides that the deputies of the German Bundestag 'shall be representatives of the whole people, not bound by orders and instructions and shall be subject only to their consciences'. Article 88 of the Constitution Act of the Netherlands provides that: 'The Staten-General represents the whole Dutch nation', while Article 96 declares that 'The members vote without the burden of mandates issued by the nominees or the electorate'.

Dutch constitutional writers have pointed out that the Constitution clearly indicates that parliamentarians represent the whole nation and that they exercise a free mandate in the national interest. The Netherlands too has a system of proportional representation. Both the French and Swiss Constitutions embrace the free mandate theory. Article 91 of the Swiss Constitution provides that: 'Members of both Councils shall vote without instructions.' Article 27 of the French Constitution provides that: 'Any mandatory instructions shall be null and void. Members of Parliament shall vote according to their own personal opinion.'

The imperative mandate theory specifies that members of Parliament are obliged to act in accordance with the mandate of those voters who elected them as their representatives. It is important, therefore, to note that the debate over representation is between those who argue that an MP, once elected, is free to exercise his or her own judgment, and those who believe that an MP has as far as possible, to reflect the wishes of his or her voters/electorate. The issue of the reflection of the wishes of the *party* does not arise even in the imperative mandate theory.

THE MERITS OF THE FREE MANDATE THEORY

There are several reasons why the free mandate theory, sometimes referred to as the theory of uninstructed representation, is to be preferred to the imperative mandate theory or the theory of instructed representation. There are several weaknesses in the imperative mandate theory. Firstly, it is impracticable, as it is impossible for voters to be aware of the MP's views on all issues. Also, new issues are bound to arise in the course of the parliamentary term. Secondly, it is immoral, for it demands the sacrifice of the judgment and conviction of the representative in favour of the judgment and conviction of others. Thirdly, it will adversely affect the quality of the legislature. Persons of superior intellect and integrity are unlikely to seek election to a place in which they are not free to think for themselves or to vote according to their consciences, but merely function as a reflecting mirror for the views of others. This will ultimately be detrimental to the nation. It promotes, furthermore, parochial interests to the detriment of the national/common interest, and it undermines one of the most important functions of the legislature in a representative democracy, which is to be a *deliberative* assembly. The imperative mandate theory completely ignores this vital aspect by assuming that the member has arrived at his or her final conclusion on a matter before parliamentary deliberation commences. Edmund Burke explained this often neglected, but important, role of Parliament:

> Parliament is not a congress of ambassadors from different and hostile interests; which interests each must maintain, as an agent and advocate, against other agents and advocates; but Parliament is a deliberative assembly of one nation, with one interest, that of the whole; where not local purposes, not local prejudices, ought to guide, but the general good resulting from the general reason as a whole. You choose a member indeed, but when you have chosen him, he is not a member for Bristol, but he is a Member of Parliament.[19]

Appadurai, explaining the dangers of ignoring the deliberative function of Parliament, observes:

> Indeed, as Burke rightly saw, it would result in an absurd state of affairs in which the determination precedes discussion, in which one set of men deliberates and another decides, and where those who form this conclusion are far away from those who hear the arguments.[20]

It seems clear, therefore, that the free mandate theory enables Parliament to realise its full potential as the paramount law-making institution, and as an effective check on the executive branch of government. That is why the free mandate theory has been accepted in most liberal democracies.

JUDICIAL RECOGNITION OF THE FREE MANDATE THEORY

The free mandate theory is clearly a part of the British constitutional tradition. The imperative mandate theory was expressly rejected by the Court of Appeal in *Osborne v. Amalgamated Society of Railway Servants*[21], where Farwell LJ referred approvingly to a speech of Edmund Burke:

> But authoritative instructions, mandates issued which the member is bound blindly and implicitly to obey, to vote and to argue for, though contrary to the clearest conviction of his judgement and conscience; these are things utterly unknown to the laws of this land . . . You choose a member indeed; but when you have chosen him, he is not a member of Bristol, but he is a Member of Parliament.

This view was affirmed by the House of Lords in *Amalgamated Society of Railway Servants v. Osborne.*[22] D. Judge in *British Representative Theories and Parliamentary Specialisation* states that in 1947 the House of Commons rejected the proposition that a member of Parliament could be bound contractually to act in a certain manner.

The free mandate theory was recognised in two important cases in Zimbabwe and South Africa. The importance that the judiciary attached to the theory, as vital for the independence of Parliament and its effective functioning as a check on the executive, can be seen in the judgments. In *Chikerama v. The United African National Council*[23] members of a political party had been nominated on a party list through a system of proportional representation, to become members of the legislature. They had entered into an agreement under which they pledged to vacate their seats if they withdrew their support from the political party that nominated them. The members subsequently resigned from the party which nominated them and the party sought a declaration that their seats be declared vacant. The Appellate Division of the Zimbabwe High Court, refusing to grant such a declaration, stated that the wide wording of the pledges given were unenforceable as they were contrary to public policy. The Court also accepted the free mandate theory and observed:

> The contract in question calls for the resignation of the member if for any reason he ceases to be a member of the respondents' party. There might be the best and most commendable of reasons for a Member to resign from his party. His party might so drastically change its principles and its policies as to make resignation from it the only proper and honourable course for him to take. To take an extreme example, the leaders of the party might decide to collaborate with the terrorists or to indulge in subversive activities, leaving him no option

but to resign from it. In such a case it would not be he but the leaders themselves, seeking to unseat him, who would be 'unfit for membership of the House' and deserving of expulsion.[24]

A similar approach was adopted by the South African Appeal Court in the case of *Du Plessis v. Skrywer,*[25] where a political party sought to force a member of the then Namibian National Assembly to vacate his seat on the ground that he had resigned from that political party. The Court considered the role of members of Parliament and declared unequivocally that they had the right to vote according to their consciences. The Court stated that since the National Assembly in Namibia could pass laws in the national interest, this implied that members should exercise the freedom to speak and vote when considering parliamentary business irrespective of party prescriptions regarding policy and principles. It is significant that the court also referred to the *Privileges and Competencies of Parliament Act* in support of its conclusion that a member is free to vote according to her or his conscience. Furthermore Rumpff CJ observed that: 'The members of the legislative assembly can, in my opinion, not be seen as representatives of the nominating parties or societies, but only as representatives of the people of the area.'

Thus the tradition that a member of Parliament, once elected, is free to vote according to her or his conscience and according to her or his conception of the national interest, has been asserted by political and legal authorities throughout the world, and in liberal democracies where *both* the simple plurality and proportional representation systems have been practised. This is because they have appreciated the pivotal importance of an independent member of Parliament for the preservation of a vibrant Parliament and ultimately for a free society. Proportional representation is a method by which MPs are elected to Parliament. However, once elected, other more important considerations pertaining to the effective functioning of Parliament as an institution override or trump what some perceive as the 'logic' of the system. Klaus von Beyme in *Political Parties in Western Democracies* observes that:

> Most parliamentary democracies lay great stress on individual freedom for Members of Parliament . . . All the Western democracies see the Member of Parliament as independent of instruction, and nowhere has he been subjected by law to order from his voters . . . The independence of Members of Parliament has had to be defended not only against voters but also against the parliamentary party. But party discipline which emerged in many democracies as the parties gained in strength, has never been institutionalised.[26]

The final point made by von Beyme is significant. Most political authorities have acknowledged the enhanced role of the political party and its increasing control over MPs in modern democracies, but such a development has invariably been cited as a weakness, a dangerous trend, or a political reality, not as something positive or as a principle to be institutionalised. It is indeed unfortunate that in Sri Lanka, on the other hand, this is referred to as an inevitable consequence of the electoral system of the country, exalted to the status of a doctrine and legitimised in the Constitution.

The constitutional provisions relating to the freedom of conscience of members of Parliament in Sri Lanka, therefore, need to be changed. It is submitted that the Supreme Court, through a process of creative constitutional interpretation, should have whittled down the scope of these provisions. A combination of various approaches could have been adopted to achieve this objective. The Court could have stressed the essence of representative democracy by doing the very opposite of what Kulatunga J did in *Dissanayake et al. v. Kaleel*; it should have read Article 99 (13) subject to the 'basic feature' set out in Article 4(a), which reads: ' The legislative power of the People shall be exercised by Parliament, consisting of the elected *representatives* of the *People* and by the People at a Referendum [emphasis added].'

The Court could have cited, as in the South African case, constitutional and legislative provisions dealing with the powers and privileges of members of Parliament that confer on Sri Lankan MPs the same rights and privileges enjoyed by their counterparts in the British House of Commons. The Standing Orders of the Sri Lankan Parliament hardly refer to political parties, and the procedures laid out suggest clearly the *individual responsibility* borne by members of Parliament in the conduct of their parliamentary duties.

Creative and bold constitutional interpretation is not alien to Sri Lanka's constitutional jurisprudence. In the well-known case of *Liyanage v. the Queen*[27] the appellate courts virtually read the doctrine of separation of powers into the Constitution that existed from relatively slender constitutional foundations. H.W.R. Wade commented that:

> The implications read into the Constitution are to be viewed as an exercise in creative judicial activism rather than an exercise in juristic logic. He that seeketh findeth. More generally, the decision illustrates how, given an appropriate political climate, sophisticated and imaginative judicial review can modify the text of the Constitution which embodies few express guarantees or prohibitions.[28]

The cases discussed above were sufficiently important to justify another '*Liyanage*'. The judges in *Liyanage* were aware of the far-reaching consequences of their decision and the implications for constitutionalism. It seems, unfortunately, that the judges in the 'expulsion cases' were not.

9

The Structural Weaknesses of Representation in Macau

Jorge Costa Oliveira and Arnaldo Gonçalves[1]

Macau was the first European settlement in the Far East, the Portuguese having arrived in 1557. The territory is composed of a small peninsula named Macau, and the islands of Taipa and Coloane, the total land area being 16 square kilometres. Unlike Hong Kong, a territory that was ceded to the British after the 'Opium War', Macau emerged from an understanding with China. Currently, the territory of Macau's situation is defined in the Portuguese Constitution and in the 'Joint Declaration of the Government of the People's Republic of China and the Government of the Republic of Portugal on the Question of Macau' (usually called the Sino-Portuguese Joint Declaration) signed in Beijing on 13 April 1987. This Declaration states that Macau forms part of China's territory and that the government of the People's Republic of China shall resume sovereignty over Macau on 20 December 1999.

Since 1976 Portugal has accepted that Macau is Chinese territory under Portuguese administration. This situation will last until 1999, when China will resume its sovereignty over the territory and Macau will become a Special Administrative Region of the People's Republic of China. Under the terms of the Sino-Portuguese Joint Declaration, Portugal is responsible for the administration of Macau during the 'transition period' leading up to 20 December 1999.

Macau's legal system is based on the Romano-Germanic branch of continental European law. It is characterised by the fact that laws proper are, by far, the most important source of law, and the relevant legislation is inserted into specific legal codes known as the five 'big codes': the Civil Code, the Commercial Code, the Civil Procedure Code, the Criminal Code and the Criminal Procedure Code.

Macau's constitutional organisation has undergone major changes during the territory's history. Initially, there was a system of 'mixed jurisdiction' (from 1557 to 1822), followed by a 'colonial period' (1822 to 1976) and latterly a 'transition period' (lasting from 1976 until 19 December 1999). Chinese control begins on 20 December.

A constant feature of Macau's history has been the ongoing co-operation displayed by Portugal and China. In addition to this, Macau has always enjoyed a high degree of autonomy. Its geographical location, traditional openness, and economic, social and cultural environment have attracted and facilitated the coexistence of extremely varied cultures, languages and religions. The 1991 General Population Census indicated a total resident population of 356 000 inhabitants, with an estimated increase to 381 000 by the end of 1992. Of the population 95% are ethnic Chinese who speak Cantonese, and the other 5% are people of Portuguese origin and of other nationalities. Chinese and Portuguese are both the official languages of Macau, but the use of Portuguese remains extensive in the legal system, the courts and the administration. English is mostly used for commerce and business.

Although China will resume full sovereignty over Macau at the end of the century, Macau shall maintain its present legal system and a somewhat similar political system based on the predominance of the executive and a high degree of power concentrated in the representative of the 'central' outside government.

THE PRESENT FORMAL POLITICAL SYSTEM

The Constitution of Macau comprises parts of the Portuguese Constitution that apply directly to Macau, a constitutional law called the Organic Statute of Macau and other parts of the constitutional Portuguese framework that apply indirectly through the Organic Statute. Under the Organic Statute, Macau is a collective person of internal law whose organs of self-government are: (1) the governor; and (2) the Legislative Assembly. The governor is nominated by the President of the Portuguese Republic, holds the executive powers and also enjoys a wide range of legislative powers.

The Legislative Assembly holds wide legislative powers and a core of instruments to control the activity of the governor and the administration, in general. As head of the executive, the governor:

1 conducts the territory's general policy;
2 supervises the whole public administration;

3   issues administrative regulations;
4   guarantees the freedoms of the residents and the independence of the courts;
5   manages the territory's finances;
6   defines the structure and the rules of operation of the monetary and financial markets;
7   may refuse the entry of aliens, in accordance with the law.

The governor is assisted by seven under-secretaries, one for each main area of the administration, appointed by the Portuguese president upon a proposal of the governor. The under-secretaries are vested with very broad delegation of powers, and within certain limitations they may subdelegate them to the directors of public departments under their supervision.

Briefly, we can represent the organic structure of Macau's Administration in Figure 9.1.

In the law-making process the governor is assisted by the Consultative Council. This Council consists of five members appointed by the governor from among Macau residents of recognised merit and prestige in the local community; and five elected—of whom two are appointed by the Municipal Assemblies (Macau and Taipa/Coloane Islands) and three are elected by the representatives of social interests of the territory, through functional constituencies. This body may advise the governor on all matters of government, although in practice it is heard only in the law-making process.

Another body of self-government of Macau is the Legislative Assembly. It has powers to enact laws, and to control the governor and the under-secretaries' policies and activities. The Legislative Assembly is composed of 23 members designated as follows: (1) seven appointed by the governor from local residents of recognised merit and prestige in the local community; (2) eight elected by direct and universal suffrage based on lists presented by civic associations or nomination committees; and (3) eight elected by indirect suffrage, through functional constituencies representing economic, labour, professional and cultural, educational and social interests.

This particular system of representation comes from the specific status of Macau as Chinese territory, and is deeply connected with the traditions and idiosyncrasies of Chinese society. As noted above, Macau has two municipalities. Their main functions are to provide services for the local communities that go beyond the functions and activities of the institutional government. The role of the municipalities is clearly not very relevant at the moment, considering the small dimension of the territory.

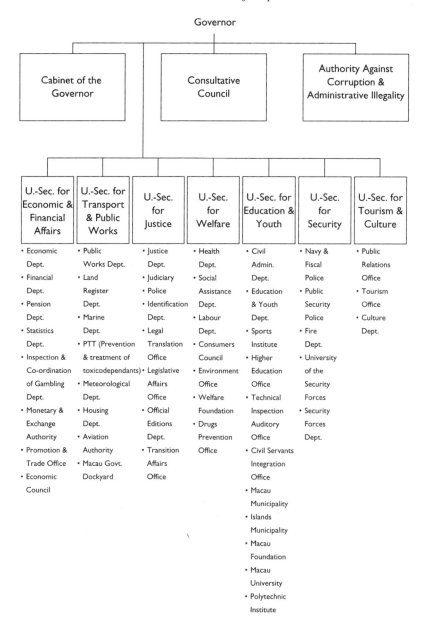

Figure 9.1   Macau's administrative structure

THE ROLE OF REPRESENTATIVES UNTIL RECENT TIMES

Until recently there have been three kinds of representatives in the political system of Macau:

1   the governor, representing the interests of Portugal;

2   the Legislative Assembly, representing local interests, which is basically a chamber where the leaders of the Macanese (that is, inhabitants with Portuguese ancestors or of Portuguese culture) community and the local Chinese businesspeople can make their voices heard; and

3   several 'informal representatives' of Mainland China interests, with close ties to the political institutions of the People's Republic of China.

'Informal representatives' include entrepreneurial associations—such as the 'Exporters' Association', the 'Textile Manufacturing Association' and the 'Industrial Association'—organised under the umbrella of the Commercial Association, whose chairperson is usually considered the leader of the local Chinese community. Dr Ma Man Kei, who was chairperson in 1993, performed these functions, among others, as well as those of 'effective member' of the Chinese People's Political Consultative Conference, the 'multi-party' co-operation body in the political system of the People's Republic of China.

Other 'informal representatives' of Mainland China interests are the *kaifongs* or neighbourhood associations. There are approximately 24 *kaifongs* associated in the 'General Union of the Neighbourhood Associations of Macau'. The majority of these *kaifongs* were established after the regrettable incidents of December 1966.[2] Their activity is centred on providing support to the local/neighbourhood communities in an overpopulated town. They have concentrated their main efforts on housing, where they have tried for many years to fill the gap arising from the absence of ongoing policy relating to this area within the administration. Although the administration has invested significantly in these fields the *kaifongs* still influence decision making on these issues, and are often consulted by the executive.

THE CURRENT ROLE OF REPRESENTATIVES

In the last few years, the system of political representation has changed very quickly. Firstly, the composition of the Legislative Assembly has changed. Most of its members are Chinese and, in most cases, either belong to the 'informal representatives' of Mainland China interests or have close ties with Mainland interests. This is exemplified by the case of several local businesspeople whose activities (and income) are directly dependent on investments in Mainland China, on joint ventures with public companies on Mainland China, or on credit provided by Mainland public banks or subsidiaries.

At the same time, the role of the Macanese community has changed. Although the president of the Legislative Assembly is considered to be from among this group and two of its pre-eminent members are now under-secretaries (for Administration and Education and for Health and Social Matters), the fact is that the role of the Macanese community has been decreasing in the relevant decision-making centres, especially after the death in 1992 of Dr Carlos Assumção, the former president of the Legislative Assembly.

Furthermore, China has already stated that the localisation of the top posts in the Civil Service should be done using Chinese, not Macanese. On the other hand, a new actor has appeared on the stage: the Sino-Portuguese Joint Liaison Group.

THE JOINT LIAISON GROUP

The Sino-Portuguese Joint Declaration stipulates, in Article 4, that a Sino-Portuguese Joint Liaison Group should be set up in order to ensure the effective application of the Sino-Portuguese Joint Declaration and to establish the appropriate conditions for the full resumption of sovereignty by China over Macau on 20 December 1999.

The Joint Liaison Group (JLG) should not interfere in any way whatsoever with the 'Portuguese administration of Macau' over the normal course of government activities during the transitional period, since it is also stipulated in the Joint Declaration that, until 19 December 1999, the Portuguese government will be fully responsible for the administration of Macau. However, it is very difficult to separate the areas the JLG is 'allowed' to include on its agenda of mutual consultations and discussions. As time goes by it is understandable that the Chinese side has been trying to have a greater say in decision making in order to guarantee a smooth transition to full Chinese sovereignty.

As the year 1999 approaches, the number of matters submitted for consultation within the JLG has been increasing, as has the intensity of consultation. In fact, the JLG discusses many issues that are within the sphere of competence of the 'Portuguese administration of Macau'. And new and unexpected problems are emerging from this situation, the most important reflecting the lack of an institutional forum for local businesspeople. The increasing number of consultations in the JLG may lead to a lessening of the role of the Legislative Assembly in law making. This is the main reason that a new consultative body, The Economic Council—where the most relevant and powerful local businesspeople advise the governor— has recently been set up.

THE STRUCTURAL WEAKNESSES OF REPRESENTATION IN MACAU

A lack of a sense of belonging

Because 95% of Macau's population are ethnic Chinese who migrated to Macau on specific occasions, the patterns of participation and representation are similar to those existing in other overseas Chinese communities spread around the world. The first massive influx of Chinese immigrants occurred during the time of China's war with the Japanese in the 1930s. The population of Macau increased from 157 000 in 1927 to 245 000 in 1939, and decreased to 170 000 after 1960. A second wave of Chinese immigration occurred in the late 1960s, during China's Cultural Revolution, and a third after 1978, when the PRC adopted reform policies and relaxed emigration controls.

Half of the present population of Macau thus entered the territory in the last 15 to 30 years. Prior to the 1991 Census some 50 000 illegal immigrants 'invaded' Macau in search of better jobs and conditions of living, forcing the authorities to adopt more effective means of controlling immigration. Recent polls suggest, however, that many local residents are considering moving to yet another country or territory. This highly mobile population lacks a sense of belonging, and does not regard the territory of Macau as its home.

Although the population of Macau watches the same TV channels, reads almost the same newspapers and shares the same global culture as the population of Hong Kong, it 'produces' a markedly different output in political terms. For instance, since electoral registration is not compulsory, only about 5% of the residents of Macau have completed their registration. It might be that people predominantly interested in cultivating business opportunities do not want to earn the disapprobation of Mainland China authorities by participating in political activities of which they disapprove. Indeed, what worries China is not only the existence of strong democratic parties (like the 'United Democrats' in Hong Kong) but also the very transformation of what are supposed to be the 'business cities' of Hong Kong and Macau into 'political cities'. A clear perception of this point explains why the residents of Macau do not 'get involved in politics'.

Sociological background

Interestingly, Chinese migration into Macau has fostered traditional forms of representation, normally assumed by the customary heads of the community, the eldest sons, and based on the traditional structure of the family in Chinese society. In fact, the organisation and representation of power in Macau should not be seen separately from this sociological background. Thus several traditional values of Chinese society—including social and group conformity, which arise from the Confucian norms of filial piety and the pursuit of maintaining harmony—are also present in Macau's society.

The Chinese community in Macau reflects values and traditions that support the hierarchical structure of interpersonal relationships (*guanxi*), within the framework of a society marked by considerable distance between those who wield extensive power and those who wield none. It favours a clear and strong leadership style in which benevolent and respected leaders are not only considerate of their followers, but also able to take skilled and decisive action. Consequently, it is no surprise that the centre of power in the Chinese community is occupied by the political representative of Mainland China on the one hand, and by the patriarchs of the entrepreneurial community on the other hand.

The first centre of power is the New China News Agency (usually called *Xinhua*), which is the local branch of the Hong Kong and Macau Affairs Office of the State Council. It operates as an unofficial local 'embassy' of the Mainland and, simultaneously, as a 'shadow government' exercising a constant and growing pressure on the executive and legislative bodies. The second centre of power is occupied by leaders of the local Chinese community notable for their personal charisma and prestige, such as Mr Stanley Ho the gambling tycoon, and by the chairpersons of the entrepreneurial associations. At the same time these entities represent not only economic power but also the 'rich and famous' model, which is pursued as an ultimate goal by the local residents for whom it is one of the dominant cultural values.

The vast majority of the residents of Macau are only familiar with the system of Mainland China, and as in Mainland Chinese society Macau's people and citizens hope and desire that their leaders—who are the representatives/emanation of power—act in conformity with the general good, and govern in accordance with the interests of the majority. But they place almost no pressure on the representatives they have elected.

And since in Macau there are no political parties as such but merely civic associations that are set up during election campaigns, there is no praxis of political participation and checking of representation to which all political actors must conform.

AFTER 1999

Since the prevailing values in Macau's society are based on the long-standing traditions of Confucianism it is hardly likely they will undergo significant transformation, despite the political changes that are destined to affect the territory in the next several years. Values such as conformity, and the maintenance of harmony and *guanxi*, will continue to play a strong role in Macau and to influence the mechanisms of political representation.

Most of the variables that will have an impact on Macau's future are already visible. The Basic Law of the Macau Special Administrative Region of the People's Republic of China sets up a model based on China's mistrust of Hong Kong and Macau after their reaction to the events of 3–4 June 1989 in Tiananmen Square. The Basic Law establishes a model founded on 'autonomy with supervision' based on the predominance of the chief executive, who is to be a long-time local resident appointed by the Central People's Government of the People's Republic of China. The balance between local/regional interests and central/Beijing interests is still not clear. However, autonomy should be perceived not as a 'gift' from the central authorities but as something that is gained or won daily through the actions strengthening the differences in the systems that are to operate in Macau and Hong Kong.

Given the differences between the Chinese societies of Hong Kong and Macau noted above, it is likely that Macau shall enjoy less autonomy—and therefore shall need less 'supervision'. If the people of Macau attempt some form of ethnic assertiveness that does not support cross-cultural accommodation, Macau's existence as a singular entity in the Pearl River Delta may be endangered. The People's Republic of China evidently hopes to achieve 'successful' reunification with Hong Kong and Macau while it works towards 'reunification' with Taiwan, and any possibility of 'derailing' shall be tackled firmly.

It is not possible to foresee how the future system shall be balanced, particularly among the several 'centres of power' within the Chinese local community. Nevertheless, it is more than probable that Macau's economy will continue to depend on flows of capital from the outside, namely from Mainland China and from Hong Kong. Hence, if the degree of economic dependence continues, it is reasonable to assume that political dependence will follow and that Macau will remain a 'non-political city', with political institutions and practices reflecting traditional Chinese institutions and values which are difficult to analyse by Western approaches.

10

The Case of Voting in the Indonesian People's Consultative Assembly

Satya Arinanto

FROM PROCLAMATION TO INDEPENDENCE

On the morning of 17 August 1945, Soekarno (1901–70) read the Proclamation of Independence[1] to a small group outside his residence in Jakarta, the city that became the capital of Indonesia. The establishment of a government for the newly proclaimed Republic proceeded rapidly. At its first meeting on 18 August 1945, the Panitia Persiapan Kemerdekaan Indonesia (PPKI, or the Committee for the Preparation of Indonesian Independence)[2] added six people to its membership: Soebardjo, Kasman Singodimedjo (the commander of the Jakarta Peta garrison), Soekarno, Wikana and Chairul Saleh.[3]

The expanded Committee elected Soekarno and Hatta as respectively president and vice-president of the Republic of Indonesia. It appointed a commission of seven (Soekarno, Hatta, Professor Soepomo, Soebardjo, Otto Iskandar Dinata, Mr Muhammad Yamin and Mr Wongsonegoro) to finalise the national Constitution, which had been drafted in the month before the Japanese capitulation.[4] This was completed within a week, and though considered temporary, was immediately promulgated. The Constitution provided latitude for wide-scale social, economic and political change, and soon became a revolutionary symbol of great power, a harbinger of the good life that would follow the overthrow of alien control.[5]

Indonesian department heads formerly under the Japanese administration were speedily declared for the new government. The first cabinet of the new Republic, which under the Constitution was responsible to President Soekarno, included men who had worked with the Japanese (such as Soebardjo), and others who had not (such as Sjarifuddin and Soerachman).[6] On 29 August, the Committee for the Preparation of Indonesian Independence was dissolved by Soekarno and replaced by the Komite Nasional Indonesia Pusat (KNIP—Central Indonesian National Committee). The KNIP was to serve as an advisory body to the president and his cabinet, and had no legislative function of its own.[7] To this new body Soekarno, assisted in his selections by Hatta, appointed 135 members (including those of the Committee for the Preparation of Indonesian Independence), whom they deemed to be the outstanding Indonesian nationalists and the most important leaders of the major ethnic, religious, social and economic groups in Indonesia. They did not merely select amenable political stooges, but chose men and women of whom nearly all commanded wide popular support as outstanding leaders of Indonesian society.[8]

The 1945 Constitution, which is still in effect, recognised the right to equality before the law,[9] the right to express an opinion,[10] and the right to association.[11] It also guarantees the freedom of every inhabitant to adhere to his or her own belief,[12] the right to receive education,[13] and economic rights,[14] among others.

A HETEROGENEOUS AREA15

The nature of Japanese wartime occupation that had encompassed Southeast Asia varied considerably among the several countries affected and had different political consequences. After Japan's defeat, the courses to independence followed by these states diverged widely. Indonesia and Vietnam for example, asserted their independence through revolutionary anticolonial wars.[16] Subsequent to independence the political character of these states has continued to be significantly affected by a wide range of relationships with outside powers. The range of contemporary political systems in Southeast Asia is strikingly varied, encompassing a spectrum quite as broad as the differing cultures and divergent historical conditions that have profoundly influenced their character.[17]

HISTORY AND GEOGRAPHY18

Indonesia comprises more than 13 600 islands, 6000 of which are inhabited, and five of which (Sumatra, Kalimantan, Irian Jaya and Java) account for nine-tenths of the nation's land area. Its area is more than 1 904 000 square kilometres (approximately 736 000 square miles),[19] and its population (179.3 million in 1994) makes it the fifth-largest country in the world. The patterns of history are everywhere the creatures of geography. Indonesia's location and archipelago nature, the calmness of its seas, the ruggedness of its mountains, and the volcanic fertility of its soil, have profoundly affected the civilisation of which today's Indonesia is the heir.[20] Its population is unevenly distributed, with almost two-thirds living in Java and Madura, on just 7% of Indonesia's land area.[21]

This country is situated on the trade route between China on the one hand and India, Western Asia, and Europe on the other. Indonesia has thus for millennia been the centre of trading empires and the recipient of a diversity of external cultural influences,[22] including invasions from sea travellers, Chinese and Indian merchants and priests, Arab traders, and the Portuguese. Most recently occupied by the Japanese, Indonesia has been more heavily influenced by the Dutch.

CULTURAL AND BIOLOGICAL DIVERSITY[23]

National integration is a matter of particular concern in Indonesia because of the great diversity of both its geographical environments and its peoples. Durning suggests that Indonesia possesses greater cultural and biological diversity than any other country.[24] The basis of cultural protection in Indonesia is the 1945 Constitution, Article 32 of which states that the government shall promote the national culture of Indonesia. The Elucidation of this article states:

> National culture is the culture which develops as the fruit of the character of all the Indonesian people. Old and traditional culture is found in all the regions of Indonesia as the climax of culture, considered to be national culture. Cultural efforts must be directed towards the advancement of civilization, culture and unity, not rejecting new material from foreign cultures which could develop or enrich the culture of our own nation, as well as elevate the standards of the Indonesian nation.[25]

This explanation is important in understanding the culture of democracy in Indonesia. In the name of national unity the government always tries to ensure that the People's Consultative Assembly avoids the use of voting in its decision-making process. It prefers the use of consensus rather than voting, especially during such an important session as that which elects the president and the vice-president.

THE STATE PHILOSOPHY AND THE POLITICAL STRUCTURE26

The five principles

The five principles of the Indonesian state philosophy are:

1   *Ketuhanan yang Mahaesa* (Belief in God the Almighty);
2   *Kemanusiaan yang adil dan beradab* (A just and civilised humanity);
3   *Persatuan Indonesia* (Indonesian unity);
4   *Kerakyatan yang dipimpin oleh hikmah kebijaksanaan dalam permusyawaratan/perwakilan* (Democracy that is guided by inspirational wisdom in consultation/representation); and
5   *Keadilan sosial bagi seluruh rakyat Indonesia* (Social justice for all the people of Indonesia).

This philosophy is meant to encourage individual commitment to the precepts, because only with this commitment can Indonesia continue to function as a unified nation. Thus both Presidents Soekarno and Soeharto have repeatedly emphasised the importance of every citizen's commitment to *Pancasila*.[27]

Since its birth in 1945, the Indonesian state philosophy of *Pancasila* (*Panca* means 'five', and *sila* means 'principle') has changed in emphasis, with the emphasis at present on *Demokrasi Pancasila* (democracy based on *Pancasila*), the antithesis of Western democracy. The term 'Western democracy' here refers to a system in which voting is the key to the decision-making process. *Pancasila* democracy denies voting such a role as the key to the decision-making process.[28]

The state institutions

Basically, the Indonesian political structure comprises one highest state institution and five high state institutions. The highest state institution is Majelis Permusyawaratan Rakyat (MPR, or the People's Consultative Assembly). The five high state institutions are:

1   Presiden (the President),[29]
2   Dewan Perwakilan Rakyat (DPR, or the House of People's Representatives),[30]
3   Dewan Pertimbangan Agung (DPA, or the Supreme Advisory Council),[31]
4   Badan Pemeriksa Keuangan (BPK, or the Board of Auditors),[32]
5   Mahkamah Agung (MA, or the Supreme Court).[33]

According to the Decision of the Majelis Permusyawaratan Rakyat Sementara (MPRS, or the Provisional People's Consultative

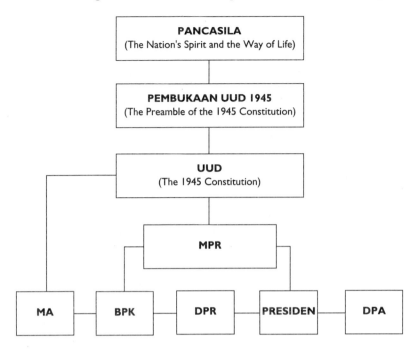

Figure 10.1   Indonesia's constitutional structure

Assembly) No. XX/MPRS/1966[34] which is still in effect to date,[35] the Indonesian political structure is as shown in Figure 10.1.[36]

THE SYSTEM OF STATE GOVERNMENT

Indonesian constitutionalism describes the working of these high state institutions as 'Sistem Pemerintahan Negara', or the system of state government. The 1945 Constitution provides:[37]

1   Indonesia is a State based on law (*rechtsstaat*). This means that the state of Indonesia is based on law, not on mere power (*machtsstaat*).
2   The Constitutional System. The government is based on the constitutional system (basic law) and does not have the nature of absolutism (unlimited power).
3   The Supreme Authority of State is in the hands of the People's Consultative Assembly (*Die gesamte Staatsgewalt liegt allein bei der Majelis*). The people's sovereignty is held by one body, named the People's Consultative Assembly, as the embodiment of the entire Indonesian People (*Vertretungsorgan des Willens des Staatsvolkes*). This Assembly establishes the Constitution and stipulates the broad outlines of State Policy. This Assembly

appoints the Head of State (President) and the Vice Head of State (Vice-President). It is this Assembly which holds the supreme executive power, whereas the President must implement the State policy in accordance with the broad outlines which have been established by the Assembly. The President, who is appointed by the Assembly, is *subordinate* and responsible to the Assembly. He is the 'mandatary' of the Assembly; he is obliged to execute the decisions of the Assembly. The President is not equal to (*neben*), but subordinate to (*untergeordnet*) the Assembly.

4   The president is the supreme executive of the government of the State under the Assembly. Under the People's Consultative Assembly, the president is the supreme executive of the government of the State. In carrying out the government of the State, power and responsibility are concentrated in the president.

5   The president is not responsible to the House of People's Representatives. Beside the president is the House of People's Representatives. The president must receive the approval of the House of People's Representatives to form legislation (*Gesetzgebung*) and to establish the State's budget of receipts and expenditures (*Staatsbegrooting*). Therefore, the president must cooperate with the House, but the president is not responsible to the House, which means that the president's position is not dependent upon the House.

6   The ministers of State are the president's assistants. The president appoints and discharges state ministers. The ministers are not responsible to the House of People's Representatives. Their positions are not dependent upon the House, but dependent upon the president.

7   The power of the head of State is not unlimited. Even though the head of State is not responsible to the House of People's Representatives, he or she is not a 'dictator', meaning that his or her power is not unlimited. It has been explained that he or she is responsible to the People's Consultative Assembly. Aside from that, he or she must pay sincere attention to the voice of the House of People's Representatives.

THE MPR AND THE DECISION-MAKING PROCESS

The 'Consultative' Assembly

The fourth principle of the state philosophy: 'democracy that is guided by inspirational wisdom in consultation/representation' is embodied in the highest state institution, Majelis Permusyawaratan

Rakyat (MPR, or the People's Consultative Assembly). The name itself indicates it is a 'consultative assembly', and not a 'voting assembly'. This institution is the repository of popular sovereignty. The basis is Article 1 clause (2) of the 1945 Constitution, which states: 'sovereignty is in the hands of the people, and is fully enforced by the MPR.'

Constitutionally, MPR is the highest and the most important institution in the Indonesian political structure. However, the 1945 Constitution reserves only two basic provisions for this organ (Articles 2 and 3), and only briefly mentions this organ's function elsewhere.

The basic functions and membership

According to the 1945 Constitution, the basic functions of this institution are to draw up a constitution and to determine the general policy of the nation (Article 3), and to elect the nation's president and vice-president (Article 6.2). The document embodying general policy of the nation is named *Garis-garis Besar Haluan Negara* (*GBHN*, or *Main Outlines of the Nation's Policy*).

Under the present political constellation, it is unlikely that the MPR will replace the 1945 Constitution. The general feeling is that this Constitution strongly reflects the spirit of unity that existed when everyone had but one interest—the independence of Indonesia.[38]

If a new constitution were to be drawn up, it would surely reflect the interests of many groups that have grown powerful since independence. In such a case, the new constitution would eventually become a compromise document, and its everlasting durability would be in question. In view of all these factors, particularly the necessity and desire to maintain the nation's unity, the current governing elite, military and civilians have repeatedly expressed the necessity of retaining the 1945 Constitution.[39]

Article 2 clause (1) of the 1945 Constitution states that membership of the MPR includes members of the DPR (House of People's Representatives), and representatives from the regions and groups, as determined by the General Election Law. There are altogether 1000 members in the MPR. This includes all 500 members of the DPR, and a further 500 executive appointees from among representatives from the regions and groups.

The elected and appointed members within the MPR are divided into five *Fraksi* ('Fractions'):

1   F-ABRI (armed forces);
2   F-KP (development Functional Group);
3   F-PP (development union);

4   F-PDI (Indonesian Democratic Party); and
5   F-UD (regional representative).

In fact, the only elected members of the MPR are those from the DPR, but since in the DPR itself the government has the right to appoint 100 members (75 from the armed forces and 25 from non-military functional groups), the total elected members of both the DPR and the MPR number only 400.

The political parties

A series of electoral laws have reduced the number of political parties that participate in Indonesian elections. At elections in 1955, conducted under the 'old order', there were 28 parties. In 1971 the number of parties was reduced to ten. On the basis of Law No. 3/1975 regarding Political Parties and Golkar, passed in preparation for general elections in 1977, this number of parties was further reduced to three. The Partai Persatuan Pembangunan (PPP, or Development Union Party) and the Partai Demokrasi Indonesia (PDI, or Indonesian Democratic Party) are political parties; and Golongan Karya (Golkar, or Functional Group), the third 'political party' consists of the military, bureaucrats, civil servants and professional groups. The PPP comprises three former Islamic political parties (Partai Muslimin Indonesia, Partai Syarikat Islam Indonesia, and Perti), while the PDI consists of the five former non-Islamic political parties (Partai Nasional Indonesia—established by Soekarno in 1927—the Catholic Party, the Protestant Party, IPKI, and Murba).

VOTING VERSUS CONSENSUS: THE 1988 EXPERIENCE

The 'consensus model' used in the MPR is also preferred in the DPR. If a unanimous decision is not reached, then a Bill is referred to the Steering Committee of the House. If the Committee also fails to generate a consensus, then the Bill is referred back to the floor for a decision either to withdraw or to invoke majority vote. Some scholars argue that this method is based on traditional values concerning decision making. The MPR has never had to vote when selecting the president and the vice-president, since there has never been more than one candidate nominated for each of these positions until 1988.

According to MPR Decree No. II/MPR/1973 regarding the Mechanism to Choose the President and the Vice-President, the president and the vice-president must co-operate. Thus, though Article 6 clause (2) of the 1945 Constitution states that the vice-president is also elected by the MPR (the same mechanism with the president), the candidate for the vice-president must in practice be approved by the president-elect. This 'unwritten law' has applied since Soeharto first held the presidency in 1967.

The MPR elected the vice-president for the first time in 1973. At that time, the late Sri Sultan Hamengkubuwono IX was elected as the vice-president. In 1978, the MPR elected the late Adam Malik as the vice-president, then Umar Wirahadikusumah (in 1983), Soedharmono (in 1988), and Try Sutrisno in 1993 (for the term 1993–98).

During the general session of the People's Consultative Assembly in 1988, attention was focused on the election of the vice-president, because of special circumstances. At one time Soeharto stated that he might not complete his fifth full term (1988–93). Since in the case of his early retirement the vice-president would have to take power,[40] the position of the vice-president was crucial. The influence of Soedharmono—the general chair of Golkar at the time of Golkar's electoral victory of 1987—grew remarkably, and he was nominated for the position of vice-president in 1988. Although he eventually won, his nomination was by no means smooth.[41] At the time President Soeharto did not propose any names, but mentioned five requirements for a vice-president: commitment to *Pancasila* and the 1945 Constitution, personal capability, links with a major sociopolitical organisation, and acceptance by various factions. Apparently Soedharmono was a more likely candidate than his rival, H. J. Naro, who was nominated by the People's Progress Party. But a few days before the vote President Soeharto was reported to have stated that the minority candidate should step aside in order to preserve national unity, and H. J. Naro, understanding that he had no other choice, withdrew from the contest.

The nomination of H. J. Naro by his party was nevertheless a sign of progress for democracy in Indonesia since there had not been, as noted above, any time previously when there was more than one contestant for the positions of president and the vice-president. When the PPP nominated Naro for the position of vice-president, only to have the nominee withdraw for lack of support from President Soeharto, it cannot be said that the MPR relied on Constitutional Article 6 (2). Rather than electing the president and the vice-president, it in reality merely installed the only candidates.

Soeharto later noted that he intended to serve a full term. This announcement perhaps pacified the military leaders who were afraid that Soedharmono would easily become the president. Nevertheless, the election of Soedharmono was significant in the sense that this was the first time during the New Order era that a vice-president was also the leader of a political organisation. Some observers argued that this might commence a new tradition in which the leader of the ruling party would become the future president of the country as well.

With the election of Soedharmono as vice-president, the question arose whether he could retain the general chair of Golkar at the same time. If he did, he would have a lot of power, a matter of concern among his opponents. Since there was no regulation that stipulated that the vice-president of Indonesia could not hold concurrently the position of general chair of Golkar, Soedharmono could theoretically remain as the general chair. But the National Congress in 1988 appointed Wahono, the former governor of East Java, to replace Soedharmono; this decision was supported by the military, because under Soedharmono's leadership Golkar had included more civilian leaders of the organisation. He also opened up Golkar membership to those Muslims who were ex-PPP leaders.

Soedharmono was perceived to be building a personal powerbase at the expense of military interests. Not surprisingly, prior to the Fourth National Congress, the military had ensured that a large number of military men were serving as regional leaders of Golkar. Campaigns were launched and military personnel were installed to head Golkar at regional level, and by the time of the Fourth National Congress the military dominated Golkar leadership at the regional level, a clear attempt to prevent Soedharmono's re-election as the general chair.

CONCLUSION

Article 2 clause (3) and Article 6 clause (2) of the 1945 Constitution stipulate that voting is not prohibited. Article 2 clause (3) states 'all decisions of the People's Consultative Assembly shall be determined by a majority vote'; while Article 6 clause (2) states 'The president and the vice-president shall be elected by the People's Consultative Assembly by a majority vote'. In fact, the MPR tends to use consultation and consensus rather than voting in its decision-making process, especially in the important sessions such as the election of the president and the vice-president.

The consensus method is generally claimed to have authority as a traditional value, but if we look into the historical background there seems to be little evidence that decision-by-consensus was once the rule rather than the exception. Indonesia has therefore never really experienced a democratic method of making decisions, whether by consensus or voting. Golkar, as the dominant faction in the People's Consultative Assembly, has been reluctant to use the voting system.

Will the Indonesian people really have democracy in their decision-making process? To answer this question is not an easy matter. The most important factor in Indonesian politics today is the president, because the president's power in the 1945 Constitution is very considerable.[42] The effectiveness of the work of the other four high state institutions (the BPK, the DPA, the DPR, the MA) and the highest state institution (the MPR) depend fully on the president. This reality is not a good thing for the future of democracy in Indonesia, especially if the military government remains in power.

11

Anti-Hopping Laws: The Malaysian Experience

Tommy Thomas

Freedom of association is one of the most fundamental rights in a free society. The freedom to mingle, live and work with others gives meaning and value to the lives of individuals and makes organised society possible. The value of freedom of association as a unifying and liberating force can be seen in the fact that, historically, a conqueror seeking to control foreign peoples invariably strikes first at freedom of association in order to eliminate effective opposition. Meetings are forbidden, curfews are enforced, trade and commerce are suppressed and rigid controls are imposed to isolate and thus debilitate the individual. Conversely, with the restoration of national sovereignty the democratic state moves at once to remove restrictions on freedom of association.[1]

Common law jurisdictions that are blessed with a written constitution usually have the advantage of an express constitutional provision guaranteeing the right of an individual to form associations. The constitutional protection of the right to form associations has traditionally been the yardstick by which laws enacted to deal with the consequences of a member of a legislative assembly resigning from his or her political party (popularly known as anti-hopping laws) are measured. Such a constitutional provision, in other words, has become the juridical source by which the constitutional legitimacy of such laws is tested. Conversely, countries like the United Kingdom, which do not have a written constitution and where Parliament (and not the constitution) is supreme, have no similar mechanisms for the testing of laws for their constitutional validity.

Because Malaysia has a written Constitution, this is the starting point for a discussion on the effect of anti-hopping laws.

THE CONSTITUTIONAL POSITION

Malaysia's first involvement with a colonial power occurred with the capture of Malacca by the Portuguese in 1511. The Dutch replaced the Portuguese in 1641, and the British presence in Malaysia first manifested itself in 1786 with the arrival of Sir Francis Light in Penang. In the aftermath of the Napoleonic wars, Britain and Holland agreed in 1824 to carve up their Eastern possessions, and Malaya, Singapore and areas of Borneo became parts of the British sphere of influence, while Indonesia belonged to the Dutch. Direct British involvement in Malaya lasted until 1957 when Malaya (the predecessor of Malaysia) achieved independence.

The independence negotiations between Britain and Malaya led to the appointment of an Independent Commonwealth Commission in March 1956 to draft a Constitution. Lord Reid of the House of Lords, and by common consent one of the greatest judges in the United Kingdom this century, was appointed chairman, the other members being Sir Ivor Jennings,[2] Sir William McKell,[3] Mr B. Malik[4] and Mr Justice Abdul Hamid.[5] The Reid Commission Draft Constitution, which was substantially adapted to form the original Federal Constitution, was heavily influenced by the system of parliamentary democracy of the Westminister model, and the language used followed verbatim in many instances the Constitution of India, which had been adopted some seven years previously. The Malaysian courts at least pay lip service to decisions of the Supreme Court of India in the interpretation of the Federal Constitution, and to a lesser extent to decisions in other common law jurisdictions. Hence, a comparative approach to the interpretation of the Federal Constitution not only yields intellectual nourishment but also provides practical utility.

Although the original Constitution has been amended some 40 times in less than 40 years since independence, with the result that the Reid Commission Draft is difficult to recognise today, the provisions that bear upon the issue of anti-hopping laws remain in their original state. Nine Articles forming Part II of the Federal Constitution provide for the fundamental liberties of subjects. Among them is Article 10, which reads (insofar as is relevant):

1. Subject to Clauses (2), (3) and (4)—
    . . .
    (c) all citizens have the right to form associations.
2 Parliament may by law impose—
    . . .

(c) on the right conferred by paragraph (c) of Clause (1), such restrictions as it deems necessary or expedient in the interest of the security of the Federation or any part thereof, public order or morality.

3   Restrictions on the right to form associations conferred by paragraph (c) of Clause (1) may also be imposed by any law relating to labour or education.

One can make the following observations on a plain reading of Article 10. First, the right to form associations is a fundamental right conferred on citizens (not on non-citizens, nor on non-natural persons). In my view, the choice of the word 'fundamental' in Part II was deliberate, and its effect, crucial, because it demonstrates that the founders felt these were not 'mere' rights or liberties but entrenched and inalienable rights that cannot be alienated, abolished or abridged altogether; and that the restrictions of such fundamental rights by Acts of Parliament should not be of such a magnitude, scale or nature as to have the practical effect of destroying or abolishing them. Rather, such restrictions should be minimal, limited and proportionate.

Second, there must be implied within Article 10 an equal right not to form an association or to join an association and a right to leave an association at any time without suffering prejudice or detriment.

Third, such a right, although fundamental, is not absolute. Thus, Parliament may by law impose restrictions. Only Parliament (and no other body) may impose such restrictions. Parliament is defined in Article 44 of the Federal Constitution to mean the 'Yang Di-Pertuan Agong' (the constitutional monarch) and two Houses of Parliament (the Senate and the House of Representatives). Parliament is the legislative authority of the whole of the Federation and is to be contrasted with the legislative assemblies of the thirteen constituent States that make up the Federation. These legislative assemblies cannot impose restrictions on freedom of association.

Fourth, Parliament's right to impose restrictions is not absolute. Rather, it is expressly limited in Article 10 (2) (c) to three circumstances:

1   security of the Federation (or any part thereof);
2   public order; or
3   morality.

Fifth, the express reference in Article 10 (3) to 'any law relating to labour or education' does not, in my view, increase Parliament's rights. It seems to be merely stating two illustrations where such restrictions may be imposed. In other words, restrictions with regard to labour or education should also satisfy the requirements of Article 10 (2) (c) mentioned above.

Finally, any law imposed by Parliament by way of purported restriction of the freedom to associate is vulnerable to constitutional challenge in the courts pursuant to Article 4 (1) of the Federal Constitution, which provides that the Constitution is the supreme law of the land and any law passed by Parliament or a legislative assembly that is inconsistent with the Constitution shall, to the extent of such inconsistency, be void; such task being entrusted to the judiciary.

CASE LAW

The October 1990 general elections saw the emergence of one of the opposition parties at the federal level as the party with the most seats in the Kelantan State Assembly. PAS (an Islamic party) thus formed the State government, with Barisan Nasional (the National Front), which has ruled Malaysia without a break since independence, relegated to the role of the opposition party in that State. In April 1991 the Kelantan State Assembly passed a law in these terms:

> Article XXXLA (1): If any member of the Legislative Assembly who is a member of a political party resigns or is expelled from, or for any reasons whatsoever ceases to be a member of such political party, he shall cease to be a member of the Legislative Assembly and his seat shall become vacant.

In July 1991, two members of PAS resigned from the party and joined UMNO, a constituent party in Barisan Nasional. Their seats were declared vacant and by-elections were held in August 1991, at which the said two members standing on the Barisan Nasional ticket lost the elections. They, thereafter, challenged the Kelantan law as being inconsistent with Article 10 (1) (c) of the Federal Constitution and to that extent void under Article 4 (1) of the Federal Constitution. Their case gave the first opportunity to a Malaysian court[6] to consider the scope and nature of the fundamental freedom of association.

In *Nordin bin Salleh v. The Kelantan State Assembly* both the High Court[7] and the Supreme Court[8] held that the State law was unconstitutional and struck it down; in consequence, the two members were restored to their positions in the State Assembly. Both courts were heavily influenced by Indian case law on the corresponding Article 19 in the Indian Constitution. Articles 19 and 10 are substantially phrased in similar terms, with two significant exceptions. First, in India, State legislatures too could enact restrictions on the freedom to form associations. Second, any restrictions there must be 'reasonable'. In that sense, the Indian legislatures have less freedom than the Malaysian Parliament, for they have to ensure that any restrictions imposed are reasonable. Conversely, the courts in India seem to have greater room to manoeuvre because the term 'reasonableness' connotes some objective criteria, whereas the wording 'such restrictions' as 'Parliament deems necessary or expedient' in the Malaysian Constitution imposes a greater subjective element. However, both Malaysian courts in the *Nordin bin Salleh* case did not seem to attach too much weight to semantic niceties in the language of the two articles, although express reference was made in the judgments to their differences.

The Malaysian courts followed in the *Nordin bin Salleh* case two principles laid down by the Supreme Court of India. First, the principle established in *O. K. Ghosh v. E. X. Joseph*[9] that any restriction to disassociate from an association would make the guaranteed right under Article 19 (1) (c) (or 10 (1) (c)) ineffective and illusory. Secondly, the test applied in *Maneka Gandhi v. Union of India*[10] for determining whether a statute infringes a fundamental right; that is, if the effect of the statute on the fundamental right is direct or inevitable, then *a fortiori* the effect must be presumed to have been intended by the statute.

Our courts also considered at some length the decision of the Full Bench of four judges of the High Court of Jammu and Kashmir in *Mian Bashir Ahmad v. The State*.[11] The facts in that case and the State law that was being challenged there were very similar to the *Nordin bin Salleh* case. Two judges held that the restrictions were reasonable while two other judges determined that the State law was unconstitutional. By virtue of a procedural rule peculiar to Jammu and Kashmir, the view upholding the validity of the State law prevailed. Obviously, neither view is binding on a Malaysian court. Both our courts preferred the latter view.

Gunn Chit Tuan SCJ (as he then was) was robust on the conditions that must be satisfied before Parliament could impose restrictions:

> I cannot, by any stretch of imagination, see how a restriction on the membership of a legislative assembly, which infringes a citizen's right to form associations under Article 10 (1) (c) of the Federal Constitution, can be deemed necessary or expedient in the interest of Malaysia or any part thereof, public order, morality or even labour or education.[12]

As an aside, what was heartening to Malaysian constitutional lawyers was the ready acceptance by both courts of the dicta expressed by Lord Wilberforce in *Minister of Home Affairs v. Fisher*[13] that a constitution should be construed with less rigidity and with

more generosity than Acts of Parliament, and as *sui generis* calling
for principles of interpretation of its own. In consequence, this
liberal method of interpreting the Constitution has now become
part of the laws of Malaysia, and is a welcome development.

From a constitutional standpoint, the courts were absolutely
correct in striking down the Kelantan law. Article 10 of the Federal
Constitution is as clear as it can be on the matter—in fact very little
can be said by way of submissions to support the constitutionality
of such a State law in the light of the express language in Article
10. As the Kelantan law results in prejudice to a member of a
political party if he or she leaves that party because the member
will then lose his or her seat in the Legislative Assembly, the law
infringes that member's freedom of association. One can therefore
readily appreciate the robustness of approach taken by Gunn Chit
Tuan SCJ, who saw the matter in simple terms because it was plain
and obvious to him.

THE POSITION ELSEWHERE

Perhaps the leading Privy Council decision is *Collymore v. Attorney
General*,[14] an appeal from Trinidad and Tobago. In delivering the
judgment on behalf of the Privy Council, Lord Donovan stated that
the constitutional freedom of association provided in Section 1 (j)
of the Constitution of Trinidad and Tobago was not sufficiently wide
as to strike down a law that curtailed the right of members of a
trade union to go on strike, and that the abridgement of the rights
of free collective bargaining and to strike were acceptable abridge-
ments of the right of freedom of association.

Although freedom of association is not explicitly protected in
the Constitution of the United States of America, the judiciary has
impliedly held that it is a necessary derivative of the First Amendment's protection of freedom of speech, the right of the people to
peaceably assemble and freedom to petition. The general principle,
as developed in the First Amendment jurisprudence of the Supreme
Court, is that of freedom 'to engage in association for the advancement of beliefs and needs'.[15]

In Canada, the Charter of Rights and Freedoms is given constitutional status pursuant to the *Constitution Act*, 1982. Section 2 (d)
of the Charter provides that everyone has the fundamental freedom
of association. In *re Public Service Employee Relations Act*[16] the Supreme
Court of Canada held that this guarantee of freedom does not
include, in the case of a trade union, a guarantee of the right to
bargain collectively and of the right to strike. In *Black v. Law Society
of Alberta*[17] the Alberta Court of Appeal held that a rule enacted by
the Law Society of Alberta prohibiting a lawyer practising in the

province of Alberta from entering into a partnership with another lawyer practising in another province in Canada was unconstitutional because it violated Section 2(d) of the Charter, which protects the formation of an association for the earning of a livelihood.

THE PROBLEM IN INDIA

My limited research on developments in some common law jurisdictions suggests that only in India has there been a reported decision on the constitutionality of an anti-hopping law. One striking feature of the *Mian Bashir*[18] case is the volume of evidence presented to the court with regard to defections in India, both at federal and State levels. By the time the case was heard (1982), numerous books and articles had been published in India on the grave problems caused by defections and the threat they posed to the very functioning of parliamentary democracy; some of these publications were tendered as evidence. Such evidence included the following facts:

1   that between 1967 and 1972, 60% of elected legislators (at all levels) defected at least once;
2   that a majority of the 51 administrations that took office between March 1967 and December 1970 fell because of defections;
3   that administrations in Mysore, Uttar Pradesh and Gujarat fell within one week of their formation after the 1971 mid-term elections;
4   that in Bihar at least 85 legislators changed sides twice, and some of them even four times;
5   that during a one-year period after the 1967 general elections, defections in the States from Congress totalled 175 and to Congress 139;
6   that between 1967 and 1970, some 900 legislators were involved in defections—of these 155 were rewarded with office, of whom 84 secured cabinet posts;
7   that the position did not improve between 1978 and 1980—in each of these four years the number of defections at the State level were 41, 57, 69 and 74; and
8   that in only one known case[19] did a defector resign his seat upon defection and contest the ensuing by-election, which he won.

The judgments were also strewn with references to malpractices such as multiple floor crossings, the role of money and other dishonourable inducements, personal aggrandisement of legislators and rank opportunism. The judgments of the four judges, which run to about 66 pages, reveal the very sorry state of Indian politics, especially at the State level, for about 35 years after independence. The political landscape cannot be disregarded when one reviews the constitutionality of a law that is enacted solely to prevent such defections in order to enable parliamentary democracy to function properly and in the manner contemplated by the founders of the Indian Constitution. To be fair, the four judges were acutely conscious of the political backdrop; what is interesting is that they were evenly divided on whether a law enacted to deal with this problem passed the test of constitutionality.

THE POLITICAL DIMENSION

Both Malaysian courts in the *Nordin bin Salleh* case referred to the political background of the defection problem in India which was referred to in the *Mian Bashir* case. In the Supreme Court, Lord President Tun Hamid Omar observed:

> The position in this country cannot, however, be said to be similar to the position in India then, for the background events to which we have briefly referred have no parallel here. Certainly, no attempt whatsoever was made either by the introduction of evidence or even by way of argument to establish the contrary.[20]

There is little doubt that although defections have occurred at federal and State levels in Malaysia, particularly in the East Malaysian State of Sabah (formerly known as North Borneo), the scale and magnitude of the problem comes nowhere near that outlined in the *Mian Bashir* case. The political reality in Malaysia has thus to be considered in order to properly appreciate the provisions in the Constitution and the State laws.

Between 1957 and 1972 Malaya, and subsequently Malaysia, was governed by the Alliance Party, which was a partnership of three parties—UMNO, MCA and MIC—representing the three major races in the country—Malays, Chinese and Indians. In 1972, the Alliance Party was replaced by the Barisan Nasional (National Front), which is a grand coalition of about ten parties, including the three constituent parties of Alliance. Barisan Nasional has won every general election since its establishment and won handsomely at general elections in 1995. One cannot exaggerate the overwhelming dominance execised by the Alliance/Barisan Nasional governments since independence; perhaps the only parallel would be the PRI Party in Mexico. Their dominance also extends to forming governments in all the States except Kelantan and Sabah, which have seen other parties in seats of power from time to time.

Barisan Nasional's ascendancy is not restricted to politics. With the advent of the New Economic Policy (NEP) in 1971 its tentacles have reached all economic and financial sectors of the nation. The mass media is heavily slanted to it. The centralisation of power is such that the prime minister (and leader of Barisan) is in an enviable position as far as patronage is concerned. Appointments by the prime minister are not limited to traditional positions of government or administration, but also include heads of public and national corporations. Likewise, because of the state's regulatory power over commercial and financial matters, the minister of Finance also has tremendous power and influence over senior appointments in banks, insurance companies and the like.

The whip system in party politics is another significant factor. Discipline has always been imposed on all legislators by all Malaysian political parties. Every issue seems to attract a three-line whip. Very few instances, if any, have occurred in Malaysian parliamentary history where members of Parliament have been allowed to vote according to their conscience. Every issue seems to be partisan and to be voted upon along party lines.

This in turn is linked to the phenomenon that the electorate seems to be voting for the party and not the candidate. With the exception of a very small number of parliamentarians who have commanded personal influence, the voting pattern hitherto uniformly appears to indicate that the electorate is not particularly concerned about the identity of the candidate; only the party that has permitted him or her to stand on its ticket matters.

These factors may help to explain why the problem of defections has not assumed Indian proportions. There is really no incentive for a Malaysian politician who belongs to the Alliance/Barisan coalition to defect. He or she belongs to the successful party; he or she chose to join it in the first place and no material advantage will accrue to the politician by defecting to the opposition party, which seems doomed to remain forever in a state of opposition. On the other hand, the leader of every opposition party in Malaysia must at all times remain vigilant to ensure that the party's ranks are not depleted. If statistics are compiled on defections in Malaysia, I am confident that they will demonstrate that the position of defections has hurt the opposition parties far more than the ruling party. This will also explain why Parliament and State legislatures of eleven States have never enacted anti-hopping laws. In Kelantan and Sabah they have been passed by a non Barisan Nasional government: PAS in Kelantan and PBS in Sabah.

The worst case of mass political defection in Malaysia occurred in February 1994 after the State elections for 48 seats in the Sabah Legislative Assembly. The PBS Party led by Joseph Pairin Kitingan won 25 seats while Barisan won 23 seats. In these circumstances, it was absolutely clear that the Sabah governor had no option but to invite Kitingan to form the State government. The governor feigned illness, with the result that one witnessed the unseemly sight of Kitingan himself camping outside the governor's palace for 36 hours. Kitingan was finally sworn in as chief minister. Exercising an unusual provision in the Sabah State Constitution, Kitingan immediately nominated six persons to be appointed to the Assembly; this meant that his government had 31 seats out of 54, which was a comfortable majority by any yardstick.

Defections of alarming proportions during the first few weeks of his administration saw Kitingan's majority evaporate on a daily basis. Within a month of taking office he was compelled to resign because he no longer commanded the confidence of the majority of the members of the Assembly, and the Barisan government took office. Thus the Sabah electorate, which had elected a PBS government, saw it toppled by defections in less than a month. It was a shameful episode which tarnished parliamentary democracy in Malaysia. Allegations of 'money politics' in the mass media did not help the image of politicians who seemed to be in a hurry to bail out of a sinking ship to join Barisan.

CONCLUSION

The problem of defections cannot be resolved by constitutional means. As stated above, Article 10 of the Constitution, as presently worded, does not permit a law to be enacted to deal with defections. Thus one would have to amend the Constitution to achieve this objective. In my view, the defection problem has not reached such dramatic proportions as to warrant an amendment of the Constitution, particularly if it has the effect of impinging upon a fundamental freedom.

Defection is a political matter and has to be resolved by political means at the political level. In a parliamentary democracy, the electorate (at least once in five years) has the ultimate say. The electorate should make known its views on the matter; if members of the electorate are sufficiently concerned about defections they should vote against candidates who they think are participating in the game of defections—to some extent it *is* a game, and it resembles musical chairs. The Malaysian electorate may not at present be sufficiently mature to take such a collective stand, and only time will tell whether they eventually will. On the other hand, perhaps the Malaysian electorate and society have the government and the politicians they deserve. This is in contrast to mature political systems such as exists in England, where defections are not a problem. Even if it is a problem there, the solution in England would not lay by force of law but by the power of the ballot box.

Perhaps 'money politics' is unknown there. Despite the record of political defections in Malaysian politics, and in particular the unscrupulous opportunism displayed by Sabah politicians early in 1994, the law and the Constitution have little role in resolving the essentially political problem of defections in politics.

12

Anti-Defection Law in India

Anil Divan

The Indian Constitution has a federal structure with 26 States and six Union territories governed by the central government. The Union Legislature has two Houses of Parliament: the House of the People (Lok Sabha) and the Council of States (Rajya Sabha). The former consists of about 535 members directly elected by adult franchise from different territorial constituencies. The Rajya Sabha consists of over 230 representatives elected by members of the State legislatures. Apart from the Parliament, each State would have a Legislative Assembly, and some States are bicameral and have a Legislative Council. Thus the directly elected members in the State assemblies would number more than 4000. The political executive at the centre functions on the parliamentary model. The president of India is the constitutional head, like the English monarch. He or she has to act on the advice of his or her Council of Ministers, headed by the prime minister of India. Thus the Council of Ministers must enjoy the confidence of the Lok Sabha, and can be voted out by a no-confidence motion. The State assemblies also function on similar lines, but the Council of Ministers is headed by a chief minister. The chief minister's government must command a majority in the State legislatures or it can be voted out of power.

With so many State assemblies, the legislatures are a fertile ground for defections or crossing of the floor, known as 'hopping' from one side to the other.

BACKGROUND

A ministerial post is a coveted position. In view of major economic and regulatory powers enjoyed by the government, the scope for corruption and kickbacks is unlimited. The lure of office and the consequent illegal economic advantages are a temptation that very few legislators can resist, and in the 1970s the problem of defections reached alarming proportions. In local Hindi parlance the legislators were called '*Ayaram*' and '*Gayaram*'—persons who cross the floor (or hop) again and again. In view of rising public criticism Parliament set up a committee to investigate the malaise of defection and make a report. To quote from the report:

> Following the fourth general election in the short period between March, 1967 and February, 1968 the Indian political scene was characterised by numerous instances of change of party allegiance by legislators in several States. Compared to roughly 542 cases in the entire period between the First and the Fourth general election (about 17 years) at least 438 defections occurred in these 12 months alone. Among independents 157 out of a total 376 elected joined the various parties in this period. That the lure of office played a dominant part in decisions of legislators to defect was obvious from the fact that out of 210 defecting legislators of the State of Bihar, Haryana, Madhya Pradesh, Punjab, Rajasthan, Uttar Pradesh and West Bengal, 116 were included in the Councils of Ministers which they helped to bring into being by defections. The other disturbing features of this phenomenon were: multiple acts of defection by the same person or set of persons (Haryana affording a conspicuous example); few resignations of the membership of the legislature or explanations by individual defectors; indifference on the part of the defectors to political proprieties, constituency preference or public opinion; and the belief held by the people and expressed in the Press that corruption and bribery were behind some of these defections.

Subhash C. Kashyap, who was secretary-general of Lok Sabha (the House of the People) from 1980 to 1990, states in his book *Anti-Defection Law*:

> Between the fourth and fifth general elections in 1967 and 1972 from among 4,000 odd members of the Lok Sabha and the Legislative Assemblies in the States and the Union Territories, there were nearly 2,000 cases of defection and counter-defection. By the end of March, 1971 approximately 50 per cent of the legislators had changed their party affiliations and several of them did so more than once . . . some of them as many as five times. One MLA was found to have defected five times to be a Minister for only five days. For some time, on an average almost one State Government was failing each month due to changes in party affiliations by members. In the case of State Assemblies alone, as much as 50.5 per cent of the total number of legislators changed their political affiliations at least once. The percentage would

be even more alarming if such States were left out where Government happened to be more stable and changes of political affiliations or defections from parties remained very infrequent. That the lure of office played a dominant part in this 'political horsetrading' was obvious from the fact that out of 210 defecting legislators of the various States during the first year of 'defection politics', 116 were included in the Councils of Ministers in the Governments which they helped to form.

After Indira Gandhi's assassination in October 1984 her son Rajiv Gandhi called for elections in December 1984. He swept the polls on a massive sympathy wave. This was his first venture into electoral politics. He rapidly enacted the Anti-Defection Law as a shield to retain his own power and prevent dissidents. The Constitution (52nd Amendment) 1985 was his answer to defections. It amended Articles 102 and 191 of the Constitution and also added the Tenth Schedule. These are the Constitutional provisions regarding disqualification of legislators on the ground of defection. Article 102 (2) that was inserted in the Constitution provided that 'a person shall be disqualified for being a member of either House of Parliament if he is so disqualified under the Tenth Schedule'. Similarly Article 191 was amended to include Subarticle (2), which provided that 'a person shall be disqualified for being a member of the Legislative Assembly or Legislative Council of a State if he is so disqualified under the Tenth Schedule'.[1]

The Objects and the Reasons of the 52nd Constitution Amendment Bill were stated thus: 'the evil of political defections has been a matter of national concern. If it is not combated it is likely to undermine the very foundations of our democracy and the principles which sustain it . . . this Bill is meant for outlawing defections.'

The Tenth Schedule broadly provides for (1) the grounds for disqualification; (2) exceptions and exemptions; (3) the machinery for decision making; and (4) jurisdiction of the courts. The grounds of disqualification are (a) if a legislator voluntarily gives up his or her membership of the political party by which he or she was set up as a candidate; or (b) if he or she votes or abstains from voting in the legislature contrary to any direction issued by the political party to which he or she belongs without obtaining permission (however, the party may condone his or her acts within fifteen days); (c) if a member elected otherwise than as a candidate of a political party joins any political party after his or her election.

Exceptions to disqualification are broadly threefold. Firstly, an exception is made if there is a split in the political party (the political party here consists of the members of that party in the legislature only). A split to earn an exemption from disqualification has to be of not less than one-third of members of the original party. If the group is one-third or more it is a new, original political party. Secondly, if there is a merger of the political parties in the legislature the member who joins the new party or refuses to join the new party does not incur disqualification. However, the merger must be supported by not less than two-thirds of the members. Thirdly, if a member is elected as a Speaker or as the chairman he or she may in view of such a position voluntarily give up membership of the political party because of his or her occupation of the office of Speaker or chairman. On ceasing to be Speaker or chair he or she can rejoin the original political party.

This giving up of membership or rejoining does not incur disqualification. The authority that is to decide whether there is a disqualification or not is the Speaker or the chair. However, when a Speaker/chair's disqualification is under contest, the matter has to be decided by a member elected by the House. As far as the jurisdiction of the courts is concerned the constitutional amendment by paragraph 7 of the Tenth Schedule provides: 'Notwithstanding anything contained in this Constitution, no Court shall have any jurisdiction in respect of any matter connected with the disqualification of a Member of a House under this Schedule.' Parliament was attempting to completely oust judicial review and keep the decision of the Speaker or chairman beyond the pale of litigation and controversy.

JUDICIAL DECISIONS

Several cases relating to defections have reached the Supreme Court of India, the apex court in the judicial hierarchy. All of them have emanated from decisions relating to defections concerning State legislators. Not a single case has reached the courts from any controversies arising in Parliament, which is the central legislature. However, the law laid down in the above cases would equally govern the interpretation of the Anti-Defection Law as embodied in the Tenth Schedule to Parliamentary Defections.

The questions that have been agitated in the court are, broadly: (1) the constitutional validity of the entire Tenth Schedule; (2) the finality of the decisions of the Speaker or the chair; (3) the powers of the court to judicially review the decisions of the Speaker or chair; and (4) whether the Speaker and chair are bound to submit to the jurisdiction of the courts and the contempt powers of the courts.

THE PUNJAB ASSEMBLY CASE2

This case resulted from the floor-crossing or 'hopping' that arose not out of love of lucre but because of political differences. A political accord was reached between the central government led by Mr Rajiv Gandhi and moderate Sikhs led by the then Chief Minister Mr Surjit Singh Barnala. Because of political differences Barnala's party (Shiromani Akali Dal) split, and 27 members formed a break-away group. The incumbent Speaker did not disqualify them, thus recognising the split. Later a new Speaker was elected and he issued notices against the breakaway group for their disqualification. These members sought a ruling from the High Court of Punjab.

In the High Court, the entire Tenth Schedule was challenged as being unconstitutional. However, the High Court struck down as unconstitutional paragraph 7 of the Tenth Schedule, which ousted the jurisdiction of the courts. The ground was that there was no ratification of the amendment by the State assemblies, and that a constitutional amendment that ousts the jurisdiction of the higher courts requires ratification by State assemblies. Paragraph 6 was read down so as not to exclude judicial review by the High Court or the Supreme Court. The rest of the Tenth Schedule was upheld.

The ratio laid down in the judgment of the Supreme Court in *Zihota Hollohon v. Zachillhu*[3] (which is the most exhaustive judgment on the point) may be summarised as follows:

1 Paragraph 7 of the Tenth Schedule is declared invalid and unconstitutional because of lack of ratification by State assemblies. Whenever powers or jurisdiction of the High Court and the Supreme Court are tinkered with, the amendment requires ratification by State legislatures. As the 52nd Amendment Bill did not undergo the process of ratification, paragraph 7 was declared to be unconstitutional.

2 The rest of the Tenth Schedule was declared to be valid and constitutional. Paragraph 7, which was struck down, was regarded as severable.

3 The argument that every elected legislator must vote according to his or her conscience and on occasions not follow the party whip was urged in support of a democratic right—freedom to vote, and also to vote according to one's conscience. The court held that under Indian conditions there was no vice in the Tenth Schedule that would subvert democratic rights. In fact it was held that the anti-defection provisions were salutary and would strengthen the fabric of Indian parliamentary democracy by curbing unprincipled and unethical political defections.

4 The decision of the Speakers or chairpersons on disqualification of a member was regarded as an adjudicatory function, and such a function was equated with the function of a tribunal. As a result judicial review was permissible and could not be excluded.

5 The High Courts and Supreme Court under their constitutional powers of judicial review could set aside such decisions by

Speakers/Chairpersons on grounds such as mala fide or non-compliance of rules of natural justice, or even on the ground of perversity. The above decision was reached by a majority of three against two. The minority of two judges held the entire 52nd Amendment that inserted the Tenth Schedule as unconstitutional and as an abortive attempt to amend it. The ground was lack of proper presidential assent after obtaining the required ratification from State legislatures.

An interesting controversy arose between the Supreme Court of India and the Speaker of the Manipur Assembly, Shri Borobabu. The Speaker took up the stand, under the Indian Constitution, that the privileges of the State legislatures are those enjoyed by the House of Commons when the Constitution of India was brought into force, in January 1950. There are provisions in the Constitution by which the courts do not interfere with the legislative process and procedures and similarly the legislatures do not discuss or interfere with court proceedings. It is only after a law is enacted that the question of judicial review could be appropriately raised and decided. The contention of the Speaker was that the matter of deciding on defections fell within legislative privileges and was an internal matter, and he would not submit to jurisdiction or follow the orders of the Supreme Court. The Supreme Court took a different view of its own powers, and having held that the Speakers acted as Tribunals while deciding the question as to disqualification by defection, they were in that capacity bound to follow the Court's orders. In fact the Supreme Court was on the point of issuing notices for contempt against the Speaker, but ultimately the Speaker relented and submitted to the Court's jurisdiction.

LOOPHOLES AND POSSIBLE REFORMS

The Anti-Defection Law was rushed through Parliament when the Rajiv Gandhi government had a massive majority. He wanted to prevent defections from his own party which would threaten his position as prime minister. The motivation, like most political motivations, was for protecting his own powerbase rather than improving the system.

The loopholes that need to be plugged are as follows:

1   There is no precise definition of terms such as 'political party', 'split' or 'merger'. When a defection is threatened the normal *modus operandi* is to expel some disloyal members so that those members may not be counted to achieve the one-third members required for a split. The balance of members who are expelled cannot then defect in order to defeat or destabilise the government.

2   Independent members who have come without support of any party are prevented from joining a political party. This is in contrast to the one-third group being permitted to cross floors on the basis of a split.

3   Before threatening defection there is a flurry of activity and many members are expelled. Whether such expulsion is legal or illegal is not being decided by the Speaker/chair.

4   Unlike an independent judicial body such as an election tribunal or court the jurisdiction is exercised by the Speaker or the chair. Their approach is neither objective nor judicial and they lack judicial experience. The decisions betray a partisan approach and are coloured by political considerations, party loyalties and affiliations, and their personal interest. If the Anti-Defection Law is to have greater impact the decisions will have to be made in a more objective, disinterested and judicial manner, and should ideally be left to an independent judicial forum.

CONCLUSIONS

The 52nd Amendment is a step in the right direction. It has to a considerable extent controlled the daily defections that were once witnessed in the Indian political scene. The Supreme Court's interpretation of the amendment and the provisions as to defection have considerably enlarged the power of judicial review. It means that a large slice of power has passed to the higher judiciary. An interesting constitutional controversy arose when the central government led by Prime Minister V. P. Singh lost a no-confidence motion and resigned on 7 November 1990. The succeeding Prime Minister Mr Chandra Shekhar belonged to V. P. Singh's party, but walked out of it, claiming more than one-third of the original group to avoid disqualification. The matter was carried to the Speaker, but before the Speaker gave his decision the Chandra Shekhar government—having won a vote of confidence on the floor of the Lok Sabha with the support of the opposition led by Rajiv Gandhi—was in office from 16 November 1990. On 11 January 1991 when the Speaker gave his ruling, the government was well and truly in the saddle. The Speaker's ruling was to give the benefit of the doubt to most of the members who had changed loyalties as a group, thereby ensuring the continuance of the new administration. The Speaker's decision was never challenged in the Supreme Court, but if it had been, momentous questions would have arisen. The Court's decision would have either knocked out or kept in place the new administration. This illustrates how the Court's powers have been greatly enlarged—an awesome power to unseat governments and disqualify ministers.

PART III
The Constitutional and Legal Framework

13

The Japanese Constitution and Representative Democracy

Akira Osuka

Representative democracy means that 'the representatives of the people' take part in government of the state on behalf of the people as sovereign. The Constitution of Japan provides in its preface that 'Government is a sacred trust of the people—the powers of which are exercised by the representatives of the people'. Therefore, representative democracy is a fundamental principle of government in Japan. This chapter shows how it is incorporated in the Japanese Constitution.

As the central function of representative democracy is provided through Parliament, the system is often called 'parliamentary democracy'. Section 43 of the Constitution stipulates that 'Both Houses shall consist of elected members, representative of all the people', and it is clear that the representatives of all the people are the 'members' who are 'duly elected representatives in the National Diet'. This is very significant in two ways.

Firstly, 'representatives of all the people' refers not to specific electoral districts but to the whole of Japan. Secondly, as Section 15 provides 'Universal adult suffrage is guaranteed with regard to the election of public officials', and as Section 44 provides 'The qualifications of members of both Houses [shall not be discriminated] because of race, creed, sex, social status, family origin, education, property or income', representatives of the people should be elected not by an election with any kind of qualification but by a universal election. And Section 51, which provides 'Members of both Houses shall not be held liable outside the House for speeches, debates or votes cast inside the House' is also important in light of the embodiment of representative democracy, because it protects freedom of speech in the Diet, together with certain exemptions from common legal responsibilities generally imposed on all the people.

Secondly, the provisions concerning the cabinet government system are also important. Section 67 provides that 'The Prime Minister shall be designated from among the members of the Diet by a resolution of the Diet'. Section 68 provides that 'The Prime Minister shall appoint the Ministers of State. However, a majority of their number must be chosen from among the members of the Diet', Section 66 provides that 'The Cabinet, in the exercise of executive power, shall be collectively responsible to the Diet', and Section 69 provides that 'If the House of Representatives passes a no-confidence resolution, or rejects a confidence resolution, the Cabinet shall resign en masse, unless the House of Representatives is dissolved within ten days'. These provisions are all illustrations of the cabinet government system. Generally speaking, cabinet government is a system in which the organisation and continuation of the cabinet requires the confidence of the Diet. The Japanese Constitution does not adopt an exact separation of powers, but subjects the cabinet to supervision by the Diet, to ensure that executive power is not exceeded. Thus the actual operation of representative democracy can be safely maintained in the constitutionally ordered structure of the cabinet, the Diet, and the people.

But some questions about representative democracy persist. The first concerns the relationship between representative democracy and popular sovereignty. As the Constitution proclaims in its Preface that 'sovereign power resides with the people' and refers in Section 1 to 'the people with whom resides sovereign power', popular sovereignty is clearly stated as being the fundamental principle of government. Popular sovereignty refers to the principle that the people themselves play the central role in all spheres of government. But there is also the question as to the relationship between popular sovereignty and representative democracy, and this second question focuses on the contents of three constitutional provisions that deal directly with democracy. The Constitution provides in Section 96 that

> Amendments to this Constitution shall be initiated by the Diet, through a concurring vote of two-thirds or more of all the members of each House and shall thereupon be submitted to the people for ratification, which shall require the affirmative vote of a majority of all votes cast thereon, at a special referendum or at such election as the Diet shall specify.

Section 95 provides that 'A special law, applicable only to one local public entity, cannot be enacted by the Diet without the consent of the majority of the voters of the local public entity concerned, obtained in accordance with law'. Finally, Section 79 provides that 'The appointment of the judges of the Supreme Court shall be reviewed by the people'. Since these provisions require direct participation of the people in specified governmental matters, the Constitution seems to suppose direct democracy to that extent. But does this imply a contradiction with the notion of representative democracy?

A third question, and one which is quite contemporary, concerns the role of political parties. Today political parties exert great influence on both the people and the members of the Diet. But this leads to problems concerning the limitations placed on the choices open to the people, and the constraints that are placed on the political activities of members of the Diet.

THE PRINCIPLE OF REPRESENTATIVE DEMOCRACY

Representative democracy and popular sovereignty

The first question concerns the relationship between popular sovereignty and representative democracy, both of which have been developed in Western democratic countries. For example, in France before the French Revolution began in 1789, the members of 'States General (*États Généraux*) were legally constrained to abide by orders issued by the groups from which they came.[1] In other words, a representative of a particular group had no liberty to express his own view, and if he acted against orders, would have been forced to resign. Today, this kind of relationship is called 'mandatory delegation' (*mandat impératif*).

The French Revolution violently overthrew the antiquated socio-economic order of the *ancien régime* and deprived the monarch of absolute power. For the first time, the French citizens themselves acquired political power, and the political idea advocated at that time was the principle of popular sovereignty. However, the French Constitution of 1791 adopted the principle of so-called 'national' sovereignty (*la souveraineté de la nation*). The term 'nation' is used to describe the sovereign people in the sense of the nation as an abstract notion of all the people, including even the monarch. Since the adoption of such a notion conceptually did not enable the means for its application in reality, and could not facilitate the exercise of actual sovereign power, actual representatives inevitably were needed. Further, as the people could not give any mandatory delegation to their representatives, the representatives were able to act in the Parliament without any constraints. In this way, the representatives became independent of the people as sovereign, and hence there was no necessity, in principle, for universal election. Restricted elections were administered, based on special limitations according to the amount of one's tax and property. Therefore 'national' sovereignty was a mere surface principle conferring legitimacy on the representatives who exercised the actual power. Furthermore, there was no legal duty imposed by the electors apart from the political relationship. Such a representative relationship is generally called 'pure representation' *(le gouvernement représentatif pur)*. In this way, the original model of representative democracy was formed, and it gradually spread to other Western countries.

On the other hand, soon after the Revolution in France, the theory of sovereignty of the 'people' *(la souveraineté du peuple)* appeared. This theory assumed that the sovereign power resided in the 'people', an entity that consisted of all the adults, and assumed that individual adults actually exercised the sovereign power. Theoretically, it follows that the people should take part in government and determine its policies, and hence the only ruling principle should be direct democracy. Therefore, not only a universal election system but also a mandatory delegation system, a recall system, and so on were, as a matter of course, required. In this sense, the theory of 'popular representation' *(le gouvernement représentatif populaire)* emphasises not legitimacy—which is given to the representatives—but the actual power itself which is exercised by the people as sovereign. But such an ideal popular sovereignty has not yet been realised in the world.

The system of 'pure representation' developed into 'semi-representation' *(le gouvernement semi-représentatif)* through the progress of democracy, especially through the male universal election system which evolved in the middle of the nineteenth century in Western countries. This institution was founded on the idea that the electors' will should be reflected as correctly as possible, and it is now accepted in many countries. The 'semi-representation' model has an affirmative aspect, in that the electors' will should be realised through a universal election. However, it also has a negative aspect, in that mandatory delegation is prohibited. There then arises a relationship between the notions of sovereign theory and 'semi-representation'. In France it is generally thought that sovereignty can be based either on the 'national' or the 'popular' theory of sovereignty.

In the light of these theories, how does representative democracy relate to popular sovereignty in Japan? The Japanese Constitution provides that representatives of the people shall be the elected members of the Diet (Section 43), that election shall be universal election (Sections 15 and 44), and that referendums shall be held on three special occasions. Therefore, the Constitution supposes 'semi-representation'. But at the same time, this 'semi-representation' has significance solely in the political sense; that is to say, the representatives of the people in the Japanese Constitution still remain of the classical type which is founded on the theory of 'national' sovereignty. Therefore, the will of the people (the electors' will) at best can be realised through an actual election and actual political process. This is so because, firstly, it is natural to think in the light of the historical process of representative democracy. Secondly, because the Japanese Constitution stipulates that Diet members as representatives of the people shall be the representatives of all Japanese people, it is quite inconsistent with this Constitution to interpret such Diet members as being the partial representatives of some people. Thirdly, if immunity for speeches delivered in the Diet is purportedly to ensure full political freedom, partial representation would contradict this. Fourthly, the idea of 'semi-representation' should be realised solely through an actual election and politics, and should not be claimed to establish a certain legal relationship as an institution in the constitutional meaning. Fifthly, the Constitution intends to control executive power (which is now on the increase), but not by the direct democratic control of the Parliament. Finally, sovereignty of the people thoroughly excludes minors from the definition of sovereignty and immediately connects with direct democracy.

Representative democracy and direct democracy

If the ideal of democracy is briefly expressed in the famous phrase 'government of the people, by the people, for the people', it is direct democracy that is the most appropriate system. And if this is so, why do many countries nowadays adopt not direct democracy but representative democracy? The first reason for it is that direct democracy could only be maintained in small countries. The second reason is that people neither have enough time to spend on political activities nor become sufficiently politically aware to do so. The third reason is that, as German history in the Nazi period clearly demonstrates, people often tend—without due deliberation—to be swept along a wrongful course by the tide of contemporary events. Because of these aspects, the Japanese Constitution does not adopt direct democracy.

This leaves us with the question as to why there are three provisions pertaining to direct democracy written into the Constitution. It is obvious that these provisions are a mere supplement to the institution of representative government. Referendums on constitutional amendment are provided for in Section 96. Amendments to the Constitution are so important and serious a matter that the people should directly participate in their determination. Nevertheless, Section 96 still has supplementary significance, for the initiation of amendments is not allowed to the people. Local referendums as provided for in Section 95 are only to be held when the special Bill is particularly concerned with a certain local entity. While the popular review of the Supreme Court justices is indeed a direct democratic provision, it is also at best an elaborate mechanism for the will of the people to be reflected as much as possible.

Representative democracy and the party state

Once democracy is rooted in the people and a universal election system is introduced, political parties are organised to give effect to their own interests, and to ensure that their own representatives enter the Diet. The state that adopts a cabinet government system will in fact be managed by the political parties (will be a 'party state'), because the cabinet usually consists of the political party or parties that constitute the majority in the Diet. A political platform and public pledge at an election come to have more and more importance these days, but at the same time they come to restrain not only the various choices of the electors but also the free activities of Diet members. As a natural consequence, we have to think whether reinforcement of such restraints binding representatives to party decisions might be against the ideal of representative democracy.

Party discipline might present, on one hand, a certain threat to representative democracy. But on the other hand, under 'semi-representation' such a restraint is expected as a matter of course, because political parties play an important role in connecting the Diet to the people. So, it is not incompatible with Sections 43 and 51 to reinforce this restraint or to dismiss from party membership any representative who does not comply. However, it would be unconstitutional, I think, to enact such legislations that all the Diet members should belong to a particular party, or that a person removed from any party or who changes his or her own party shall be deprived of his or her status as a Diet member.

POLITICAL RIGHT OF THE PEOPLE

Suffrage and eligibility

As mentioned above, elections are very important in 'semi-representation'. The meaning of 'elections' here is the choosing of public officials by the people as an electorate. Though the political right is not innate in itself, it is a very important and fundamental human right. But this political right is now deemed to have a 'quasi-innate character'. Suffrage and eligibility for election are considered as being the most important of the political rights. Generally speaking, suffrage means having the status or qualification to belong in the electorate, and eligibility means having the status or qualification to become an official or to hold public office.

The Japanese Constitution provides in Section 15 that 'The people have the inalienable right to choose their public officials and to dismiss them . . . Universal adult suffrage is guaranteed with regard to the election of public officials'. Section 44 states 'The qualifications of members of both Houses and their electors shall be fixed by law', and Section 47 states 'Electoral districts, method of voting and other matters pertaining to the method of election of members of both Houses shall be fixed by law'. This raises the question of why the Constitution lays down the existence of representatives in such a way, when the right to choose or dismiss public officials is 'inalienable'. While those who advocate the theory of 'sovereignty of the people' emphasise the possibility of imposing mandatory delegation upon public officials on the basis of Section 15, this theory is not compatible with the Japanese Constitution. Section 15 declares merely an ultimate confidence in the officials is conferred by the people under the popular sovereignty principle, because the people can only take part in the government indirectly, namely, through election of the Diet members and local government members. As to dismissal, only Supreme Court justices might be dismissed; others cannot be dismissed.

Now we have reached the question of the legal character of suffrage, concerning which there are four theories: (1) that an election is a public obligation in which people participate as individual members of an electorate; (2) that the electorate as a whole exercises its own power as a body of the state; (3) that an election has a dual aspect derived from fundamental human rights and public obligations; or (4) that an election is an individual right stemming from popular sovereignty. Of these theories, only the third is compatible with the idea of representative democracy, and this is now a commonly held view. Suffrage has two dimensions, one being that the people exercise a constitutional right to vote, the other being that the people perform a public obligation. The reason the Constitution admits the legislature some discretion concerning elections follows from the latter dimension. By contrast, the eligibility to vote and to stand as a candidate for the Diet emphasises the exercise of the individual rights aspect of the constitutionally protected provisions.

Other political rights

Considering political rights broadly, there are other rights besides suffrage and eligibility, including the right to petition. Freedom of speech (Section 21) has come to carry weight for its special function in the political process. Non-economic liberties are guaranteed more carefully than economic liberties because freedom of speech exists at the core of the non-economic liberties that are essential to democracy. In other words, to reflect the will of the people, it is necessary to secure the freedom of criticism against the government of the day, thereby securing a majority rule which presupposes respect for minority views.

These days, moreover, such freedom of political speech should be protected for another reason. The exercise of freedom of speech requires information, and so the state should never obstruct the free flow of information. In modern societies where much information is exclusively possessed by the media and the state, the people must press for the disclosure of much more information about them than these institutions hold. Freedom of speech is thus now considered to range from negative liberty (the freedom to know) to affirmative rights (the right to know). For this reason the right to know carries much weight as a political right in contemporary democratic processes, but it is also generally considered that to establish the obligation of the government to disclose some pieces of information calls for specific legislation. Section 21 itself guarantees only negative freedom to remove state interventions and is insufficient to compel the government to undertake affirmative action. Furthermore, the assertion of the right to know about the media must be considered with much more caution than the assertion of the right to know about the state, because the media is itself a private body which is fundamentally permitted to exercise the freedom of speech.

THE ELECTORAL SYSTEM

The principles of the electoral system

There is one final aspect of representative democracy to be considered: the electoral system. The Japanese Constitution provides in Section 47 that details about the election system shall be fixed by statutes, but this does not grant broad legislative latitude to the Diet, as the basic principles are definitely laid down in the Constitution. The first principle is universal election (Sections 15 and 44), which prohibits restrictions being placed on elections as they were in early modern times. The second principle is equal election, which emphasises the equal value of each person's suffrage. The Constitution provides in Section 14 that 'All of the people are equal under the law and there shall be no discrimination in political, economic or social relations because of race, creed, sex, social status or family origin'. According to a proviso of Section 44 dealing with elections for the Diet, all persons, as sovereign, are to be treated as equal in democratic society. Therefore, an election that classifies people or gives twofold votes to one person cannot be permitted. The equal election principle requires not only the mere formality of 'one vote for one person' but also substantially equal weight for each vote. This is currently important given the tendency for disproportionality between the numbers of residents in electoral districts in relation to the numbers of Diet members returned. In a judicial doctrine of the Supreme Court, equal value of vote has allegedly been guaranteed, but in that doctrine disproportion is allowed to the extent of three to one at the national level. This is a serious problem, because in view of the notion of equal election disproportion should be corrected within a ratio of at least two to one, preferably corrected to as close to a one to one ratio as possible. But in some cases a little deviation would be permissible, for each electoral district has its own traditional, particular background.

The third principle is secret election. The Constitution provides in Section 15 that 'In all elections, secrecy of the ballot shall not be violated. A voter shall not be answerable, publicly or privately, for the choice he has made'. This provision is intended to secure one's freedom to vote in accordance with one's free will. It is especially important that the less powerful in society have such freedom, and it is also important because it seeks to ensure the fairness of elections.

The current electoral system

The electoral system for the House of Representatives in Japan has long adopted the medium constituency system. Under this system, each prefecture is divided into a number of electoral districts, from which between two and five candidates are the Diet members (the present total number of the House of Representatives is 511). On the other hand, the election of the House of Councillors is based on the local electoral district system and the proportional representation system. The number of members returned through the district system ranges from two to eight (for a total of 152), while the proportional representation system is made up of only one district, namely, the whole of Japan (for a total of 100 members). The proportional representation system confers the Diet seats in proportion to the votes each party acquired, and the seats won are respectively distributed to each candidate, who is strictly bound to the ranking list of his or her own party. Political parties prepare such a candidate list, with rankings, in advance, and the seats are given in accordance with that order.

The merit of the large constituency system and the medium constituency system is that the range of choice widens and various candidates can stand for the Diet. But the greater merit of both systems is that fruitless votes—so-called 'dead votes'—will certainly decrease, because the success of the election can be achieved even if the votes gained are not relatively many. The merit of the proportional representation system is also significant in that various minorities can get their own seat, because the proportion of all seats distributed is much in accordance with the actual proportion of votes gained.

But there are some possible demerits in both systems. For example, the voters tend to become indifferent to politics since the relationship between candidates and voters is not very close. In addition, a great deal of money tends to be spent due to the large size of each constituency. Also, plural candidates who belong to the same party often share the same electoral fate—whether as winners or losers.

The chief disadvantages of the proportional representation system are that many small parties somehow get seats and destabilise the political situation, and that the choice offered to people is likely to be bound to the candidate-ranking done by each party, especially under the system of the so-called 'absolutely bound list', tending to distort the original intent of democratic elections.

In this way it can be seen that each system has its own merits and demerits. Japan has recently discussed its electoral system following an agreement between the then Hosokawa administration and LDP (Liberal Democratic Party), which resulted in the passage of the 'Political Reform Act' through the Diet in January 1994.

Electoral reform and its problems

This reform Act is the most notable event in the course of recent political changes in Japan. Its distinctive feature is that it reintroduces the single-member constituency system for the first time after World War II, and combines the single-member constituency system with the proportional representation system. Japan's system for electing members of the House of Representatives now comprises a mixed system consisting of the single-member constituency system and the proportional representation system. The full number of seats is raised to 500, comprising 300 single-member constituency representatives and a further 200 representatives elected by proportional representation. There are by definition 300 single-member constituencies, and the proportional representation system has a further eleven electoral districts whose seats are proportionately decided according to the votes polled for the respective parties. The merits of the single-member system are that the relationship between candidates and the people can be closer; that choices between policy options can be argued more vigorously; that the political situation should stabilise; and that candidates' movements can be monitored more easily in smaller districts, minimising the potential for illegal expenditure on electoral campaigning.

At the same time there are many defects in the single-member constituency system. First of all, fruitless votes will certainly increase, allowing larger parties to get an undeserved number of seats in relation to votes gained. Second, since the single-member constituency system has only one seat per electoral district, competition will become so keen that bribery (corruption) will be committed. Third, one Diet member of one electoral district can only represent the will of the residents living there. Furthermore, since one electoral district is small in extent, a leading figure of that area is so likely to control the election that it becomes increasingly difficult for newcomers to stand for the Diet.

This newly reformed institution consists of two systems, but eventually only the single-member system will work, because the will of the people at the national level cannot be reflected correctly through the operation of the proportional representation seats. It is generally agreed that future politics will be increasingly managed by the political parties following the introduction of the single-member system, and that the various political groupings may be reorganised into two large parties. But this probable change will evolve exclusively around the existing parties, because under the new system new parties or candidates who seek to win seats on behalf of new parties shall be treated as individual rather than party-affiliated candidates, not as candidates of the new party, but as individual candidates. Therefore, future political reorganisation will focus on the existing parties. Whether political stability exclusively led by two big parties is better than vital politics brought about by various parties or vice versa is a question the Japanese people are now asking about the future of their system of representative democracy. They feel themselves to be at a crossroads, and at a serious turning point in the evolution of their political system.

14

The Constitution and Representative Democracy in Bangladesh

Amir ul-Islam

Representation through electioneering in the area known as Bangladesh dates to the mid nineteenth century, when a restricted franchise was introduced at local government level in Bengal. But the election as an institution did not take firm root in the society, which basically remained traditional and in which representation of the people in the system of governance was marginalised under colonial rule. It took almost a century to develop the legal framework for the representative system. Until the *India Act* of 1935 representatives were mostly nominated rather than elected to the native and provincial legislatures. The people of Bangladesh have participated in provincial and later national elections since 1937 under British, Pakistani and independent rule, but experience with elections has been both infrequent and unfortunate. Following the malpractices of the Pakistan era, interference with the conduct of or the consequences of elections became the rule rather than the exception in independent Bangladesh. In the post-independence era the journey of representative democracy in Bangladesh has been neither smooth nor steady. The people have rarely been able to effect their will through elections, which have been more often twisted, manipulated and mutilated. Rather than being an instrument of representation, elections have been perceived as a device for ascending to or for remaining in power—which has more often been acquired through means other than elections.

The purposes for which elections have been held have varied depending upon the interests and wishes of the rulers, and have hardly depended upon the will or the interests of the people; and their regularity and frequency have been anything but steady or consistent. The motivations of the major actors have always failed to make the electors the main focus of the process, and there has always been much controversy not only about the freeness of elections but also about their efficacy and procedural fairness. It is ironic that after the creation of Pakistan following elections in 1946 (including the part now known as Bangladesh), no national election was held on the basis of adult franchise until 1970.

ELECTIONS AND POLITICAL TREACHERY

The history of Bangladesh is full of treacherous acts and events, the train of which has been traced by Mr Justice Shahabuddin Ahmed in his celebrated Judgment concerning the 8th Amendment of the Constitution. This Judgment recalls how, after the election was won in 1946 on the basis of the Lahore Resolution, the majority population of what was then East Bengal was reduced to a minority, and a 'State' was reduced to a province. The Judgment also points out how an elected Constituent Assembly was dissolved without any lawful authority; how an elected prime minister was dismissed by a governor-general not having any legal power to do so; how the historic election process of 1946 was frustrated; and how the will of the people exercised through an election was defeated through conspiracy and treachery. The Judgment further shows how the attempt to frame the Constitution of Pakistan was sabotaged again; how general elections scheduled to be held in 1959 were pre-empted by a military takeover by the then Commander In Charge of the Army, General Ayub Khan; how after a long struggle the only general election held in 1970–71 was frustrated by the imposition of a most unjust and treacherous war upon the unarmed people; and how through great sacrifice the people won the war of liberation with the purpose of establishing democracy.

REPRESENTATION IN POST-INDEPENDENCE BANGLADESH: THE CONTRADICTION BETWEEN THE CONCEPT AND THE REALITY

In giving themselves a Constitution the people of Bangladesh also vested the entire power of the Republic in the people, to be exercised in accordance with the Constitution. There had thus been a drastic change in the role and concept of representation in the nation's life. During the colonial era under the British, elections were perceived as part of the scheme of familiarising the local inhabitants with governance, while in the period under Pakistan's regime, elections became a mechanism for legitimising a military-bureaucratic regime.

But the changing role of elections under the Bangladesh Constitution needs to be considered in its proper perspective. Unless the electoral process can allow people to freely choose their government, and to participate in governance and bring the desired changes in policies, the concept of power belonging to the people as contained in the Constitution becomes inefficacious and almost nugatory. In most of the elections held so far the people have been considered as passive voters, and the main actors have been the political parties, their leaders and their candidates. Success or failure of any party or candidate has depended on their ability to gather the winning number of votes in any manner fair or foul.

The only exceptions to these comments have been the elections of 1970 and 1991. The political reality of the present day is far from that contemplated in the Constitution, the fundamental tenet of which is that all powers belong to the people, who are the real actors in the election process. It is the fundamental mandate of the Constitution that all powers are to be exercised on behalf of the people; but the people are excluded from the process of exercising these powers in various ways. It is said that the Constitution is the supreme law of the land, but the same is trampled on and violated with impunity by those who are bound by the oath to defend it. Article 7 of our Constitution has postulated a basic framework under which powers on behalf of the people are to be exercised, but the very Constitution was replaced by military decree by those who on various occasions took power through unconstitutional means. Article 7 provides as follows:

(i)   All powers in the Republic belong to the people and their exercise on behalf of the people shall be effected only under, and by the authority of, this Constitution.

(ii) This Constitution is, as the solemn expression of the will of the people, the supreme law of the Republic, and if any other law is inconsistent with this Constitution that other law shall, to the extent of the inconsistency, be void.

OBJECTS OF ELECTION UNDER THE CONSTITUTION

The main objects of elections are to facilitate popular participation in public affairs in order to strengthen empowerment of the people; to provide for orderly succession in government by the peaceful transfer of power; to allow for the ultimate exercise of sovereign power and authority of the people through the people's chosen representatives; and to effect change in policy. Since the people as a whole cannot act in the day-to-day running of the affairs of the Republic, they need to act through their agents, namely the elected representatives. It is therefore fundamental that the system through which such representatives are chosen must include free and fair elections, acceptance of the electoral verdict and the accountability of the government to the people. The reality of electioneering remains far removed from the ideals summarised above.

DISILLUSIONMENT AND THE DEMAND FOR A NEUTRAL ADMINISTRATION

In 1990 a pro-democracy movement unseated military leader, President Ershad, and in 1991 the nation's first genuinely free election was won by Khaleda Zia, widow of President Ziaur Rahman, whose earlier assassination had brought her into politics. In view of the abuse and hypocrisy, treachery and sabotage that has been experienced in Bangladesh's recent electoral history, the opposition parties subsequently commenced a boycott of the new Parliament, calling for its dissolution, and for the appointment of a neutral caretaker government until a new Parliament could be elected through free and fair elections conducted under a neutral administration. Over the next two years opposition leader Sheikh Hasina led the opposition in orchestrating general strikes which disrupted the economy, the government and the Parliament. All opposition members, including Awami League deputies, resigned from parliament on 28 December 1994. General elections were held twice in Bangladesh in 1996, as the country continued to struggle for stable and constitutional governance.

The demand for a caretaker government which arose following the restoration of democracy in 1990 was based on a widespread perception that the elections had been 'engineered' by the previous, autocratic, regime. The electoral system's credibility had been destroyed in the course of the militarisation of politics. Instead of the reversal of this trend following the restoration of democracy in 1990 people witnessed repetitions of earlier abuses.

The need for a caretaker and for a neutral government for the interim period was no doubt a legitimate and a popular demand, as the people and particularly all the opposition political parties believed that such a government could ensure the neutrality of administration, security forces, police, law-enforcement agencies and the media on the one hand, and the prevention of abuses of state patronage and public power by any particular party or group on the other.

During the period of crisis there were proposals for an interim national government headed by the prime minister, which did not find favour with the opposition. Demands were also raised for the establishment of an interim government under the Ombudsman, although the office of Ombudsman was not yet established. Yet another option that was discussed was the establishment of a permanent committee of elders selected by the Speaker in consultation with the leader of the House and the opposition. While the government was ready to form a national government under Prime Minister Zia consisting of equal numbers of members in the cabinet from both the sides, they could not agree to any Constitutional changes.

In the search for a solution without making major constitutional changes the French model may provide an interesting study. A provision in the Constitution of the Fourth Republic in France, until amended in 1954, provided that in the event of dissolution of the Assembly by a government in power the prime minister and the minister of the Interior should lose their posts. The former was to be replaced by the president of the Assembly, who would appoint a new minister of the Interior with the consent of an all-party Bureau of the Assembly, and would also bring into the government one member of each group in the Assembly not already represented in the government. It is quite possible that a similar formulation will not be perceived as any loss of face by any party. Rather, it can be accepted as a convention to be incorporated, if agreed, as part of the Constitution at some future point in time. To have an interim government headed by the Speaker upon the dissolution of Parliament, with equal numbers of members in the cabinet from both the party in power and that in opposition would not entail any change in the Constitution.

As a matter of fact, if one looks closely, it is possible to find provision for the element of caretaker government even under the present Bangladesh Constitution. Suppose, on the advice of the prime minister, the Parliament is dissolved today or is dissolved at the end of five years. Then, as under the present dispensation, Begum Khaleda Zia the present (1995) prime minister is expected to continue in office under Article 57 (3) of the Constitution, which provides that 'Nothing in this Article shall disqualify the Prime Minister from holding office until his successor has entered upon office'.

This article thus enables the prime minister to continue in office until her successor enters upon office after the holding of a general election within three months of the dissolution of Parliament. Begum Khaleda Zia's government thus becomes a caretaker government as soon as the Parliament is dissolved, merely for the purpose of handing over the power to her successor in office. So the concept of a caretaker government is a prevalent concept which is already in the Constitution. What the opposition wants is to make the caretaker government neutral and free from party influence.

After the dissolution of the Parliament, neither the prime minister nor any other minister will any longer represent his or her constituency as an MP, nor is there any responsibility attached to the cabinet to remain accountable to the Parliament. In other words, there is no accountability for the caretaker government even if it is headed by the party leader, as is usually the case during the existence of the Parliament. No mischief will be done to the entire structure and balance in the Constitution if, instead of the prime minister, the Speaker heads the interim government for a limited purpose and for a very limited time.

These proposals should be considered free from party or group interests, as it is through collective wisdom that an appropriate solution can be found. It is therefore of utmost importance and urgency that the entire nation and the people, along with all political parties, be involved in consultations through national media and through dialogue and debate. In order to secure a free and fair election and to restore the election as an institution, the following practices may be considered through change of law where necessary, and by making provisions in the Constitution and electoral laws as may be required:

1 A national commitment at all levels for free and fair elections by having:
   (a) all government agencies and civil servants directed to remain neutral and to co-operate with an independent Election Commission to ensure and oversee free and fair elections as part of their duties,
   (b) a vigilant press and media under a neutral administration, which gives equal and equitable coverage to all the parties,
   (c) a campaign to educate the public about free and fair elections, and to ensure full access to information on public issues,
   (d) a citizens' vigilance committee, and
   (e) foreign and local observers for monitoring the election.
2 An independent judiciary to interpret electoral laws and to exercise writ jurisdiction, as part of judicial review in order to ensure strict compliance with the law by the contestants, and to ensure fair and just implementation of electoral laws. The judiciary should not console itself with the pious hope that electoral fraud and violation of laws can be corrected and remedied later through legal challenges. Furthermore, the Chief Election Commission and the returning and presiding officers should be granted extensive powers, while not being allowed themselves to

succumb to hidden influences, or to think themselves above the law or judicial review.

3 An honest, upright, competent, non-partisan Election Commission consisting of three members chosen through extensive consultation among the major political parties and citizens' organisations, having an efficient and trained administration and independent budgetary support to run free and fair elections.

4 Adoption of measures to limit the cost of electoral campaigning and banning the influence of arms (legal and illegal), muscle and money in the election process, giving consideration to the following key points:

(a) regulation of campaigns in the constituencies,

(b) provision by the state of printed publicity materials in exchange for a security deposit from each candidate of an amount (e.g. T. 15 000) in order to reduce the number of frivolous candidates,

(c) organisation of some meetings by the Chief Election Commission,

(d) provision of budgetary support for parties in proportion to the votes obtained by each party at the preceding election, and a requirement that all parties fully disclose their campaign income and expenditure (without, however, being required to name the source),

(e) regulations making false propaganda, and campaigning in the name of religion, electoral offences,

(f) fair allocation of time on radio and television to all political parties,

(g) strict maintenance of law and order during both the campaign and polling.

5 Instead of counting the votes at each centre, arrangements can be made to seal the boxes and, having obtained the signatures of agents and of the presiding officer and polling officers, to secure the boxes at District Headquarters in front of the candidates, their agents and the press.

6 An education program for voters should be developed, and the people's vigilance should be organised through groups, NGO's and human rights organisations.

7 Close links should be built between law-enforcement agencies, security forces and the police, under the Chief Election Commission.

8 Complaints against election-related violence and breaches of electoral laws should be registered, and investigated fully.

9 Election disputes should be processed speedily and efficiently.

10 Prosecutions for electoral offences and election-related violence should be made quickly.
11 A code of conduct having the binding force of law should be devised for political parties and candidates.
12 Electoral campaigning should be prohibited in the 72 hours preceding the election.
13 The Chief Election Commission should arrange for the posting of campaign materials to all voters.
14 The list of voters should be prepared according to the Census, and should be updated annually.
15 A strict register of births and deaths should be maintained.
16 An identification card should be introduced.

On election day the people must feel that they are in control of their own destiny, and not at the mercy of the political parties. Ultimate belief in the people and in the people's sovereign power as is envisaged in the Bangladesh Constitution would be the guarantee for their freedom and their free choice. As Robespierre once said: 'Let the people speak, for their voice is the voice of god, the voice of reason and of the general good.'

In order that the people can speak freely and can make free choices, the necessary social conditions must be created. One of the most important causes of the people's ignorance is the people's misery. Robespierre said: 'The people will become enlightened when they have bread and when the rich and the government will have ceased to hire perfidious journalists and venal speakers to mislead them.' J. L. Talmon in his book *The Origin of Totalitarian Democracy* (London, Secker & Warburg, 1952) has suggested that Robespierre was saying: 'That as long as the people were hungry and dominated and misled by the rich, their recorded opinions could not be taken as reflecting the true will of the sovereign.' It is the free will of the people that therefore has to be exercised through elections in order to realise the sovereignty and prosperity of Bangladesh.

15

Democracy and Representation in the Special Administrative Regions of Hong Kong and Macau

Yash Ghai

In this chapter I propose to examine the system of representation that will be established in Hong Kong and Macau after the transfer of sovereignty over these regions to the People's Republic of China (PRC). Their constitutional systems will be determined by the Basic Laws that have already been promulgated by China's National People's Congress (NPC). The Basic Laws will have to be read in the context of the Chinese Constitution, although considerable doubt remains as to the relationship between the Laws and the Constitution. The two territories will enjoy a special status under the Constitution as Special Administrative Regions of the Republic, with considerable autonomy of their powers and institutions. Aspects of the colonial systems of administration influenced China's thinking on the institutions of the regions, particularly that aspect which emphasised the dominance of the executive at the expense of the legislature. However, it was not possible to entrench that dominance unchanged, due to the existence of considerable pressure—especially in Hong Kong—for a significant measure of democracy. The result is a curious and complex system of representation and equally complicated relations between the executive and the legislature. It would take up too much space to elaborate on this system here. However, some key aspects of the system are discussed below. The discussion is preceded by an exploration of the controversy over the degree of democratisation as the negotiations for the new constitutional order were underway, as that provides the context for the system that will be established in 1997 (for Hong Kong) and 1999 (for Macau).

DEMOCRACY AND DEMOCRATISATION AND THE TRANSFER OF SOVEREIGNTY

Most of the discussion on democracy took place during the drafting of the Basic Laws (as the people were excluded from the negotiations of the Joint Declarations). Curiously, the Joint Declarations established detailed economic, monetary and social policies but said little about the system of government (inverting the normal situation whereby a constitution sets up the system of government, and policies are then the outcome of the political process). It was thus clear that the primary purpose of the Declarations (and of the Basic Laws that were to follow) was to entrench existing economic and social systems, and indeed it was argued by certain conservative business lobbies (and subsequently by China) that the design of the political system must be such as promotes the economic system. At the time that Francis Fukuyama was celebrating the end of history, they contended that the success of the market (the matrix of the economies of Hong Kong and Macau) would be threatened by democracy. Those who supported democratic options were broadly sympathetic to the economic and social goals in the Declarations, so that their backing of democracy was based less on it as a framework for decision making than as a necessary adjunct to regional autonomy.

The public understanding (based on the texts of the Declarations and on assurances by the UK and China) seems to be that democratic options were available. Even those who disapproved of them realised that they could not be postponed forever. To a large extent therefore, given the antediluvian nature of the colonial political systems, the debate was concerned with the pace of democratisation—it was widely assumed that one could not move from the stone to the satellite age in a single direct leap. But the discussion of the pace centred on the methods of elections, and there was limited engagement on the relationship between the executive and the legislature. Nor was there much discussion of factors or policies that would make a success of democracy, perhaps because these territories—particularly Hong Kong—were considered good candidates, with high literacy rates; ethnic homogeneity; economic prosperity; an active non-state sector; a large and vigorous press; a cosmopolitan and plural society; and small, compact land areas. However, to get a fuller flavour of the debate, it is necessary to turn briefly to the views of the main protagonists.

Neither of the departing colonial powers had much interest in democracy. Portugal itself was a dictatorship until 1976, and the leaders of the revolution were more concerned to establish democracy at home than worry about its considerable colonial empire, which disintegrated in the face of local dissidence or rebellion and the Portuguese reluctance to engage in a phased decolonisation. In relation to Macau, Portugal was anxious to hand it back to China rather than try to democratise it. Having disavowed sovereignty over Macau, Portugal was willing to go along with China in a leisurely pace of political change. Nor were there domestic pressures for democratisation—the Macanese, who had enjoyed a privileged position in the colonial order, would stand to lose from it, and the local Chinese leaders took their cue from China and consequently opposed democratisation. There were no political parties, and no effective lobby for democratisation.

The British position was more complex. Until the talks with China on the transfer of sovereignty (and well after it realised that Hong Kong must be returned) it had little interest in democratisation (so that even in the middle of 1984 Hong Kong's constitutional system resembled that of a nineteenth-century African colony). Britain's favourite excuse for this unmitigated gubernatorial rule— that China would not have approved of any moves towards democracy—may indeed have been a factor, but it is clear that Britain found the system congenial for other reasons. It ensured a privileged position for British commercial interests, the co-optation of rising Chinese entrepreneurs, a cosy existence for bureaucrats, and above all the dominance of the market (in which the system was so effective that—as I explore below—many businesspeople came, under British encouragement, to believe that the market and democracy were mutually antagonistic).[1] Nor did Britain have to respond to public pressures for democracy.

However, faced with the imminence of the transfer of power, Britain showed an interest in a limited degree of democracy. It must have been concerned with public and parliamentary reaction in the UK (and more widely) to the unprotected transfer of nearly 6 million of Her Majesty's subjects to a Communist regime. Anxious, meanwhile, to exclude these same subjects from entry to the UK, it may have considered that a high degree of autonomy exercised democratically in Hong Kong would both reduce pressures on them for emigration and morally justify their exclusion. It may also have felt that as the period of transition was upon it during which China would seek to assert more and more influence, it would need to mobilise legitimacy (and allies) in Hong Kong through democratisation.[2] (I do not discuss here another theory explaining new-found British interest in democracy, which has been put out by the Chinese and has the imprimatur of Lee Kuan Yew, that it is part of a Western

conspiracy to undermine China—and other Asian burgeoning economies—by destabilising their societies).[3]

At the same time, the imminence of Chinese sovereignty complicated the new-found task of democratisation. Not only were
twelve years too short a time to transform a thoroughgoing colonial
system (in which its subjects had not even formed a political party
or association) into a viable democratic system, but also Britain
could not decide independently on the aims of political development (having been rebuffed at attempts at a parliamentary system),
and was somewhat directionless. Nor was there, despite everything,
much public enthusiasm for democracy, and as a colonial power
Britain found itself in the unusual role of mobilising public opinion
for democracy rather than resisting it (and discovered that it was
not so suited to it!). But the fundamental difficulty was a major
contradiction: Britain had fought hard, in the Joint Declaration, to
secure its right to rule Hong Kong during the transition period, for
which it required an effective executive which commanded the
support of the legislature. Democratisation may well lead to higher
proportions of legislators who were not committed to support the
government or not beholden to do so—the prospect of a legislature
that bureaucrats could not control was anathema to them.[4] The
government was not really willing to give up any of its powers, and
there was no prospect that the governor's status or authority would
be diminished in any way, ruling out any prospects of real accountability to the legislature (although the Green Paper of 1984 had
contemplated a diminishing role for the governor as in other
instances of decolonisation). A further element in the contradiction
was a consultative role for China through a Joint Liaison Group
(JLG) established in the Joint Declaration.[5] 'Consultation' turned
more and more into joint decision making on numerous matters
that would, even under the Basic Law, fall within the autonomy of
Hong Kong. China made co-operation on transition issues—on
which Britain became more and China less keen—contingent on
acceptable British behaviour on a wide front of issues, particularly
democratisation, which became a more urgent matter at all levels
of British policy after the Tiananmen Square massacre. The British
dilemma is obvious: the greater the number of decisions made in
the JLG, the less is the consolidation of democracy; and yet the
greater the friction existing between Britain and China, the more
threatened is British authority.

Britain found itself negotiating with too many parties with
conflicting interests, compounded by the fact that Britain had also
to conduct its bilateral relations with China regardless of its Hong
Kong interests. China's commercial opening to the outside world
lured Western states to it with visions of immense riches, and Britain

was no less keen to reap the rewards of investments in and trade with China. For many in Britain, particularly the mandarins in the Foreign Office and some businesspeople, Hong Kong became an irritant. The perception in Hong Kong was that Britain had sold Hong Kong down the (Pearl) river, in order to repair its bilateral relations with China so as to protect its bigger commercial interests. For a long time British policy was determined by Foreign Office bureaucrats (popularly but hardly affectionately known as the 'China Mafia') whose principal approach was said to be the appeasement of China. In these calculations democratisation had a low priority.[6] Tiananmen Square brought major shifts of policy, signified by the replacement of Governor Sir David Wilson, brought up in the ethos of the China Mafia, by the politician Christopher Patten, former British cabinet member and chair of the British Conservative Party (although the triumph of politicians over mandarins was short lived).[7]

The colonial administration had relied for legitimacy on the ideology of an efficient and impartial administration, together with the rule of law, which it claimed were unique in the region and were responsible for the great economic success of Hong Kong.[8] The rationality and even-handedness of the administration had laid the foundations on which a market economy had flourished. Thus in essence, as mentioned above, legitimacy came from economic success, and that in turn derived from the market. But the administration did not entirely disregard the political dimensions; one of its boasts was that it had established an extensive and well-functioning system of advisory and consultative bodies to inform itself of public opinion and to involve knowledgeable public leaders in policy making. There are over 400 boards and committees, on which sit members of the public, that offer advice to the government. There is indeed much to be said for this form of participatory democracy, but unfortunately board and committee members are for the most part appointed by the government from a small section of the population, creating a big overlap in membership (and reinforcing the interests of the section already well represented in the Legislative and Executive Councils). The government has been criticised for ignoring the views of the committees when it does not suit it.[9] As we shall see, the rationale of an efficient administration underpinning the market and the specific form of public participation through consultation have continued to overshadow the debates on democracy.[10]

The Chinese position on democratisation was likewise complicated by various factors. Its own political system is highly undemocratic and authoritarian, with an unelected executive which is not responsible to any elected body, and with no protection of civil and political rights (despite the language of its Constitution). But China was then going through a modernisation phase in which it emphasised law and, under allegedly pro-democracy leadership, took some tentative steps towards liberalisation through elections at lower levels with more than one candidate per post, and discussions on the separation of the apparatuses of the Communist Party and the government.[11] But there was very considerable opposition to these measures within the Communist Party, and China decided that it would pursue economic and technological modernisation without political reforms—a decision that was both symbolised and strengthened by the use of armed forces in Tiananmen Square in 1989. Under the circumstances China was unsympathetic to the aspirations in Hong Kong for greater democracy; it feared both the example, for its own people, of a democratically run Chinese government (some Hong Kong people were saying that Hong Kong should become a Special Democratic Region of China) and the support that Hong Kong people might offer the democratic movement on the Mainland. By the time the Basic Law was being drafted, there was considerable anxiety among the Chinese leaders about the succession to Deng Xiaoping—succession being just as fraught in the communist regime as in the imperial system—and therefore a corresponding reluctance to accept an open-ended political system in Hong Kong.

These worries reinforced another Chinese preoccupation—that of instability and even rebellion in Hong Kong, both in the transitional and post-transitional periods.[12] China was anxious to control developments in Hong Kong and Macau and feared that democracy would introduce uncertainties and bring to power leaders that might not be amenable to it.[13] Pointing frequently to the collapse of democracy (and the ensuing 'anarchy') in former British imperial possessions, it cautioned against a hasty move to democracy. At the same time it was anxious not to alienate the people of Hong Kong and had said that it would accept a local consensus (although it became increasingly partisan itself and in the end disregarded a consensus reached by Hong Kong's leaders). It allied itself increasingly with Hong Kong's commercial elite, who were opposed to democracy, and in collaboration with it tried to deflect demands for democracy into forms that would maintain the dominance of the elite and weaken the impact of democracy.

Opinion within Hong Kong was inchoate and divided. Along a continuum, I will discuss the views of the conservative business community, who were supported by professionals, and of the 'liberals' who supported a faster process of democratisation. I make no attempt, for a variety of reasons, to assess the degree of public support each view commanded, since there were no referendums or elections based on the issues that divided the people.[14] There was no common understanding of democracy or its institutional implications. Opinion also changed during the period under consideration. For similar reasons I make no attempt to locate these views within the class structure of Hong Kong. Thus although I ascribe the conservative view to the 'business community', it would be wrong to imply that this community was a monolith. Moreover the business community found powerful support among the most active sections of the working class (represented by trade unions who support China, as opposed to those that support Taiwan—the major division within the labour movement), who for years had toed the line of the Chinese Communist Party and were now opposed to democratisation or social welfare. Thus we had the curious situation of the Communist Party and trade unions joining with the business community in promoting the entrenchment of the economic and political privileges of the latter.

The business community's views were determined by two separate but related considerations. The first was to maintain the market system (including its privileged economic and political positions) and the second was to ensure that China would respect the autonomy promised to Hong Kong. It maintained that democracy would disrupt the market system, as it would generate pressures towards social welfare which politicians would be unable to resist and which would in turn increase the costs of production and make Hong Kong uncompetitive. It would also lead to less rational and less responsible decision making, with confrontation (and playing to galleries) replacing an honest search for consensus. The business community proposed that a person's right to participate in decision making should be related to his or her abilities and achievements, so that, for example, one person may have more votes than another (and some presumably would have none); in Hong Kong these qualities were measured by one's economic success.[15]

The business community had a rather special understanding of the relationship between the market and politics. There has always been a swashbuckling quality to the market in Hong Kong. The older British firms had a preference for a laissez-faire economy, and in the course of time it became the ideology of the government. The ideology hid the close and cosy relations between the government and business leaders, and resulted in a particularly skewed distribution of incomes, disadvantaging the working class. As the Chinese firms began, in the 1980s and 1990s, to replace British firms in the commanding heights, they shared the same interest in intimacy with and therefore influence over the government and in keeping public expenditure low, but otherwise they seem to have little commitment to a laissez-faire economy. Undoubtedly they believe in the rights of property and contracts, but they probably have even less interest than their British counterparts in the rule of law.[16] The growing Chinese presence in Hong Kong's economy and Hong Kong's investment in China (which specially benefit Hong Kong Chinese firms) have driven some sort of a wedge between them and other firms, but in general the business sector ritually pays homage to the rule of law (at the same time as it denounces the human rights movement). Presumably, as in the West in the nineteenth century, it regards democratisation as a threat to the rule of law. Such bourgeoisie as Hong Kong has does not seem to share the view of its counterparts elsewhere that the market is inextricably linked to democracy and human rights, but espouses instead the views made fashionable by Lee Kuan Yew and Mahathir bin Mohamad—and recently, by the Chinese leaders—that authoritarian governments are necessary for the market economy, at least in Asia.[17]

The business community considers that China will tolerate the autonomy promised to Hong Kong in the Basic Law only so long as Hong Kong is economically successful and can contribute to its own development. Democracy will therefore erode the chances of autonomy. Democratisation will threaten autonomy in another way—it will lead either to instability or to a kind of politics (and the possibility of involvement of Hong Kong in Chinese politics) that will irritate China and lead to its intervention in the internal affairs of Hong Kong (this argument carries little conviction since the business community has already facilitated increasing Chinese involvement in Hong Kong politics).

The instrumental view of liberals or democrats is the exact opposite. They see only democracy as standing between China and Hong Kong's autonomy. In the absence of democracy, the political system—especially with the extensive powers of the executive appointed by China—will be open to the manipulation of China. The business leaders will be co-opted and other groups ignored as under the British. Democracy will also help to reinforce the sense of identity of the Hong Kong people—another basis for valuing and maintaining autonomy. But the liberals also value democracy for a reason exactly opposite to that of the conservative group—they see democracy as modernising the economic system of Hong Kong. It will help to ensure a more equitable balance between capital on one hand and labour and consumers on the other. Only in this way will there be a firm commitment to the economic system, and thus a guarantee of its survival.

An examination of the Joint Declaration and the Basic Law shows that the conservatives were more influential than the democrats. In the former they were able to entrench an economic system marked by low taxes and no-deficit budgeting, with a high degree of separation of its economic instruments from China. In the latter, they were able to secure an indefinite postponement of full democracy, and to ensure that in the meantime their political influence would remain dominant. The reason they succeeded gives a good insight into the nature of the Hong Kong system and may provide clues for the future. Conservatives were particularly influential during the heyday of British control (especially with their membership in the Legislative and Executive Councils), and were able to stall British initiatives towards democratisation in the early 1980s (most analysts blame China for aborting these initiatives, but little noticed is the opposition from within the Executive Council, which was decisive even before discussions began with China).[18] During the drafting of the Basic Law, the business community organised a pressure group (the so-called 'group of 89') to oppose democratisation and ensure a powerful executive largely unaccountable to the legislature. Their strategy was to influence the Chinese directly in private meetings.

On the other hand, the democrats were oriented towards mass action, organising the distribution of pamphlets, signature campaigns and marches. They were driven to these tactics partly because they did not have access to inner sanctums of British or Chinese power, but also because they believed it was necessary to make people aware of the issues and that they would be able to demonstrate a measure of support for democracy that neither of the sovereign powers could ignore. They had overestimated the commitment of both governments to public opinion; and in the case of China at least, the demonstration of public support may well have had the opposite effect—that of hardening attitudes towards democratisation and compelling China to promote the anti-democracy coalition through the well-known tactics of the United Front.

Thus these developments were not only a setback for democracy, but showed the persistence of the colonial style of politics, whereby key people were co-opted through nomination to select bodies, and in their turn obtained favours through kowtowing to the authorities. Policies were made in small cabals; there was little prior public announcement of issues to be decided, much less any discussion of issues. Repository of so much patronage, China could weaken a political group, however numerous its membership, by merely refusing to speak to its leaders. It remains to be seen to what extent such tactics would retard democratisation in a society renowned for being pragmatic and self-seeking.[19] I now turn to the framework within which politics will be conducted and power exercised after the transfer of sovereignty.

DEMOCRATISATION UNDER THE BASIC LAWS

Representation

Before discussing the forms of representation, a preliminary clarification is necessary as to who will be entitled to representation. Since Hong Kong and Macau will be integral parts of a larger state, the citizenship of that state may be expected to determine entitlement to political rights. Yet there are two factors that require that Chinese citizenship should not be a decisive or exclusive criterion. First, in order to preserve their autonomy, some substantial connection with the Special Administrative Region (SAR) is necessary for those claiming citizenship (as is essentially the case now in the territories). Second, in order to preserve their cosmopolitan and international character (which is particularly important for their economies), it may be necessary to facilitate the participation in public life of foreign residents. Logically, the sole criterion should be a minimum period of residence in the SAR, but the conclusion is seen to run counter to the imperative of sovereignty. The result is the establishment of various categories carrying different degrees of entitlement. The principal category is that of a permanent resident of the SAR. It covers: (1) Chinese citizens born in the territory before or after the establishment of the SAR; (2) Chinese citizens who have resided in the territory for a continuous period of seven years before or after the establishment of the SAR; (3) persons of Chinese nationality born outside Hong Kong of parents covered in categories (1) and (2); (4) other persons who have ordinarily resided in the territory for a continuous period of seven years before or after the establishment of the SAR and have taken it as their place of permanent residence; and (5) persons under 21 years born in the territory of a person in the preceding category. The following would also qualify as permanent residents: in Hong Kong, those who had a right of abode before the establishment of the SAR; and in Macau, Portuguese born in Macau who have taken it as their place of permanent residence.[20] Thus the category of permanent citizens is subdivided into those who are also Chinese citizens, and others. Chinese citizenship law is based on ethnic origins, so that indigenous Chinese will become citizens (except for those who have acquired a foreign citizenship, since its law does not allow dual nationality).[21] Another distinction, which is more widely applicable in Hong Kong than Macau, is between Chinese nationals depending on whether or not they have a right of abode abroad.[22] There is also the category of non-permanent residents of each SAR, those who are qualified to obtain an identity card but who have no right of abode.

The Basic Laws provide for at least three forms of representation. The first of these is in the NPC—'to participate in the work of the highest organ of state power' (Article 21). The number of seats and the method of selection are to be specified by the NPC.[23] Only those residents who are Chinese nationals are eligible for election or voting (or 'to participate in the management of state affairs').

The NPC is a large body (it has over 2000 members) which meets once a year for about 10 to 14 days. It has been seen largely as a 'rubber-stamping' body, and on the rare occasions on which some members have shown an independence of mind (as recently in relation to the Three Gorges Dam project), an effective hearing is denied. The principal function of the NPC is to ratify key decisions of the Communist Party. Its Standing Committee (which has about 200 members and meets several times a year) acts in practice as the legislature. Hong Kong and Macau NPC members would be eligible to a seat on the Standing Committee, in which they would exercise somewhat greater powers. However, decisions on most matters are made within committees of the Communist Party, and the role of the Standing Committee, as with the NPC, is formal. In any case, Hong Kong and Macau members will be a very small proportion of the total membership, who are amenable to party discipline, so that they would be able to exercise little influence on policy.

The second form of representation is within the government of the Special Administrative Regions, which is headed by the Chief Executive. This post is the lynchpin of the political system. Who may be appointed to it? He or she must be a Chinese citizen of at least 40 years of age, who is a permanent resident with a continuous residence of not less than 20 years in the territory and who has no right of abode in a foreign country (Article 44 in Hong Kong, Articles 46 and 49 in Macau). The appointment is for five years, and the post may not be held for more than two consecutive terms.

How is the Chief Executive to be appointed? In each case the appointment is made by the Central People's Government of the PRC. There is no provision for a veto or reference back of a nomination presented to it, so it may be assumed that its role is formal. The procedures for the nomination of a candidate to the PRC is similar for Hong Kong and Macau for the foreseeable future, but the long-term aims are different. Both Basic Laws say that he or she 'shall be selected by elections or through consultations held locally'. Each Basic Law provides for the methods of choosing the first and subsequent Chief Executives, which in essence follow the same principle; that is, election by a specially constituted committee. In Hong Kong the membership of the committee, the initial one to be appointed by a Preparatory Committee set up by the NPC and subsequent ones to be elected by corporate groups themselves, is drawn in equal proportions from (1) the industrial, commercial and financial sectors; (2) the professions; (3) labour, grassroots, religious and other sectors; and (4) former political representatives in Hong Kong or deputies to the NPC or the Chinese People's Political Consultative Conference. In Macau there is a slight weightage in favour of the first category (30%) at the expense of the last (20%). For the first Chief Executive, the method of selection of the candidate—as between consultations or elections—is left for further decision, but for subsequent appointments the committee would designate a candidate through a secret ballot on a 'one person one vote' basis. To enter the contest, a candidate has to be nominated by a substantial number of members (100 in Hong Kong out of 800 members, and in Macau 50 out of 300).

These methods are to be followed up to ten years after the establishment of the SAR. Thereafter an amendment is possible, but it would require the consent of the NPC after it has been endorsed by two-thirds of the Legislative Council and by the Chief Executive. However, it would appear that a member of the Council cannot propose an amendment since he or she is not qualified to introduce a motion or a Bill relating to the 'political structure' or 'the operation of the government' (Article 74 for Hong Kong and Article 75 for Macau). The ultimate aim, but only for Hong Kong, is specified as selection by universal suffrage upon nomination by 'a broadly representative nominating committee in accordance with democratic procedures' (Article 45). However, the move to this method is to be made in accordance with 'the principle of gradual and orderly progress', the specific method in each period to be specified 'in the light of actual situation' in the HKSAR. These cautious provisions are reinforced by a veto of the NPC on an amendment. Nevertheless, the statement of the ultimate principle may strengthen the hand of pro-democracy lobbies in Hong Kong, and although there is no similar provision in Macau, movement towards greater democracy in Hong Kong may strengthen the case for change there.

The third form of representation is the Legislative Council. (I do not discuss local government organs for they have no political or executive power). In Hong Kong it would consist of 60 members; in Macau, starting from a membership of 23 for the first Council, it would increase to 29 by the third legislature. For Macau it is specified that a majority of members will be elected (Article 68), while for Hong Kong the principle is that the Council shall be 'constituted by elections' with the ultimate aim of the elections of all the members by universal suffrage (Article 68). Thus it is possible to have non-elected members in Macau, while in Hong Kong— although all members must be elected—various forms of elections are possible (the Chinese refusing to accept that 'elections' in the Joint Declaration meant direct elections by universal franchise). The duration of a legislature, unless sooner dissolved, is four years.

Each has three categories of members (although all the categories are not the same). The proportion between them varies over a period of time (the Basic Laws providing explicitly for the first three legislatures). The first Hong Kong legislature would have twenty members directly elected from geographical constituencies, ten elected by an electoral college, and 30 elected by functional constituencies. The directly elected members increase in number to 24 and then to 30, those elected by the electoral college decrease to six and then cease, while the number of functional members remains constant. In Macau the number of directly elected members starts at eight and progresses to ten and twelve; indirectly elected members start at eight and increase to ten, while members appointed by the Chief Executive remain constant, at seven. Neither 'functional' nor 'indirectly elected' is defined; presumably these terms are to be understood by reference to existing practice—a point I return to in a short while. Thereafter (the year 2007 for Hong Kong and 2009 for Macau) the composition of the legislature may be changed on the approval both of two-thirds of the Council and of the Chief Executive (but as with the amendment regarding the selection of the Chief Executive, members of the Council will not be able to propose an amendment). China has to be notified of the change but has no veto over it. However, for Hong Kong it is specified that the change must be 'gradual and orderly'.

The right of franchise is equally broad in the two territories; all permanent residents may vote (Article 26 in both cases).[24] However the picture is more complicated as far as the right to stand for the Council is concerned. In Hong Kong it is restricted to Chinese citizens who are permanent residents without the right of abode in a foreign country, except that up to 20% of members may be citizens with such a right, or non-citizen residents (Article 66). In Macau it is sufficient that they are permanent residents. Presumably candidacy for functional (or indirectly elected) seats would additionally require membership of or links to a relevant interest group.

Some obvious conclusions follow from this brief description of the electoral system. The first is the rather cautious unfolding of the political system from the meagreness of the Joint Declarations; and the second is that the Basic Laws provide merely for the continuation rather than the end of the transition period leading up to a fully democratic system. Several important details, particularly on the system of voting, have yet to be determined. These are the responsibility of the legislatures of the SAR, but in practice China is likely to influence the decisions (now that the 'through train' concept for Hong Kong has been abandoned, under which the system set up by the last colonial Legislative Council may have survived). It may, for example, have a particular interest in proportional representation rather than plurality for the direct elections if it considers that its supporters enjoy limited popularity (already its advisers have expressed an interest in the New Zealand type of mixed electoral system).[25] As for the selection of the Chief Executive, it is clear that the business community and its allies, the professions, will have a decisive say.

Functional constituencies will play a key role for the foreseeable future. They will constitute half of the Hong Kong legislature, and the electoral college to elect ten and then six members will be dominated by representatives of similar interests. The importance of functional members will be enhanced by the procedures of the Legislative Council whereby any private Bill or motion (including an amendment to a government Bill) will have to be passed by separate voting of the functional members and the others (Annex II of the Basic Law) (which is intended to put a brake on progressive initiatives). In Macau they will hold the balance between the elected and the appointed members; but in practice they are likely to be allied with the appointed members (thus constituting a majority), just as the Hong Kong members elected by the Election Committee are likely to be supporters of the Chief Executive.[26] The reason for this is that functional constituencies will dominate the selection of the Chief Executive. Of the Election Committee 75% (a slightly higher proportion in Macau) will consist of representatives of functional constituencies; and the remaining 25% comprising representatives and former representatives of various bodies in Hong Kong and China, will probably have emerged through previous nomination or support of functional constituencies. It is therefore important to establish the character of functional constituencies.

Functional constituencies were first established in Hong Kong in 1985 as part of the initial tentative steps towards greater representativeness. They replaced in part nominated members who had for decades been appointed by the governor from business and professional sectors. The functional constituencies have represented this bias: five of the original twelve constituencies were given to business sectors, and the other seven went to professions (most of whom, like lawyers and engineers, were expected to ally with business—only two went to labour).[27] By 1991 their number had increased to 21, largely by subdividing business and professional constituencies and increasing their salience. Thus the electorate in most constituencies became even smaller, so that the number of eligible voters in all of them totalled 104 609 (of whom only 69 825 had registered)— less than 0.2% of the population! Small electorates, based for the most part on corporate membership, meant disproportionate power to the larger firms with several subsidiaries; it has been estimated that about seven business groups controlled more than 25% of functional constituencies.[28] Such a system necessarily produced allies of a conservative government, but if the government were doubly anxious to ensure support, it could easily influence the small electorates.

There is no doubt that the Chinese and the business community favoured functional constituencies in the Basic Law for these reasons—although neither of the Basic Laws specify the nature of functional constituencies, the dominance of business and professional sectors and the provision of small electorates were underlying assumptions. The item of Patten's constitutional proposals of 1992 (enacted in 1994 for the 1995 elections) that the Chinese took most objection to was the broadening of the electorates for some of the existing constituencies (by shifting entitlement to vote from corporations to individuals) and the creation of nine new constituencies with enormous electorates—thus upsetting the entire balance of the political system under the Basic Law.[29]

The effect of functional constituencies is not only to secure the salience of conservative, economic interests, but to influence the development of the political system away from open and party politics (political parties being the main means in modern politics to mobilise and represent the people).[30] The small electorates for business and professional constituencies can be influenced through personal contacts or by relying upon corporate muscle, and political parties may even be counterproductive given the attitudes of several leading businesspeople. It is possible, under the arrangements of the Basic Laws, for a group of politicians to compete and operate without a political party; and indeed without popular support. The Liberal Party in Hong Kong does not intend to field any candidates for geographical constituencies. Nor is there any sign yet of a political party in Macau. Since, in some functional constituencies at least, the Chinese will effectively be able to decide on the winning candidates, the politics of nomination (refined into a high art by the colonial, particularly British, authorities) will persist, disabling those who seek to mobilise public support. By creating different bases of support and representation, the Basic Laws, as is their intention, will fragment the political community and weaken the Legislative Council's ability to provide an effective challenge to the administration. It may consequently fail to attract some talented people to politics, for popular politics will not be an avenue to power until there is a change in the electoral system.

The geographical constituencies will, however, provide a basis and incentive for the organisation of parties (as will the elections to local government bodies). In turn the growth of parties may influence at least some (the larger) functional constituencies. Politicians who reach the Council through party support and popular elections will have both an organisation base and a claim to legitimacy which may be used to challenge the government, especially as the Chief Executive may lack a popular mandate. The significance of these councillors will be the validity they provide to democratic principles. The very lack of their institutional power will highlight the oddities of the political system, and perhaps ultimately its unworkability—unless the executive is massively bolstered by the Chinese in contravention of the ethos of the Basic Laws. It is to that matter that I now turn.

Responsiveness and accountability

The distinguishing characteristic of the political systems of the SRAs is the dominance of the executive. Executive powers are vested in one person, the Chief Executive (notwithstanding the confusion in the Basic Laws, since similar powers are ascribed alike to him or her and the government in general). He or she nominates his or her principal officials for appointment by the PRC. The Chief Executive is assisted by an Executive Council, but its functions are advisory and consultative (in relation to proposed legislation, 'important' policies, and the dissolution of the legislature)— although if the advice is not taken, the fact has to be recorded.[31] The dependent nature of the Executive Council is emphasised by the fact that its membership is in the gift of the Chief Executive. The wide powers of the executive were seen by the business community as protection against vacillating policies and uneasy compromises.

An examination of the relationship between the Chief Executive and the Legislative Council discloses that the system is not an exact reproduction of the US-type executive presidency, as it has some quasi-parliamentary features. The Chief Executive is accountable to the Legislative Council; but accountability is specifically and narrowly defined (and is far removed from the ministerial 'responsibility' of the parliamentary system). Accountability is constituted by four obligations of the government: to implement laws; present regular policy addresses to the Council; to answer questions raised by its members; and to obtain its approval for taxation and public expenditure (Article 64 for Hong Kong and 65 for Macau). Only one of these obligations—that relating to public finance— comes armed with a sanction, since public revenue can neither be raised nor spent without the Council's approval. Temporary appropriations in case of refusal are possible, in Macau without the Council's consent, but in Hong Kong that consent may be dispensed with only when the Council is dissolved (Article 53 in Macau, Article

51 in Hong Kong)—but the picture is even more complex, as we shall shortly see. Macau, unlike Hong Kong, also provides explicitly for the Council's scrutiny of audit reports (Article 71(2))—in Hong Kong one would have to rely on existing law for this power. Explanations and answers by the government will be provided by such officials as are designated by the Chief Executive, who may forbid a public servant to testify before the Council or its committees.

There is one point—legislation—on which there can be a serious conflict between the executive and the legislature, the resolution of which invokes some parliamentary principles (and demonstrates the relative weakness of the legislature). If the Chief Executive vetoes a Bill passed by the Council (on the grounds that it does not represent the overall interests of the region), the Council may resubmit the Bill to him or her if it is passed by a two-thirds majority. The Chief Executive then has the option of signing the Bill or dissolving the Council. The Council can also be dissolved if it refuses to pass a government Bill or the budget (only in Macau is there a formal requirement to provide a public justification for the dissolution). However, if the Bill that he or she had rejected is passed again by the new Council, he or she either has to sign it or resign. The power to dissolve the Council is available to the Chief Executive only once in each term of office.

This mechanism for referring the issue to the interest groups relevant in the electoral process (it would be inaccurate to say to the people!) is tilted in favour of the executive, since the initial penalty is paid, as it were, by the councillors. But there are other considerations too that favour the executive. The very threat of dissolution often serves to ensure compliance by the members. Secondly, the executive can to a substantial extent control the introduction of a Bill by a member, since a member can introduce a Bill only with its consent if it relates to 'government policies', which can cover many sins (and absolutely cannot on 'public expenditure or political structure or the operation of the government'). Thus the chance that any great issue of public importance is involved is remote, making it unlikely that the Chief Executive would not allow the veto to be overridden. Thirdly, the need for a veto in the first instance would arise only if the executive lost the support of both classes of members (since private Bills are voted on separately in Hong Kong, while in Macau the directly elected members could not pass it on their own—an element of bicameralism that survived the far-reaching proposals of a businessman, presented with the support of the Chinese, as a further tilt towards conservatism). Fourthly, it would seem that the Chief Executive can veto once any Bills passed even those passed by a subsequent Council. So the only effective possibility, from the point of view of the Council, once the Chief Executive has played his or her master card of dissolution, is to obstruct new policies of the executive. Incidentally, this method of resolving disputes between the legislature and the executive is hardly conducive to 'stability and prosperity', which are the principal aims of the Basic Laws.

The Council's ability to invoke a crisis is limited. It can indeed mobilise the procedure for the impeachment of the Chief Executive, but only for 'serious breach of law or dereliction of duty', and thereafter has little control over the process since the matter is then referred by the chief justice to an independent committee for investigation. If its report is adverse to him or her, an impeachment motion requires a two-thirds vote of all its members, and even then the final decision rests with the Central People's Government (Article 73 in Hong Kong and Article 71 in Macau).

If this procedure smacks more of a presidential than a parliamentary system, it is open to the executive to operate the system in other ways through a more parliamentary mode. The simplest and least formal way would be to operate on a convention under which the government recognised the primacy of the views and policies of the largest party and its allies. Secondly, he or she could appoint to the Executive Council those members of the Legislative Council who come from the largest party or coalition (legislative councillors are one category of members of the Executive Council, others being officials and eminent persons). This would not only establish effective links between the executive and the legislature, but would also recognise the credentials of the more representative of the councillors. Thirdly, it may also be open to the Chief Executive to appoint his or her senior policy makers from the Legislative Council, chosen from the leading party or coalition of parties. Under the Basic Laws such persons are called 'principal officials' and are currently in charge of various policy areas. The possibility of this kind of arrangement is greater in Macau, since the principal officials need merely to be permanent residents (not citizens or without right of abode abroad) and councillors need not lose their membership if they hold another post which may be permitted by a law (Article 81 (2))—but the arrangement is less feasible since Macau has no political parties! In Hong Kong on the other hand a legislator loses his or her seat on accepting a government appointment and becoming a public servant (Article 78 (4)). However, this suggests that a government appointment by itself does not disqualify a member, and there is nothing in the Basic Law that requires a principal official to be a public servant (although the choice of the Chief Executive would be limited to politicians who are residents and who are Chinese citizens without the right of abode elsewhere).[32] Here again there would be a need to accept certain conventions about collective responsibility, since the Basic Laws vest executive power in the Chief Executive.[33]

Even if this option is open, whether it would be taken up depends in large part on the background of the Chief Executive. If he or she has been a public servant, the chances of the appointment of political principal officials are small. In any case such a scenario is somewhat hypothetical, since a Chief Executive might see his or her authority diminished if the principal officials are politicians with independent bases of their own rather than career public servants. Moreover he or she would have to be satisfied that nominations for principal officials are acceptable to China (whatever the legal position regarding their appointment)—and China is not likely to be disposed towards politically oriented councillors (probably representing geographical constituencies) and any system that gives prominence to and thus encourages political parties. The China factor is important here as in many other instances, and it is time now to examine how it affects responsiveness and accountability of the executive in the SAR.

Although China's role in the appointment of the Chief Executive is formal (I have previously argued that it has no veto), in practice it would play an active role in identifying and promoting a candidate, enough of a guarantee for his or her success. The powers and the constitutional position of the Chief Executive are crucial to Chinese control over the SAR, since control over him or her gives access to the administrative system. The importance that China attaches to its control over the Chief Executive is demonstrated by the rule that no amendment to the method of his or her selection (as opposed to that of the legislature) can be made without its approval, even if two-thirds of the Legislative Council support it. Even more dramatic is the veto China has kept for itself over impeachment. Even if an independent committee has found good cause and the Council has voted by at least two-thirds of all its members for the Chief Executive's removal, China can ignore it. This contempt for the Council shows its solicitude for its chosen candidate, and serves merely to increase his or her dependence on China. In addition, the Basic Laws require his or her accountability to China; accountability is not spelt out as in relation to the Council, and the scope of activities over which the accountability ranges is unclear. In the event of a clash of 'accountabilities', it is obvious that China will claim priority, relying upon sovereignty. China therefore neatly achieved the twin purpose of a strong executive (which it preferred because of its distrust of democratic and parliamentary politics) and control over it.[34]

In summary, the most powerful post in the SAR, the Chief Executive, in whom lies the power to respond to and initiate policy, is neither representative of nor accountable to its people. The numerous restrictions on the power of initiative of the more representative Legislative Council means that it will be unable to respond to the public, except in a negative way. Executive accountability to the legislature is narrow, and the imbalance between them means that even that accountability will be hard to exact. The dependence of the Chief Executive on China means that he or she will be more responsive to China—over whose authorities the people of the SAR have no influence. He or she will have to rely on ample powers of patronage, and the backing of China. This will attenuate the political process—a bad omen for democratisation.

16

Nepal's Experiment in Representation

Ganesh Raj Sharma

Governance through popular representation evolved gradually in Nepal before the universal adult franchise was constitutionally adopted. Historically, Nepal has an uninterrupted record of independence with its own traditions, traceable even in ancient Hindu and Buddhist Scriptures. As a multi-ethnic, multi-racial and multilingual nation, Nepal has social and cultural roots appropriate for a moderate and pluralist society. It has assimilated and reconciled influences between two ancient civilisations of Asia, and has maintained its indigenous polity. Subject to only a minimum involvement of the state, villages had historically been the primary units of the self-governing institution traditionally known as the 'panchayat'.

Even the institution of monarchy commanded allegiance on the basis of popular, rather than of divine, power. Consensus instead of conquest remained the major basis of monarchy in Nepal. After Revered King Drabya Shah was made king, Gurungs (a Tibeto-Burman people who live in the central midlands of Nepal, from Gorkha and Bagalaung to high on the slopes of the Annapurna mountains) in Liglig near Gorkha developed a tradition of electing their leader, and this had an impact on the functioning of the Shah kings, who ruled on the basis of persuasion and consent, while a body of councils represented the popular will in governance.

Following this tradition, King Prithwinarayan Shah, who unified modern Nepal in the eighteenth century, expressed his vision for the nation in his famous words: 'I observed the arrangements of king Ram Shah; I saw the arrangements of Jayasthiti Malla also. Let

the king not kill a servant in his house. Let the king see that justice
is done. Let there be no injustice in our country.' He expressed his
personal view that he wanted to make Biraj Bakheti his prime
minister but he named Kalu Pande for the job because this was
what the people desired. Despite reversals in practice, theoretically
it was a trend towards the supremacy of the popular will in governance. This was the time when major industrial democracies were
engaged in a drive to colonise countries across continents. Close to
Nepal, the French were fighting a losing battle against the British
in India. Americans were fighting for independence and the French
were preparing for their historic revolution.

The tradition of ruling through councils and popular will came
to an end after prolonged court conspiracies and the Kot massacre
of 1846. A family oligarchy now prevailed over the king, and a system
of hereditary prime ministership with absolute power over the state
continued until the Rana oligarchy was overthrown by a popular
uprising backed by the king in 1951. Meanwhile, momentous changes
accompanying the independence of India and the liberation of China
influenced Nepal as well. The liberal-minded Prime Minister Padma
Shumsher tried to introduce reforms under the hereditary prime
ministership and India's Prime Minister Jawaharlal Nehru provided
constitutional expertise to draft a Constitution. But the value of the
Constitution of 1948 was not fully tested. It was a grand compromise
that followed an attempted revolution, and was abrogated by the
Interim Government of Nepal Act of 1951. Although the 1951 Act was
intended to bring a democratic Constitution to Nepal within two
years, tensions between traditional and modernising forces delayed
the process until 1958. This interim period was in a way a period of
apprenticeship in parliamentary democracy and in the cabinet system
of government, as several advisory assemblies were constituted by
nomination, and several forms of government were tested in power.
Ultimately, the king rather than the constituent assembly, acting on
popular consensus, initiated a Constitutional Drafting Committee in
1958. It included representatives of the prominent political parties
and drew on the expertise of Sir Ivor Jennings, but unfortunately it
was, like all the other constitutions for third world countries that Sir
Ivor drafted, rejected by the body politic of Nepal also. Under the
Constitution of the Kingdom of Nepal (1958), the Parliament—
including the king and two Houses of Parliament—was sovereign.
Although the king had ample discretion to overrule the government
and the legislature, the Constitution included a system of checks and
balances.

When submitting the draft Constitution Sir Ivor explained that
'The commission had prepared a draft similar in principles to
constitutions of other countries in Asia operating the parliamentary

system of government, but with modifications which distinguish a constitutional monarchy from a federal state. The general scheme is as follows:

(1) Executive authority is vested in His Majesty, but general direction and control of administration are vested in a cabinet responsible to parliament. Because the parliamentary system is new to Nepal, and accordingly, guidance cannot be sought from constitutional convention, care had been taken to define, with such precision as the changing circumstances of government allow, the relation between His Majesty and His ministers.

(2) Parliament will consist of two houses, called in the English text the House of Representatives and the Senate. The House of Representatives will consist wholly of members elected by the electors voting in single member constituencies by secret ballot; and adult franchise is provided for. There will be a general election every five years, or more often if His Majesty dissolves Parliament on the recommendation of the cabinet. The senate on the other hand, will consist as to one half of persons appointed by His Majesty on the recommendations, and as to the other half of persons appointed by His Majesty on the recommendation of the Prime Minister. When Parliament is dissolved, the senators will retain their seats, but one-third of the senators will retire every two years. Provision is made for the House of Representatives, as the elected House, to override the senate, except in respect of constitutional amendments; and the cabinet will be collectively responsible to the House of Representatives. All legislation will require the Royal Assent, but the circumstances in which His Majesty may withhold assent are required.'

A Constitution that made for the supremacy of the Parliament had no chance of surviving in the Nepalese context at this time, and the king, exercising his inherent prerogative, promulgated a new Constitution in 1962, which emphasised a grassroots system of guided democracy. What Western democracies and particularly Britain had achieved in the years following the industrial revolution was being implemented in a traditional society which lacked the features of industrial societies.

The Constitution made for parliamentary supremacy, and therefore produced a form of village-based guided democracy. In justification of his action King Mahendra denounced the Western model of democracy as unsuitable to the genius of the Nepali people. Although he hoped to revert to fully fledged parliamentary democracy within five or seven years after consolidating democracy at the base, there followed three decades of uneasiness.

This was a period when many developing countries were attempting various forms of government. Indonesia, under the leadership of Soekarno, was experimenting with guided democracy as a path towards ameliorating the miseries of the masses. Nasser of Egypt had the same kind of vision for guided democracy. In Pakistan, Ayub Khan was also trying 'basic democracy' based on grassroots democracy with limited franchise. In all developing countries political parties were considered vulnerable to polarisation and to linkage with the forces of the Cold War, and Western democracies were more concerned with their global security than with helping the fledgling democracies of the third world. Thus there were no tears shed in the democratic world at the rejection of democracy in Nepal.

When Nepal established parliamentary democracy in 1958, disenchantment with this system had already begun to set in elsewhere. In India, Socialist leader Jaya Prakash Narayan believed it was possible to develop a partyless democracy. Disappointed by the socialist movement he had led so vigorously, he then concentrated on an alternative to the framework of Western democracy, and criticised the functioning of political parties in India, with its corroding and corrupting struggles for power:

> I saw how parties backed by finance, organisation and the means of propaganda could impose themselves on the people; how people's rule became in effect party rule; how party rule in turn became the rule of caucus and coterie; how democracy was reduced to mere casting of votes; how even this right to vote was restricted severely by the system of powerful parties setting up their candidates from whom, alone, for all practical purposes, the voters had to make their choice; how even this limited choice was made unreal by the fact that the issues posed before the electorate were by and large incomprehensible to it.
>
> The party system as I saw it was emasculating the people. It did not function so as to develop their strength and initiative, nor to help them establish their self-rule and to manage their affairs themselves. All that the parties were concerned with was to rule over the people, no doubt with their consent! The party system, so it appeared to me, was seeking to reduce the people to the position of sheep whose only function of sovereignty would be to choose the shepherd who would look after their affairs! This to me did not spell freedom—the freedom, the Swaraj, for which I had fought and for which the people of this country had fought.[1]

Such debates perhaps inspired and encouraged King Mahendra to stand against the multi-party system. The king, as a crown prince, had already expressed his annoyance by criticising political parties for not behaving according to the norms of democracy. He found himself very much more in sympathy with those who were in search of an alternative model of democracy for a developing country. It has been disclosed by a former Prime Minister, Dr Tulsi Giri, that the draft of the Constitution of 1962, which included provision for panchayats and an indirect method of election to the National

Panchayat, was forwarded to Jaya Prakash Narayan for consideration. His reactions remain unknown. But in support of that constitutional arrangement a Gandhian scholar, Shriman Narayan Agrawal, who was also India's ambassador in Nepal, has said in his recollections 'that in a small and developing country like Nepal, I saw no harm in that type of democratic system, and that even Gandhiji had pleaded for direct democracy at the base and for indirect elections upwards'.[2]

The Constitution of 1962 formalised 'Panchayat' as a system of governance on a tier basis in the first phase. Although political parties were banned the constitution remained silent about partylessness, which became a feature of the Constitution through the First Constitutional Amendment of 1967, which expanded the electoral base but kept the tier system intact.

Growing involvement of the people in the political process increased political polarisation, and made 'partylessness' practically irrelevant. In 1975 the Second Amendment to the Constitution once more broadened the electorate, and introduced a party-like body known as the Go To Village Campaign to curb conflicts, and establish harmony, between political interests and ideas.

Pressures built up within the Panchayat system as well as from outside it, and it was put to a test in a national referendum in 1980. The result favoured gradual reform in the political system. A Third Amendment was made to the Constitution in 1980, and had three major elements. First, the Rashtriya Panchayat was instituted as the national legislature on the basis of direct adult franchise. Second, the prime minister was to be elected by the majority of the members of the legislature. Third, the Council of Ministers was responsible to the House, personally as well as collectively.

However, a stipulation requiring members of the Rashtriya Panchayat to be members of a class organisation under the guidance and control of a political body of the Panchayat was a deterrent to plural political activities. Even for conciliatory politicians such as B. P. Koirala, participation in such an election was not acceptable. The motive behind the reform was preservation of the Panchayat system, whereas most political parties wanted an alternative, pluralist, political system, which the Constitution still did not allow. Thus the Panchayat system again produced political confrontation and upheaval of serious dimensions. Conscious of the alarming situation in the country, the king initiated an all-party consensus, the final result of which was the Constitution of the Kingdom of Nepal (1990), the nation's fifth Constitution in five decades.

Though essentially authoritarian, the Panchayat system contained within it gradual reforms. Numerous Supreme Court cases of the period reflect the constitutional nature of the struggle for the rights of the people as well as for institutional developments. In the apex national legislature the practices of parliamentary democracy and the accountability of the government were attempted. But the most significant democratic development occurred at the lowest unit of the Panchayat system in the form of local self-government. About 4000 villages and 36 towns were incorporated as local self-government units. These bodies provided an apprenticeship in governance, since they served to educate the masses in political issues, despite the populations widespread illiteracy. The situation showed that direct adult franchise and the partyless system were incompatible, and as such reform as had already taken place could not meet the popular demand for political parties the country faced great upheaval by 1990. The Constitution of that year was drafted with past experience in mind, and resulted in a compromise multi-party democracy and constitutional monarchy.

Nepal's Constitution is based on the principle of the separation of the powers of the state. Parliament represents the people. All executive functions derive sanction and legitimacy from parliamentary legislation. Treaty-making power has to be exercised under parliamentary ratification according to Article 126 of the Constitution. An independent judiciary, and particularly the Supreme Court, renders justice according to law, and the Supreme Court has powers to nullify unjust law by a process of judicial review. It is, therefore, not a system of strict parliamentary supremacy.

Though multi-party democracy was revived, the 1958 Constitution (which provided for a multi-party system) was not, as it was considered to lack adequate checks upon the arbitrary use of discretionary powers, particularly by the head of the state. Considerable restrictions were imposed on the executive powers of the state. Article 116 states that the Constitution cannot be amended in such a way as to contravene the spirit of the Preamble of the Constitution.

Besides other ideals, the Constitution in its Preamble declares the nature of governance:

> And whereas, it is expedient to promulgate and enforce this constitution, made with the widest possible participation of the Nepalese people, to guarantee basic human rights to every citizen of Nepal; and also to consolidate the Adult Franchise, the Parliamentary System of Government, Constitutional monarchy and the system of Multi-Party Democracy by promoting amongst the people of Nepal the spirit of fraternity and the bond of unity on the basis of liberty and equality; and also to establish an independent and competent system of justice with a view to transforming the concept of the Rule of Law into a living reality.

In the Directive Principles and Policies of the State, Article 24(4) has a provision on representation:

> It shall be the chief responsibility of the state to maintain conditions suitable to enjoyment of the fruits of democracy through wider participation of the people in governance of the country and by way of decentralisation, and to promote general welfare by making provisions for the protection and promotion of human rights, by maintaining tranquillity and order in the society.

Nepal has a bicameral legislature through popular representation. The House of Representatives is elected on the basis of universal adult franchise in one-member constituencies, and the other House, the Upper House, is constituted partly by the king's nominations—impliedly on the advice of the prime minister—and partly on the basis of indirect election from local and district tiers of the local self-government units.

Thirty members of the Upper House are elected on the basis of proportional representation according to the single transferable vote system. The House of Representatives has the more important role in choosing the prime minister, in creating legislation, and in making government accountable. On many important issues joint sessions of both the Houses are held. Ratification of treaties of vital national interest is required by the joint session of the Parliament.

Though there is an expression regarding 'wider participation of the people in the governance by way of decentralisation', the Constitution intends to let Parliament determine the extent of such decentralisation. The whole edifice of local self-government would have come to a standstill had there been no compulsion to constitute it for the purpose of electing from the local units of self-government one-quarter of the members of the Upper House. The prime minister after the first general elections had been reluctant to share his power, and this conflict between politicians seeking centralisation of power and local units seeking self-governance has been a recurring source of confrontation.

Decentralisation was not compatible with the absolute control of a party in power, which sought to work through nominated political workers, as opposed to the leaders of local units upholding the trust and pride of the elected representatives of the people. Whereas party units are dependent on the will of the leaders, leaders of the elected local units are more demanding and more assertive. The central government usually comprises a homogeneous leadership, whereas most of the local units are either non-ideological or are multi-party coalitions. Among 4000 village units and 36 town units of self-government, the general pattern is of coalitions, in situations of varied interests and ideologies. Incidentally, the same situation of coalition has been forced upon the central government by the result of elections in 1994.

The 1990 Constitution introduced major changes in the matter of representation, by combining adult franchise, the parliamentary system of government, multi-party democracy, and constitutional monarchy. Parliament under the Constitution consists of His Majesty and two Houses. The House of Representatives consists of 205 members elected by direct adult franchise. The Upper House consists of 60 members who have entered via different channels: ten who have high reputations for their prominent service in various fields of national life, nominated by the king; 35 (including three women) elected by the members of the House of Representatives on a proportional representation basis by means of the single transferable vote; and three members from each of five development regions, elected on the basis of the system of a single transferable vote by different units of local governments.

The last two general elections under the present multi-party system have been assessed as being generally free and fair by various observation groups which included persons from a number of countries. The percentage of voting in both the elections was higher than expected. In 1991 about 65% and in 1994 about 62% polling were considered generally satisfactory. Except for a few cases of violence, the situation was very peaceful throughout the election. Electoral expenditures increased, but 'big money' did not ensure success in the election. Defeat of the party in power proved that the use or misuse of government power did not affect the result: even if willing, no party had the machinery to win the election by irregular means.

The number of political parties is also undergoing change. Before the election many parties fought over election symbols, which after a Supreme Court decision were allotted to whichever party applied for them. The present Constitution has a provision regarding political organisations. Under Article 113, political parties or organisations wishing recognition from the Election Commission for the purpose of elections, have to procure more than 3% of the total votes cast in the election for the House of Representatives. In 1991 only five political parties were able to maintain more than 3% of the total votes polled, and in 1994 only four political parties were able to maintain recognition of national parties by procuring more than 3% of the total votes. Even among these four, two political parties polled higher than the others, mainly because of the first-past-the-post election system in which minority votes are wasted, and knowing the trends, voters generally chose candidates likely not only to win but also to provide an alternative government.

The first-past-the-post system of election of government creates a deadlock when a particular political party emerges without a viable government, as occurred in the Parliament of 1958. In the 109-seat House, Nepali Congress had a two-thirds majority (74 seats) and the main opposition party, Gorkha Dal, had eighteen seats only. The Communist Party of Nepal at that time had just four seats. In the 1991 election the ruling party Nepali Congress obtained a simple majority (114 seats) in the 205-seat House, while the Communist Party of Nepal (United Marxist Leninist) won 69 seats. The Nepali Congress won about 37% of the popular votes and CPN-UML about 29 percent. When it won 37% of votes in 1958 the Nepali Congress won two-thirds of the House of Representatives seats, but winning approximately the same percentage of votes in 1991 returned the party a small majority. In the recent election, although the Nepali Congress won about 33% of all votes the CPN-UML formed government after receiving a larger number of seats but approximately 30% of votes. The emergence of a third political party with a substantial number of parliamentary seats was an unexpected development. The justification for the first-past-the-post election system was that it made for a strong and stable government, but the 1991 elections resulted in the formation of an unstable coalition government for which no party was prepared.

The election system that has been adopted for the House of Representatives in the Constitution works smoothly in a two-party system. But the emergence of additional parties cannot be restricted by law. Even in more developed democracies a two-party system sometimes faces such a crisis. When David Owen formed the Social Democratic Party in the UK worries were expressed about a stable government. The candidature of Ross Perot as a serious independent presidential candidate in the United States of America was an instance of crisis or at least uncertainty in a predominantly two-party system. A large number of Americans know that they are dissatisfied with the choice offered by the two major parties, but they are less sure what they want instead. No alternative party has yet come up with a program to match the mood. The even bigger obstacle is the first-past-the-post system for the American Congress, which makes it especially hard for fledgling parties to gain seats and grow.

Accepting that approach, Nepal's recent election results indicate that voters were dissatisfied with the ruling party but were not giving great support to any specific alternative, and this divided mood of the people forced a coalition or consensus government into existence. As three major parties are competing for survival in a system suited to two-party competition, voters as consumers now have the option to preserve two of them for the next election. The other significant trend concerns the formation of a broad national outlook by voters in choosing their representatives. In a multi-ethnic, multi-racial and multi-lingual nation like Nepal, voters have reflected non-parochial choice. But the victory of the Communist Party of Nepal is evidence of a non-traditional approach to politics by the people.

A democratic method of representation in the government has a positive impact in the functioning of political parties. Earlier a large number of Communist organisations advocated a proletariat dictatorship through a violent revolution, despite Nepal lacking a proletarian class. Soon after the first general election, when the Communists emerged as the main opposition party in Parliament, the Communist Party congress declared its faith in multi-party democracy. The Communists contested the first election calling for the formation of a government of workers and peasants, but their slogan in the second election called for a government of nationalists and democrats. As the prospect of getting into power through the ballot brightened they changed in style and rhetoric to the point that now, although there are some Communist ministers and members of Parliament who have past convictions for crimes against their 'class enemies', their presence in power has not provoked any adverse reaction.

Similarly, persons who had helped the king to switch to the Panchayat system and reject multi-party parliamentary democracy have emerged as a third force in the Parliament, in the form of the Rashtriya Prajatantra Party. Its chair, Surya Bahadur Thapa—who was a prominent minister after the royal takeover in 1960 and who led the partyless Panchayat to victory in the 1980 national referendum—is now the popularly elected leader of a democratic party which is functioning in an exemplary manner. The success of the Rashtriya Prajatantra Party may derive from its long-term apprenticeship in power, and its re-emergence in democratic form is a testimony to its members' political training through various democratic institutions under the Panchayat system.

It is strange that the Nepali Congress, a party of avowed democrats who have undertaken a long struggle, failed to complete a full term in government due to internal conflict, thus achieving themselves a result that the combined parliamentary opposition had failed to bring about through the movement of a no-confidence motion in the 1994 winter session of the Parliament.

There are other political parties also who are being forced to change their earlier postures and style of functioning because of the competitive and representative political situation that now exists in Nepal. Most parties now have a non-ideological tendency, but few have democratised their own organisations. All major political parties hold similar views on economic liberalisation, privatisation and open government. They also concur on the basic norms of the Constitution.

In the period leading up to general elections in 1994, a great deal of controversy arose in the ruling party as to whether the elected members of Parliament should abide by the discipline of the leader of the parliamentary party or should follow the dictates of the central body of leadership of the party, most of whose members were non-elected. The prime minister had a mandate through popular election to implement his programs, but other influential party members asserted their position of overall leadership. Besides, the ruling Nepali Congress had a non-elected and non-statutory position of a 'supreme' leader, who very much believed that the party as well as the parliamentary unit of the party should follow his dictates because he had better knowledge of the heart and mind of the common people. As a result, the party was not able to function in the Parliament efficiently; nor could it build up its organisation to face new challenges imposed by the changed political situation in which Nepali Congress was elected into power to deliver the goods to the people. Nepali Congress thus appeared untrustworthy to the people, and proved disorganised as a party.

This controversy regarding the supremacy of leadership between the central party body and the parliamentary body of the party remained unresolved even after defeat in the general election. When elected members of the party in the Parliament were going to elect the leader of the parliamentary party the entrenched leadership of the party refused to endorse their choice. When democratic norms fail to work, traditional authority prevails, and the Nepali Congress is an interesting case of a democratic party functioning in a traditional society. Its history is one of struggle for democratic values, but always under patriarchal leadership; and in comparison, less democratic parties have functioned more democratically.

CONCLUSION

The Constitution of Nepal favours a democratic and representative form of government, and the Supreme Court has acted as the final interpreter of the law since 1951. In 1994 it settled a constitutional dispute concerning the legality of a dissolution of the House of Representatives on the recommendation of the prime minister. Although this decision made some politicians disgruntled, it was accepted by the people in a democratic spirit. The people are striving to create a new constitutional practice, and to adhere to the processes of checks and balances and accountability of the government established in the Constitution—and to take them very seriously. Nepali tradition shows a unique model of compromise and reconciliation, of change coupled with continuity, as demonstrated by the election of a Communist government in a multi-party democracy and under the monarchy. Democracy now has a favourable climate in which to progress in Nepal, unless it is disturbed by extraneous circumstances.

Endnotes

Abbreviations

AC	Appeal Court
AIR	*All India Reporter*
CAD	*Constituent Assembly Debates*
Ch.	Chancery
DLR	*Dominion Law Reports*
J	Justice
J & K	*Jammu & Kashmir Series*
LJ	Lord Justice
LSD	*Lok Sabha Debates*
MLJ	*Malayan Law Journal*
NLR	*New Law Reports*
SA	South Africa
SC	Supreme Court
SCC	Supreme Court of Canada
SCJ	Supreme Court Justice
US	United States Supreme Court Reports

1 INTRODUCTION: SYSTEMS OF REPRESENTATION IN ASIA–PACIFIC CONSTITUTIONS—A COMPARATIVE ANALYSIS

1 This was the case, for instance, with elections for the National Assembly in South Korea in 1988. See James M. West & Edward J. Baker, 'The 1987 Constitutional Reforms in South Korea: Electoral Processes and Judicial Independence', *Human Rights Yearbook*, 1:1988, pp. 135–77.

2 ibid.; Hong Nach Kim, 'The 1988 Parliamentary Election in South Korea, *Asian Survey* 29:5 (1989), pp. 480–95.

3 Fred Gaige & John Scholz, 'The 1991 Parliamentary Elections in Nepal', *Asian Survey* 31:11 (1991), pp. 1040–60.

4 Terence Duffy, 'Cambodia since the Election: Peace, Democracy and Human Rights?',15 *Contemporary Southeast Asia* (March 1994), pp. 407–32.

5 R. J. May, 'People Power and Powerful People: Regime Change and Regime Maintenance in the Asia–Pacific Region', *Observing Change in Asia:* Essays in Honour of J.A.C. Mackie, Bathurst, Crawford House Press, 194–200.

6 Quoted in Giovanni Sartori, *The Theory of Democracy Revisited*, Chatham, Chatham House Press, 1987, p. 37.

7 In Asia only Hong Kong and Macau remain as colonial states, although both are scheduled to return to Chinese sovereignty in the near future.

8 The terms of an election to be held in 1998 will play a critical role in the ultimate success or failure of the 1988 Matignon Accord—a peace accord between the French government, the Kanak Socialist National Liberation Front (FLNKS) and the Rally for Caledonia in the Republic.

9 This issue is explored further in Graham Hassall & Cheryl Saunders, 'State of Emergency in the Asia–Pacific Region', in *States of Emergency: The Asia–Pacific Experience*, eds K. S. Venkateswaran & Colm Campbell, International Commission of Jurists and LAWASIA (forthcoming).

10 See Larry Diamond, Juan J. Linz & Seymour Martin Lipset eds, *Democracy in Developing Countries, vol. 2: Africa*, Lynne Rienner Publishers, Boulder, 1988; Larry Diamond & M. Plather eds, *The Global Resurgence of Democracy*: Johns Hopkins University Press, Baltimore, 1993; Larry Diamond, Juan J. Linz & Seymour Martin Lipset eds, *Politics in Developing Countries: Comparing Experiences with Democracy*, Lynne Rienner Publishers, Boulder & London, 1990; Jyotirindra Das Gupta, 'India: Democratic Becoming and Combined Development', in *Politics in Developing Countries*, eds Diamond & Lipset, Sung-Joo Han, 'South Korea: Politics in Transition', in *Politics in Developing Countries*, eds Diamond & Lipset; K. Jackson, 'The Philippines: The Search for a Suitable Democratic Solution 1946–1986', in *Democracy in Developing Countries*, eds Diamond, Linz & Lipset; David M. Lipset, 'Papua New Guinea: The Melanesian Ethic and the Spirit of Capitalism, 1975–1986' in *Democracy in Developing Countries*, eds Diamond, Linz & Lipset; G. Marks, and L. Diamond eds, *Reexamining Democracy: Essays In Honor of Seymour Martin Lipset*, Sage, Newbury Park, 1992; Chai-Anan Samudavanija, 'Thailand: A Stable Semi-Democracy', in *Politics in Developing Countries*, eds Diamond, Linz & Lipset.

11 Elections have an impact on national economies, whether large or small. Recent elections in Nepal and Vanuatu, for instance, have been judged partly on their cost to the public purse. Elections in the Philippines have been known to have had a significant economic impact.

12 Kevin Tan, 'The Presidential Executive System in Singapore: Problems and Prospects', in *The Powers and Functions of Executive Government: Studies from the Asia Pacific Region*, eds Graham Hassall & Cheryl

Saunders, Centre for Comparative Constitutional Studies, Melbourne, 1994, pp. 37–53.

13 Gareth Porter, *Vietnam: The Politics of Bureaucratic Socialism*, Cornell University Press, Ithaca and London, 1993.

14 At the time of the 1955 elections there were 36 political parties in Indonesia, 27 of which gained seats in Parliament. President Soekarno later banned many parties, including Masjumi, and by 1960 there were just ten. In 1973 the remaining parties were required to merge: the PPP (United Development Party) was formed by four Islamic parties (Nahdatul Ulama, Indonesian Muslim's Party, Perti and Partai Sarikat Islam (PSII)), and the PDI (Indonesian Democratic Party) was formed by five non-Islamic nationalist and Christian parties. Legislation in 1975 banned all other political parties.

15 See generally: Peter King ed., *Pangu Returns to Power: The 1982 Elections in Papua New Guinea*, vol. 9, Department of Political and Social Change, Canberra, 1989; Ralph Premdas & Jeffrey S. Steeves, 'National Elections in Papua New Guinea: The Return of Pangu to Power', 23 *Asian Survey* 8 (1983), pp. 991–1006; and Michael Oliver ed., *Eleksin: the 1987 National Election in Papua New Guinea*, University of Papua New Guinea, Port Moresby, 1989.

16 Prior to the first national poll in 1955 a Constitutional Delineation Committee devised 52 single-member constituencies, 51 of which were won by the UMNO/MCA/MIC Alliance.

17 John Paxton, *World Legislatures*, Macmillan, London, 1974.

18 In his work *The Future of Democracy* Bobbio states

> There can be no objection to students being represented by students in schools, or workers by workers in factories. But once the context changes to where what is at stake are the interests of the citizen and not those of this or that interest group, citizens should be represented by citizens who are distinguished from each other on the grounds, not of the interest groups they represent, but of the different general visions they have developed which inform the way they conceive the problems. (These are general visions which each possesses by virtue of membership, not of this or that interest group, but of this or that political movement). *The Future of Democracy*, Polity, Cambridge, 1987, p. 5.

19 See Hans Thoolen ed., *Indonesia and the Rule of Law: Twenty Years of 'New Order' Government*, Frances Pinter, London, 1987.

20 *Jakarta Post*, 4 March 1992.

21 The first Somare government was defeated March 1980 by Julius Chan; the second Somare government was defeated in November by Paias Wingti; and the Wingti government was defeated in July 1988 by Rabbie Namaliu, who headed a six-party coalition.

22 *Bangkok Post*, 21 August 1995.

23 ibid.

24 *Far Eastern Economic Review*, 17 March 1994, p. 20.

25 The states of Arunachal Pradesh, Meghalaya, Mizoram and Nagaland, by amending Article 332 of the Constitution. Under the *Representation of the People (Amendment) Act* of 1987, 59 out of 60 seats in Arunachal Pradesh, 55 out of 60 in Meghalaya, 30 out of 40 in Mizoram and 59 out of 60 in Nagaland were reserved for Scheduled Tribes. The

Election Commission has identified 55 reserved seats in Meghalaya, 59 in Nagaland, 59 in Arunachal Pradesh and 39 in Mizoram.

26 In Indonesia in 1984 the largest Muslim group, Nahdatul Ulama, left the PPP to become once more a purely social, rather than political, organisation. The government scheduled 1992 parliamentary elections for 9 June, during the period of pilgrimage (*Haj*) by Muslims to Mecca, prompting Islamic leaders to warn the government that the estimated 80 000 pilgrims could not mix the act of electing with their 'holy situation'.

27 *Philippine Newsletter*, Embassy of the Philippines (Australia), January–March 1992.

2 THE CULT OF *FATUNG*: REPRESENTATIONAL MANIPULATION AND RECONSTRUCTION IN TAIWAN

1 According to the ROC Constitution, in addition to the Legislative Yuan, the national legislative organ, there are two other representative bodies, the National Assembly and Control Yuan. The Council of Grand Justices rendered Constitutional Interpretation No. 76 confirming that the Legislative Yuan, National Assembly and Control Yuan are all equivalent to Congress or Parliament in Western democracies. According to recent Constitutional Interpretation No. 325, due to a change in the nature of its appointment procedures from election to presidential nomination and confirmation by the National Assembly, the Control Yuan is now a quasi-judicial and quasi-legislative organ (similar to an ombudsman) but is no longer a representative body.

2 Article 2 of the Constitution.

3 Article 62 of the Constitution.

4 There are Taiwan delegates in the National People's Assembly of the People's Republic of China.

5 The economic success of Taiwan has been termed an 'economic miracle' or the 'Taiwan experience,' see for example Thomas Gold, *State and Society in the Taiwan Miracle* M.E. Sharpe, Armonke, NY, 1986.

6 It has been argued by the separationists that the status of Taiwan is still pending for self-determination by all residents in Taiwan. See for example Lung-chu Chen & W. M. Reisman, 'Who Owns Taiwan?: A Search for International Title', 81 *Yale Law Journal* (1972), p. 599.

7 Soldiers were awarded tickets to claim land once the Mainland was recovered. As the mission became impossible, the authority compensated the soldiers and collected these tickets through the enactment of a special law.

8 This was the beginning of authoritarian rule in Taiwan. In the mid 1980s, Edwin A. Winckler identified a transformation from 'hard' to 'soft' authoritarianism in Taiwan: 'Institutionalization and Participation on Taiwan: From Hard to Soft Authoritarianism?', 99 *The China Quarterly* (1984), p. 481.

9 Max Weber, (Guenther Roth and Claus Wittich eds), *Economy and Society: An Outline of Interpretive Sociology*, University of California Press, Berkeley, 1968, p. 213.

10 Juan Linz, 'Crisis, Breakdown, and Reequilibration', in *The Breakdown of Democratic Regimes*, eds Juan Linz & Alfred Stepan, Johns Hopkins University Press, Baltimore, 1978, p. 17.

11 Article 27 (1) of the Constitution.

12 Article 47 of the Constitution. This article was temporarily frozen by the 'Temporary Provisions Effective During the Period of National Mobilisation for the Suppressing of the Communist Rebellion'.

13 'Members of the Legislative Yuan shall serve a term of three years and shall be re-eligible' (Article 65 of the Constitution); 'Members of the National Assembly and Control Yuan shall serve a term of six years and shall be re-eligible' (Articles 28 and 93).

14 No. 31, Interpretation of the Council of Grand Justices.

15 Linz, 'Crisis, Breakdown, and Reequilibration', p. 69.

16 Nelson Polsby, 'Legislatures', in *Governmental Institution and Process*, eds Fred Greenstein & Nelson Polsby, Addison-Wesley, Reading MA, 1975, p. 298.

17 ibid., p. 299.

18 David Mayhew, *Congress: The Electoral Connection*, Yale University Press, New Haven, 1974.

19 Due to the general impression that these majority tenured representatives always supported government policies and legislative Bills, they have been known as the 'voting troop'.

20 The martial law decree was issued when the Nationalists were at war with the Communists. This state of emergency was carried over to Taiwan with the retreat of the government. Surprisingly, the decree lasted for 38 years until its revocation in 1987.

21 Before the liberalisation, licenses to new newspapers were frozen and existing presses were limited to three pieces of paper.

22 The Democratic Progress Party, formerly called Dang-Wei, announced its establishment in 1986, before the official liberalisation measure was announced.

23 The determination of Chiang Ching-kuo was most decisive. Nevertheless, both internal and external pressure also reinforced his determination. See Y. Chow & A. Nathan, 'Democratizing the Transition in Taiwan', 27 *Asian Survey* (1987), pp. 277, 283–85. See also Jiunn-rong Yeh, 'Changing Forces of Constitutional and Regulatory Reform in Taiwan', 4 *Journal of Chinese Law* 1990, p. 83.

24 Confucius once said, 'One who is old and not going to die [meaning rendering no contribution to the society] is just like a thief'.

25 According to the law, a representative who applied for voluntary retirement would receive compensation of about NT$5 million.

26 Dissenting opinion to Interpretation No. 261 by Grand Justice Lee Tze-pong.

27 Interpretation No. 261, Council of Grand Justices.

28 John Ely, *Democracy and Distrust: A Theory of Judicial Review* Harvard University Press, Cambridge MA, 1980.

29 Although the PRC has changed the number to 21.

30 Article 65 of the Election and Recall Law.

31 Article 27 of the Constitution.

3 CHOOSING REPRESENTATIVES: SINGAPORE DOES IT HER WAY

1 For a description of the Westminster model of parliamentary government, see S. A. de Smith, *The New Commonwealth and its Constitutions*, Stevens & Son, London, 1964, pp. 77–102.

2 See William Dale, 'The Making and Remaking of Commonwealth Countries,' 42, *International and Comparative Law Quarterly*. Jan. (1993) p. 67, citing the 1972 Wooding Commission set up to review the Trinidad and Tobago Constitution.

3 See 'A map up here, in the mind', *The Economist*, 29 June 1991, pp. 16–17.

4 Francis Fukuyama, 'Asia's Soft Authoritarian Alternative', *New Perspectives Quarterly*, Spring 1992, p. 60.

5 The PAP's shift from its non-ideological, pragmatic stance is best reflected by its espousal of the *Shared Values White Paper* (Cmd.1 of 1991), ordered to lie on the table 2 January 1991. It embodies five core values which the PAP government hopes will gain acceptance as the embodiment of a 'national ideology'. Critics have pointed out that the values smack of a brand of Confucianism that will appeal to ageing autocrats. These values are: nation above community and society above self; family as the basic unit of society; regard and community support for the individual; consensus instead of contention; and racial and religious harmony. An attempt to include belief in God was rejected as a sixth value.

6 See for example Fareed Zakaria, 'Culture is Destiny: A Conversation with Lee Kuan Yew', *Foreign Affairs*, March/April 1994, p.109.

7 See generally Lucian Pye, *Asian Power and Politics: The Cultural Dimensions of Authority*, Belknap Press, Cambridge MA, 1985.

8 For a latter-day variation on this singular theme, see Lim Hng Kiang, 'No Need for Opposition Checks and Balances,' *Petir*, November/December 1992, pp. 74–7.

9 PAP newcomer, then Commodore Teo Chee Hean (now rear-admiral and minister of state), canvassing for votes in the 1992 Marine Parade GRC by-elections, quoted in *Straits Times*, 12 December 1992, p. 26.

10 For a comprehensive account of the restructuring of and modifications made to the Singapore legislature, see my article, 'The Post Colonial Constitutional Evolution of the Singapore Legislature', *The Singapore Journal of Legal Studies*, July 1993, p. 80.

11 William Shakespeare, *The Tempest*, Act I, Scene ii, lines 401–2.

12 See generally G. L. Ooi, *Town Councils in Singapore: Self Determination for Public Housing Estates*, Institute of Policy Studies Occasional Paper 4, 1985.

13 The preamble to the Town Council Act provides that the town council, a body corporate with perpetual succession, is to 'control, manage, maintain and improve the common property of housing estates of the Housing and Development Board'. It is to be noted that s3(1) of the Act provides that town councils can be established in single constitu-

encies or when two or three constituencies group themselves together for this purpose.

14 Paragraph 43, Wee Commission Report. Unfortunately, the recommendation to entrench this 'inalienable right' has not been taken up.

15 Paragraph 10, Wee Commission Report.

16 See paragraphs 46 to 49 of the Wee Commission Report.

17 Paragraph 54, Wee Commission Report.

18 Paragraph 47, Wee Commission Report, Chapter III.

19 For a comprehensive account of Singaporean constitutional history, see Kevin Tan, 'The Evolution of Singapore's Modern Constitution: Developments from 1945 to the present day', 1 *Singapore Academy of Law Journal* 1 (1989)

20 Paragraph 39, *Report of the Constitutional Commission Singapore 1954.*

21 *Singapore Parliamentary Debates,* 30 March 1979, p. 296.

22 1984 *Constitutional Amendment Act* (No. 16 of 1984).

23 For an early examination of the NCMP scheme, see V. Winslow, 'Creating a Utopian Parliament', 28 *Malaya Law Review* (1984), p. 268.

24 Mr Goh Chok Tong, then defence and second health minister, in *The Straits Times,* 21 May 1984.

25 See Section 51, Parliamentary Elections Act (Cap 218).

26 Parliamentary Elections Act (Cap 218).

27 Singapore Parliamentary Debates, 1984, vol. 43, col. 1726.

28 Presidential Opening Speech 'On Building Consensus', *Singapore Parliamentary Debates,* Official Record, 9 January 1989, col. 15.

29 Goh Chok Tong, *Singapore Parliamentary Debates,* Official Record, 29 November 1990, col. 695.

30 Section 3(2), Fourth Schedule, Republic of Singapore Constitution.

31 Article 39(2), Republic of Singapore Constitution.

32 It is to be noted that the PAP employs professional managers to run their town councils, while the four opposition-led wards are directly managed and have appointed party-affiliated persons to salaried posts. The employment by opposition MPs of town council staff from their political parties, utilising public funds, has caused some controversy over the issue of political patronage. See *Straits Times,* 24 July 1993, p. 32.

33 See Francis Seow, *To Catch a Tartar,* Yale University Southeast Asia Studies, New Haven CT, 1994.

34 See, for example, Tan Cheng Bock's (Ayer Rajah Constituency) speech, Second Reading of the NMP Bill, *Singapore Parliamentary Debates, Official Record,* 29 November 1989, col. 695.

35 The composition of Singapore's population breaks down to something like 77% Chinese, 14% Malay, 7% Indians and 2% 'Others'.

36 See generally *Group Representative Constituencies: A Summary of the Report of the Select Committee, Ministry of Communications and Information.*

37 *Singapore Parliamentary Debates,* Official Record, 11 January 1988, col. 178.

38 Section 27C(2) Parliamentary Elections Act (Cap 218).

39 Section 27A(7) Parliamentary Elections Act (Cap 218).

40 As far as the opposition candidates are concerned, the electorate seems to identify quite closely with their personal electioneering, as their

political parties have hitherto lacked any coherent party program or manifesto. It is to be noted that all four opposition wards—Hougang, Nee Soon Central, Bukit Gombak and Potong Pasir—are single-member constituencies. It would seem, as the PAP incumbents in the former three wards unhappily discovered in the 1991 general elections, that riding on the PAP ticket no longer guarantees electoral victory in Singapore.

41 See Goh Chok Tong, *Parliamentary Debates*, 10 August 1991.

42 First Deputy Prime Minister Goh, Report of the Singapore Parliamentary Debates, 11 January 1988, vol. 51, col. 184.

43 Sadly, Eunos GRC lost Dr Tay Eng Soon to cancer, while Mr Ong Teng Cheong was obliged to vacate his Toa Payoh GRC seat when he presented himself as a candidate for the presidential elections.

44 The one exception was the sacrificial lamb, Andy Gan, who had to contest against the deeply entrenched Mr Chiam in the single-member Potong Pasir ward.

45 No note 45.

46 See K. Tan, 'Constitutional Implications of the 1991 General Elections', 26 *Singapore Law Review* (1992), p. 46.

47 'PAP's Teamwork', *Far Eastern Economic Review*, 10 December 1987, p. 15.

48 For an analysis of the 1991 general elections, see Dr Bilveer Singh, *Whither PAP's Dominance*, Pelanduk Publications, Pentaling Jaya, 1992.

49 The Speaker of the House stated that: 'As its unofficial leader, the House should give Mr Chiam (presently serving his third term as representative of Potong Pasir constituency) due courtesy and precedence among the opposition MPs.' Quoted in *Straits Times*, 6 January 1992.

50 Unfortunately, the first two appointees, Dr Maurice Choo and the late Mr Leong Chee Whye, were prevented from making any impact as their term lasted just nine months before Parliament was dissolved for general elections. The second slate of NMPs were law lecturer Walter Woon, surgeon Kanwaljit Soin, business entrepreneur Chia Shi Teck, business leader Robert Chua, trade unionist Tong Kok Yeo and hematologist Toh Keng Kiat.

51 *Straits Times*, 26 March 1994. It was reported that the other NMPs spoke as well, but confined themselves mainly to their special interests. Mr Robert Chua's ten questions and Mr Chia Shi Teck's five questions were directed mainly at business issues, while law lecturer Walter Woon spoke mainly on law and education.

52 Democratic Institutions and Political Culture', (2 September 1993, dialogue arranged by the National University of Singapore Society), *Commentary*, vol. 11, no. 2, 1993 pp. 7–24.

53 The present slate of NMPs are Dr K. Soin and Associate Professor Walter Woon, who are serving their second term. The newcomers are Dr Lee Tsao Yuan, deputy director of the Institute of Policy Studies, Mr Stephen Lee, president of the Singapore National Employers' Federation, Mr Imran Mohammed, a director of the Association of Muslim Professionals and Mr John de Payva, secretary-general of the Singapore Manual and Mercantile Workers' Union.

54 'Life or death for politicians in one committee's hands', *Straits Times*, 5 November 1994, p. 33.
55 *Foreign Affairs*, 109, March/April 1994, p. 119.
56 See 'Worse Than a Zero Sum Game?' *Sunday Times*, 20 March 1994, p. 2.
57 Alex Josey, *The Singapore General Elections 1972*, Singapore Eastern University Press, Singapore, 1972, p. 15.

4 CHOOSING A NEW SYSTEM OF REPRESENTATION FOR NEW ZEALAND

1 The full details for each voting system were *not* fully determined at this time. Exact details of the reform option preferred by voters in the indicative referendum (the MMP option) were prescribed in the Electoral Act 1993 before the final referendum was held which gave voters the choice between the FPP system and the MMP system.
2 Under the new Act each voter will have two votes—one for the candidate to represent the electorate (the candidate who obtains the most votes is elected), and one for the party (a party must win 5% of the vote, or an electorate seat, to be eligible for a share of the party list seats). Elections will continue to be held every three years. The New Zealand Parliament will normally have 120 members. The membership of the next Parliament will be:

- 60 general electorate seats (the number is determined by a population-based formula);
- 5 Maori seats (the number is determined by the number of voters on the Maori Roll);
- 55 party list seats.

Under MMP the final overall composition of Parliament depends on the support won by each political party in the nationwide party vote. Each party's share of the seats in Parliament reflects its share of the nationwide party vote. Political parties must be registered if they wish to nominate candidates for party list seats. Registration requires parties to have at least 500 members and to use democratic methods (in which all financial members can take part) to select their candidates. New Zealand has adopted a 'closed list' system. Parties will be required to nominate party list candidates in the order they want them elected. Voters will not be able to change the order decided upon by each party. The allocation of party list seats in Parliament will be undertaken by the chief electoral officer based on the election results. A person can stand for both an electorate seat and a party list seat. Should the candidate win the electorate seat, that candidate's name would be removed from the party list before the party list seats were allocated. In the case of a vacancy in an electorate seat a by-election is held. In the case of a vacancy occurring in a party list seat the next available person from the same party list will be invited to take the seat.

3 P.J. Downey, 'Constitutional Arrangements', *New Zealand Law Journal*, 21 October 1990, p. 341–2.
4 G. Palmer, *Unbridled Power*, Oxford University Press, Wellington, New Zealand, 1979.

5 THE CHOOSING OF REPRESENTATIVES IN KOREA

1 On the Korean form of government, see Dai-Kwon Choi, *Honbophak* (*Science of Constitutional Law*), Pakyongsa, Seoul, 1989, pp. 354–72; Dai-Kwon Choi, 'Jongchikyehyokulwihan myotkajisaengkak (1)' ('Some Thoughts on Political Reforms'), 33 *Seoul Law Journal* 1 (1992) pp. 162–71.
2 88 honka 6, 8 Sept 1989 decision of the Constitutional Court. See also 91d honma 21, 11 Mar 1991 decision of the Constitutional Court for local elections.
3 See Kye Hi-yol, 'Dangjokpyondongkwa uiwonjik' ('Change of Party Affiliation and the National Assembly Membership'), *Sabophaengjong* (*Justice and Administration*), April 1993, pp. 4–16 and May 1993, pp. 37–41; Kyong-kun Kang, 'Uiwonui dangjokbyongkyongkwa jayuwiimui uimi' ('Change of Party Affiliation by a National Assembly Member'), *Wolkan kosi*, November 1992, pp. 49–62; Mun-hyon Kim, 'Kukhoeuiwonui jongdangdaepyosong' ('National Assembly Members as Party Representatives'), *Kosikye*, May 1992, pp. 36–47; Mun-hyon Kim, 'Jonkukkuuiwon sonchulpangbopkwa myotkaji honbopjok munjae' ('The Ways of Selecting the National Assembly Members from the National District and a Few Constitutional Problems'), *Wolkan kosi*, July 1994, pp. 61–2, esp. 70–72; Man-hi Chong, 'Jongdangkukkawa honbopwonriui pyonjil' ('Party State and Transformation of the Constitutional Principles'), *Kosiyonku* (*Bar Exam and Research*), August 1993, pp. 126–39; Yon-ju Chong, 'Hyonhaengsonkojaedoui munjaejom' ('Problems in the Present Election System'), *Kosikye* (*Bar Exam Circle*), August 1994, pp. 83–98, esp. 91–3; Yong-song Kwon, *Honbophakwonron* (*Constitutional Law: A Textbook*), Bopmunsa, Seoul, 1994, pp. 945–6; Tschol-su Kim, *Honbophakkaeron* (*Constitutional Law*), Pakyongsa, Seoul, 1994, pp. 722–3.
4 Dai-Kwon Choi, 'Jongchikyehyokulwihan myotkajisaengkak (I),' pp. 171–80.
5 Dai-Kwon Choi, 'Jongchikyehyokulwihan myotkajisaengkak (II)' ('Some Thoughts on Political Reforms'), 33 *Seoul Law Journal* 2, (1992), pp. 93–125 (1992); Kwang-ung Kim, 'Jongchisonjinhwalulwihan jongchijakum, jongdang mit sonkokwanryonbopjaeui jongbipangan' ('Reform Ideas on Political Funds, Political Parties and Elections Law for Political Advancement'), in *Sinhankukui kukiongkyehyokulwihan bopjaejoligbipanghyang* (*Legislative Directions for Political Reforms of New Korea*), Hankukbopjaeyonkuwon, Seoul, 1993; *Jongehikwankyebopiaeui kaesonpanghyang* (*Reform Directions for Politics-Related Legislation*), Hankukbopjaeyonkuwon, Seoul, 1993; Kon Yang, 'Hankukui kukhoeuiwonsonkojaedoui munjaejomkwa ku kaehyokui pangyang' ('Problems in the Korean Parliamentary Election System

and Suggestions for Its Reform'), 9 *Hanyangdaehak Bophakronchong* (*Hanyang Law Review*) (1992) pp. 99–106; Hae-chan Yi, 'I yadanguron jongkwonkyochaemothanda' ('You Cannot Achieve Political Change with these Kinds of Opposition Parties'), *Sindonga*, July 1991, pp. 255–73; Chang-ju Ra, 'Jongchijakumbop' ('Political Financing Law'), *Minjokiisong*, October 1986, pp. 142–6; Wol-hwan Ku, 'Jongchijakum, ku hukmak' ('Political Funds, Their Dark Scenes'), *Wolkan choson*, December 1983, pp. 124–45.

6 Yong-do Pak and In-jae Kim, *Daetongryong kinkupmyongryopgjaedoui komto* (*A Study on Presidential Emergency Decrees*), Hankukbopjaey nkuwon, Seoul, 1993, esp. pp. 2i ff. (its appendix).

6 BACK TO THE FUTURE: PANCHAYATS AND GOVERNANCE IN INDIA

1 See S. N. Agarwal, *Gandhian Constitution for Free India*, Allahabad 1988.
2 For example, S. L. Saxena, VII *CAD*, p. 216 (5 Nov. 1948).
3 B. R. Mandloi, VII *CAD*, p. 272 (6 Nov. 1948).
4 T. Prakasam, VII *CAD*, p. 272 (6 Nov. 1948).
5 Constitution, VII Schedule List II, E–24, 26, 27, 23.
6 *Report of the Commission on Centre-State Relations*, Delhi, 1985.
7 P. S. Deshmukh, VII *CAD*, p. 252 (5 Nov. 1948).
8 R. N. Singh, VII *CAD*, p. 240 (5 Nov. 1948).
9 N. G. Ranga, VII *CAD*, p. 350–2 (9 Nov. 1948).
10 Ambedkar VII *CAD*, p. 39 (4 Nov. 1949).
11 N. Madhav Rao, VII *CAD*, p. 386 (9 Nov. 1948).
12 G. Das, VII *CAD*, p. 523 (22 Nov. 1948).
13 M. Das, VII *CAD*, p. 308 (8 Nov. 1948).
14 Renuka Ray, VII *CAD*, pp. 356–8 (9 Nov. 1948).
15 N. Madhav Rau, VII *CAD*, p. 386 (9 Nov. 1948).
16 S. L. Saxena, VII *CAD*, pp. 309–10 (6 Nov. 1948).
17 A. C. Guha, VII *CAD*, p. 256 (6 Nov. 1948).
18 M. A. Ayyangar, VII *CAD*, p. 352.
19 VII *CAD*, p. 520 (22 Nov. 1948).
20 T. Prakasam VII *CAD*, pp. 521–2 (22 Nov. 1948).
21 S. M. Ghose, VII *CAD*, p. 523 (22 Nov. 1948).
22 V. Subramaniam, VII *CAD*, p. 525 (22 Nov. 1948).
23 T. Prakasam, VII CAD (22 Nov. 1948).
24 V. Subramaniam, VII *CAD*, p. 525 (22 Nov. 1948).
25 For a survey see *Government of India's Panchayats at a Glance: Status of Panchayat Rai Institutions in India, 1988–89*, Ministry of Agriculture, Delhi, 1989.
26 See Andhra Pradesh: C. Narsimhan, *Report on the High Power Committee on Panchyat Raj* Hyderabad, 1972; Assam: K. P. Tripathy, *Report of the Study Team on Panchayat Raj* Shillong; Gujarat: Rasik Lal Parekh, *Report of the Democratic Decentralization Committee* Ahmedabad, 1960; Himachal: Hardyal Singh, *Report of the Committee on Panchayat*, Simoa, 1865; Madhya Pradesh: *Report of the Committee on Panchayat Raj* Bhopal, 1961; Maharashtra: L. M. Bongiwar, *Evaluation Committee on Panchayat Raj*

Bombay, 1971; Mysore: *Kondaji Bassapa Report of the Committee on Panchayat Raj* Bangalore, 1962; Orissa: Dinbandhu Sahu, *Report of the Gram Panchayats Enquiry Committee* Bhubhaneshwar, 1958; Punjab: Rajinder Singh, *Report of the Study Team on Panchayati Raj* Chandigarh, 1965; Rajasthan: Sadiq Ali, *Report of the Study Team on Panchayati Raj* Jaipur, 1962; Uttar Pradesh: (*Ram Murthi Report of the Study Team on Panchayati Raj* Lucknow, 1965.

27 See *Report of the Committee on Panchayat Raj Institutions* New Delhi, 1978.
28 ibid., pp. vi, 1.
29 ibid., Conclusion 31, p.183.
30 see C. Reich, 'The new property' 73 *Yale Law Journal* (1964), p. 733.
31 See 50 *LSD* (8th series), col. 29.
32 See Institute of Social Sciences, *The New Panchayat Raj in Karnataka* Delhi, 1992.
33 Founded on amendments of the West Bengal Panchayat Act 1973. See further N. Webster, *Panchayati Raj and the Decentralization of Development Planning in West Bengal*, Calcutta 1992.
34 See *Report on Panchayat Raj*, 1978, pp. 208–12).
35 See Speech, 50 *LSD* (8th series), no. 49, Col. 66 (15 May 1989).
36 *Report on Panchayat Raj*, 1978, Clause 243-D(2), p. 210.
37 For the debates see 50 *LSD* (8th series): no. 49 cols. 27–126 (7 Aug.); no. 17, cols 317–422, 424–63 (9 Aug.); no. 18, cols 414–628 (10 Aug.). See also *CLI RSD*, no. 20, cols 71–178 (14 Aug.), and 52 *LSD* (8th series): no. 16, cols 307–15, 323–402 (8 Aug.); no. 21, cols 103–222 (16 Aug.); no. 25, cols 179–308).
38 See the Committee Appointed by V. P. Singh (Delhi, 1989).
39 See *Indian Express*, 6 August 1989.
40 Per Bijoy Chakarvarty, *CLI RSD*, no. 25, col. 206 (13 Oct. 1989).
41 Rajiv Gandhi, 50 *LSD* (8th series), no. 49, col. 66 (15 May 1989).
42 See R. Dhavan, 'Panchayat Raj or Rajiv Raj?', *Indian Express*, 23 July 1989.
43 L. C. Jain, 'And soon 68th Amendment? To ban the carrying of night soil', *Indian Express*, 31 July 1989.
44 Per Rajiv Gandhi, 50 *LSD* (8th series), no. 29, col. 29 (15 May 1989).
45 See Madhav Reddi, 50 *LSD* (8 series.), col 57.
46 M. N. Buch, 'Panchayat Raj Bill: Constitutional Implications', *Indian Express*, 27 September 1989; Rajinder Sachar, '64th Amendment Bill—If Passed a Nullity Ab Initio', *Indian Express*, 18 July 1989; P. Chattopadhyaya, 'Making Panchayats Work', *Indian Post*, 28 August 1989; cf. L. M. Singhvi, 'The 64th Amendment', *Hindustan Times*, 17 May 1989.
47 Rajiv Gandhi 50 *LSD* (8th series), (no. 49), col. 44 (15 May 1989).
48 Shri L. M. Singhvi made extracts of this Report—apparently formulated by Singhvi, P. R. Qubashi, Iqbal Narain, G. Ram Reddy, Nirmala Deshpande, L. S. Tyagi, Raj Bahadur Shastri, J. C. Jetli—in his article 'Why the Amendment?', *Hindustan Times*, 17 May 1989.
49 Report of the Joint Committee, 1992: dissent of B. Jha, pp. x–xi;
50 (Report of the Joint Committee; dissent of Sudhir Ray and Dipen Ghosh, p. ix).
51 ibid.

52 ibid. p. ix.
53 ibid., p. vi.
54 ibid., pr. 25, op. vii–viii.
55 See Transcript of Debates: 1–2 Dec. 1992 (Lok Sabha); 22 Dec. 1992 (Rajya Sabha).

7 THE ELECTORAL SYSTEM OF CHINESE PEOPLE'S DEPUTIES

1 Constitution of the People's Republic of China, Article 2.
2 ibid., Article 3.
3 Xu Chongde, *Constitution of China*, Chinese People's University Press, Beijing, 1989, p. 136.
4 ibid., p. 349.
5 *Electoral Law*, Article 3.
6 ibid, Article 4.
7 Xu Chongde, *The Constitution of China*, p. 353.
8 *Electoral Law*, Article 2.
9 ibid., Article 33.
10 ibid., Article 34.
11 ibid., Article 40.
12 ibid., Article 8.
13 ibid., Article 7.
14 ibid., Article 22.
15 ibid., Article 23.
16 ibid., Article 24.
17 ibid. Article 25.
18 ibid. Article 26.
19 ibid., Article 27.
20 ibid., Article 28.
21 ibid., Article 30.
22 ibid., Article 31.
23 ibid., Article 32.
24 ibid., Article 38.
25 ibid., Article 39.
26 Local Organic Law, Articles 27, 28.
27 ibid., Article 45.
28 Representative Law, Article 2.
29 ibid., Article 8.
30 ibid., Article 13.
31 ibid., Article 14.
32 ibid., Article 21.
33 ibid., Article 25.
34 See Ho Huahui, *Comparative Constitutional Theory*, Wuhan University Press, Hubei, p. 164.

8 REPRESENTATIVE DEMOCRACY AND THE ROLE OF THE MEMBER OF PARLIAMENT: THE SRI LANKAN EXPERIENCE

1 See Article 99 of the Constitution.

2 The petitioners in this case based their challenge against their expulsion on Article 161(d)(ii) and not 99 (13). Article 161 is contained in the chapter entitled *Transitional Provisions* and dealt with the Parliament elected in 1977, before the promulgation of the new Constitution. However, the fact that the two MPs were elected under the simple plurality system, thereby precluding the operation of the myth, makes the decision of the Supreme Court all the more indefensible.

3 These Bills were particularly controversial as they were introduced in Parliament after the Indo-Lanka Accord of July 1987, which many commentators point out was signed by the Sri Lankan government under duress.

4 This was perhaps an unrealistic expectation given the political context at the time. President Premadasa wielded almost absolute control over the United National Party. The fact that there was little, if any, intraparty democracy made it difficult to stand up to the party leadership.

5 Resolution of the Working Committee of the United National Party, 6 September 1991.

6 See C. R. de Silva, 'The Overmighty Executive? A Liberal Viewpoint' in *Ideas for Constitutional Reform*, ed. Chanaka Amaratunga Council for Liberal Democracy and Friedrich Naumann Stiftung, Colombo, 1989, p. 313.

7 The abolition of the executive presidency was an important pledge of the People's Alliance government elected at the parliamentary election on 16 August 1994. People's Alliance President-elect Chandrika Kumaratunga also made it a key feature of her campaign at the presidential election of 9 November 1994.

8 Atukorale J and de Alwis J agreed with the judgment.

9 *Gunawardena and Abeywardena v. Fernando S. C. (Spl.) 50, 51/87.*

10 ibid.

11 Paul Silk, *How Parliament Works*, Longman, London and New York, 1989, p. 44.

12 Wadugodapitiya J agreed with the judgment of Kulatunga J.

13 *Dissanayake et al. v. Kaleel S. C. (Spl.) 4–11/91.*

14 See the judgment of Wanasundera J in 'In Re the Thirteenth Amendment', *Singapore Law Reports*, 312 (1987), p. 337.

15 *Dissanayake et al. v. Kaleel S.C. (Spl.) 4–11/91.*

16 ibid.

17 Wijetunga J agreed with Dheeraratne J, while Ramanathan J dissented.

18 *Tilak Karunaratne v. Sirimavo Bandaranaike et al. S. C. (Spl.) 3/93.*

19 Speech to the electors of Bristol, 3 November 1774. *The Works of Edmund Burke*, p. 159.

20 A. Appadurai, *The Substance of Politics*, OUP, Madras, 1975, p. 528.

21 (1909) 1 Ch., p. 163.

22 (1910) *AC*, p. 87.
23 (1979) 4 *SA*, p. 258.
24 ibid., p. 273.
25 (1980) 3 *SA*, p. 863.
26 Klaus von Beyme, *Political Parties in Western Democracies*, St Martin's Press, New York, 1985.
27 (1965) 68 *NLR*, p. 265.
28 22 H. W. R. Wade, *Annual Survey of Commonwealth Law*, 1966, p. 4.

9 THE STRUCTURAL WEAKNESSES OF REPRESENTATION IN MACAU

1 The views expressed in this paper are the sole responsibility of the authors and do not necessarily represent the views of any entity, nor do they bind the government of Macau, for whom the authors presently work.
2 Usually called, in Macau, '1, 2, 3', these events are the local corollary of the 'Cultural Revolution' in the People's Republic of China and consisted, basically, of demonstrations supporting the Chinese government and protesting against foreign 'colonial' rule in Chinese territory and of persecutions of citizens with Portuguese ancestors.

10 THE CASE OF VOTING IN THE INDONESIAN PEOPLE'S CONSULTATIVE ASSEMBLY

1 The original text was called the *Proklamasi* ('Proclamation'), which ended the legal order of the colonial era, and laid down the new Republic's legal foundation and the source of its national legal order. For a stimulating discussion on this subject, see J. C. T. Simorangkir and B. Mang Reng Say, *Around and About the Indonesian Constitution of 1945*, 19th ed., Djambatan, Jakarta, 1980, p. 1.
2 Muhammad Yamin, *Naskah Persiapan Undang-undang Dasar 1945 (Text of the Preparation of the 1945 Constitution)*, 1971, p. 437.
3 George McTurnan Kahin, *Nationalism and Revolution in Indonesia*, Cornell University Press, Ithaca NY, 1970, p. 138.
4 It accepted that part of the Constitution that was already completed at the meeting of the PPKI on 18 August.
5 Kahin, *Nationalism and Revolution in Indonesia*.
6 ibid., p. 139.
7 Article IV of the Transitory Provisions of the 1945 Constitution stated: 'Prior to the formation of the People's Consultative Assembly, the House of People's Representatives and the Supreme Advisory Council in accordance with this Constitution, all their authority shall be exercised by the President assisted by a National Committee.'
8 Kahin, *Nationalism and Revolution in Indonesia*, p. 140.
9 See the 1945 Constitution, Article 27.
10 ibid., Article 28.
11 ibid., Article 28.

12 ibid., Article 29 clause (2).

13 ibid., Article 31 clause (1).

14 ibid., Article 33 clauses (1), (2) and (3).

15 The broad area lying between China and India that since World War II has generally been known as Southeast Asia is one of the most heterogeneous in the world. Though it is generally referred to as a region, the principal basis for this designation is simply geographic propinquity of its component states. They occupy territory between China and the Indian subcontinent.

The political systems presently governing the lives of Southeast Asia's 300 million inhabitants have been built on considerably different cultures. The religious component alone embraces Islam, Buddhism, Confucianism, Christianity and Hinduism. Except in the case of Thailand, the politics of all these countries have been conditioned by periods of colonial rule—ranging from little more than half a century to approximately four centuries—each of which has had a distinctive character and political legacy. See Satya Arinanto, 'Indonesia', in *Asia Pacific Constitutional Yearbook 1993*, eds Cheryl Saunders & Graham Hassall, Centre for Comparative Constitutional Studies, University of Melbourne, 1994.

16 For a comparative study see Herbert Feith, *The Decline of Constitutional Democracy in Indonesia*, Cornell University Press, Ithaca, New York, 1964, pp. 1–19.

17 George McTurnan Kahin, 'Indonesia: the pre-colonial and colonial background', in *Major Governments in Asia*, ed. George McTurnan Kahin, Cornell University Press, Ithaca NY, 1963.

18 Quoted from Arinanto, 'Indonesia', in *Asia Pacific Constitutional Yearbook 1993*, eds Saunders & Hassall.

19 ibid.

20 Herbert Feith, 'Indonesia: the historical background', in *Major Governments of Asia*, ed. Kahin, p. 155.

21 Christine Drake, *National Integration in Indonesia: Patterns and Policies*, University of Hawaii Press, Honolulu, 1989, p. 6.

22 Feith, *The Decline of Constitutional Democracy*.

23 Quoted from Arinanto, 'Indonesia', in *Asia Pacific Constitutional Yearbook 1993*, eds Saunders & Hassall.

24 Alan Thein Durning, *Guardians of the Land: Indigenous Peoples and the Health of the Earth*, World Watch Institute, Washington D.C., 1992, p. 170. The nine countries with the highest cultural diversity in the world are: Papua New Guinea, Nigeria, Cameroon, Indonesia, India, Australia, Mexico, Zaire and Brazil. The term 'highest cultural diversity' here means 'countries where more than 200 languages are spoken'. The fundamental strata of the traditional cultures of nearly all the numerous peoples of Southeast Asia set them apart from those of India and China. Beyond that, there are few common denominators among the states that currently make up the area, except for roughly similar climatic conditions and broadly similar economies and economic problems.

Most numerous of the recent immigrants to Indonesia are the Chinese. They are usually distinguishable from the Malay by their lighter skin and more strongly Mongoloid appearance. Arabs represent the second most prominent group of recent migrants. Since many Arabs have intermarried with Indonesians, Indonesians are sometimes quite Arab in appearance.

25 Simorangkir and Mang Reng Say, *Around and About*, p. 93.
26 Quoted from Arinanto, 'Indonesia', in *Asia Pacific Constitutional Yearbook 1993*, eds Saunders & Hassall.
27 ibid.
28 Charles Himawan, *The Foreign Investment Process in Indonesia: The Role of Law in the Economic Development of A Third World Country*, Gunung Agung, Singapore, 1980, pp. 56–7.
29 See Articles 4–15 of the 1945 Constitution.
30 See Articles 19–23 of the 1945 Constitution.
31 See Article 16 of the 1945 Constitution.
32 See Article 23 clause (5) of the 1945 Constitution.
33 See Articles 24–25 of the 1945 Constitution.
34 See Satya Arinanto, *Suplemen: Himpunan Peraturan Hukum Tata Negara untuk Perkuliahan 'Hukum Tata Negara' dan 'Lembaga Kepresidenan'* (*Supplement: Compilation of the Constitutional Law Regulations for the Courses of 'Constitutional Law' and 'The Presidency'*) Pusat Studi Hukum Tato Negara Fakultas Hukum Universitas Indonesia, Depok, 1994, pp. 19–26.
35 See the Decision of the MPR No. V/MPR/1973 and the Decision of the MPR No. IX/MPR/1978 in Arinanto, *Suplemen: Himpunan Peraturan Hukum Tata Negara . . .* 51–53, 61–2.
36 See H. M. Ridhwan Indra and Satya Arinanto, *Kekuasaan Presiden dalam UUD 1945 Sangat Besar* (*The President's Power in the 1945 Constitution is Very Large*), CV Haji Masagung, Jakarta, 1992, p. 4.
37 See Simorangkir and Mang Reng Say, *Around and About the Indonesian Constitution of 1945*, pp. 19–21.
38 Himawan, *The Foreign Investment Process in Indonesia*, p. 58.
39 ibid.
40 See Article 8 of the 1945 Constitution.
41 For a stimulating discussion, see Leo Suryadinata, *Military Ascendancy and Political Culture: A Study of Indonesia's Golkar*, Southeast Asia Series no. 85, Ohio University, Athens, 1989.
42 See Indra and Arinanto, *Kekuasaan Presiden*.

11 ANTI-HOPPING LAWS—THE MALAYSIAN EXPERIENCE

1 J. McIntyre in Re: *Public Service Employees Act*, (1987) 38 *DLR* (4th) 161, at 216 (*SCC*).
2 Former professor of Constitutional Law, University of Cambridge. Nominated by the United Kingdom.
3 Former governor-general of Australia and nominated by its Government.
4 Former chief justice of the High Court of Allahabad. Nominated by India.
5 Former judge of the High Court of West Pakistan. Nominated by Pakistan.

6 Article 10 (1) (c) was considered in passing in *Abdul Karsin bin Abdul Ghani v. Sabah Legislative Assembly* (1980) 1 *MLJ* 171 (*SCJ*) and *Tun mustapha bin Harun v. Sabah Legislative Assembly* (1993) 1 *MLJ* 26. Both cases were not, however, determined on their merits and hence are of little precedent value.
7 (1992) 1 *MLJ*, p. 343.
8 (1992) 1 *MLJ*, p. 697.
9 50 *AIR* (1963) SC, p. 812.
10 65 *AIR* (1978) SC, p. 597.
11 69 *AIR* (1982) J & K, p. 26.
12 (1992) I *MLJ*, at p. 717 F.
13 (1980) AC, p. 319 (*PC*).
14 (1970) AC, p. 538.
15 *N.A.A.C.P. v. Alabama ex. rel. Patterson* (1958) 357 *US* 449 pp. 1488–1502. See also *Healy v. James* (1972) 408 *US* 169 pp. 266–92.
16 (1987) 38 *DLR* (4th), p. 161.
17 (1986) 27 *DLR* (4th), p. 527. The Supreme Court of Canada affirmed this decision, but on other grounds: see (1989) 58 *DLR* (4th), p. 317.
18 See *AIR* (1978) *SC*, p. 597.
19 One Shri Hardwar Lal, who defected from the Congress Party to the Swantantara Party.
20 (1992) 1 *MLJ* 697, p. 711B.

12 ANTI-DEFECTION LAW IN INDIA

1 Tenth Schedule (Articles 102(2) and 191(2))
Provisions as to disqualification on ground of defection
(Added by the Constitution (Fifty-second Amendment) Act, 1985. s. 6 (w.e.f. 1–3–1985)).
1. **Interpretation**—In this Schedule, unless the context otherwise requires,—
   (a) 'House' means either House of Parliament or the Legislative Assembly or, as the case may be, either House of the Legislature of a State;
   (b) 'legislature party', in relation to a member of a House belonging to any political party in accordance with the provisions of paragraph 2 or paragraph 3 or, as the case may be, paragraph 4, means the group consisting of all the members of that House for the time being belonging to that political party in accordance with the said provisions;
   (c) 'Original political party', in relation to a member of a House, means the political party to which he belongs for the purposes of sub-paragraph (1) of paragraph 2;
   (d) 'paragraph' means a paragraph of this Schedule.
2. **Disqualification on ground of defection**—(1) Subject to the provisions of paragraphs 3, 4 and 5, a member of a House belonging to any political party shall be disqualified for being a member of the House—
   (a) if he has voluntarily given up his membership of such political party; or

(b) if he votes or abstains from voting in such House contrary to any direction issued by the political party to which he belongs or by any person or authority authorised by it in this behalf, without obtaining, in either case, the prior permission of such political party, person or authority and such voting or abstention has not been condoned by such political party, person or authority within fifteen days from the date of such voting or abstention.

Explanation—For the puposes of this sub-paragraph,—

(a) an elected member of a House shall be deemed to belong to the political party, if any, by which he was set up as a candidate for election as such member;

(b) a nominated member of a House shall,—

(i) where he is a member of any political party on the date of his nomination as such member, be deemed to belong to such political party;

(ii) in any other case, be deemed to belong to the political party of which he becomes, or, as the case may be, first becomes, a member before the expiry of six months from the date on which he takes his seat after complying with the requirements of article 99 or, as the case be, article 188.

(2) An elected member of a House who has been elected as such otherwise than as a candidate set up by any political party shall be disqualified for being a member of the House if he joins any political party after such election.

(3) A nominated member of a House shall be disqualified for being a member of the House if he joins any political party after the expiry of six months from the date on which he takes his seat after complying with the requirements of article 99 or, as the case may be, article 188.

(4) Notwithstanding anything contained in the foregoing provisions of this paragraph, a person who, on the commencement of the Constitution (Fifty-second Amendment) Act, 1985, is a member of a House (whether elected or nominated as such) shall,—

(i) where he was a member of a political party immediately before such commencement, be deemed, for the purposes of sub-paragraph (1) of this paragraph, to have been elected as a member of such House as a candidate set up by such political party;

(ii) in any other case, be deemed to be an elected member of the House who has been elected as such otherwise than as a candidate set up by any political party for the purposes of sub-paragraph (2) of this paragraph or, as the case may be, be deemed to be a nominated member of the House for the purposes of sub-paragraph (3) of this paragraph.

3. **Disqualification on ground of defection not to apply in case of split**—Where a member of a House makes a claim that he and any other members of his legislature party constitute the group

representing a faction which has arisen as a result of the split in his original political party and such group consists of not less than one-third of the members of such legislature party,—

(a) he shall not be disqualified under sub-paragraph (1) of paragraph 2 on the ground—

    (i) that he has voluntarily given up his membership of his original political party; or

    (ii) that he has voted or abstained from voting in such House contrary to any direction issued by such party or by any person or authority authorised by it in that behalf without obtaining the prior permission of such party, person or authority and such voting or abstention has not been condoned by such party, person or authority within fifteen days from the date of such voting or abstention; and

(b) from the time of such split, such faction shall be deemed to be the political party to which he belongs for the purposes of sub-paragraph (1) of paragraph 2 and to be his original political party for the purposes of this paragraph.

4. **Disqualification on ground of defection not to apply in case of merger**—(1) A member of a House shall not be disqualified under sub-paragraph (1) of paragraph 2 where his original political party merges with another political party and he claims that he and any other members of his original political party—

(a) have become members of such other political party or, as the case may be, of a new political party formed by such merger; or

(b) have not accepted the merger and opted to function as a separate group,

and from the time of such merger, such other political party or new political party or group, as the case may be, shall be deemed to be the political party to which he belongs for the purposes of sub-paragraph (1) of paragraph 2 and to be his original political party for the purposes of this sub-paragraph.

(2) For the purposes of sub-paragraph (1) of this paragraph, the merger of the original political party of a member of a House shall be deemed to have taken place if, and only if, not less than two-thirds of the members of the legislature party concerned have agreed to such merger.

5. **Exemption**—Notwithstanding anything contained in this Schedule, a person who has been elected to the office of the Speaker or the Deputy Speaker of the House of the People or the Deputy Chairman of the Council of States or the Chairman or the Deputy Chairman of the Legislative Council of a State or the Speaker or the Deputy Speaker of the Legislative Assembly of a State, shall not be disqualified under this Schedule,—

(a) if he, by reason of his election to such office, voluntarily gives up the membership of the political party to which he belonged immediately before such election and does not, so long as he continues to hold such office thereafter, rejoin that political party or become a member of another political party; or

(b) if he, having given up by reason of his election to such office his membership of the political party to which he belonged immediately before such election, rejoins such political party after he ceases to hold such office.

6. **Decision on questions as to disqualification on ground of defection**—(1) If any question arises as to whether a member of a House has become subject to disqualification under this Schedule, the question shall be referred for the decision of the Chairman or, as the case may be, the Speaker of such House and his decision shall be final:

Provided that where the question which has arisen is as to whether the Chairman or the Speaker of a House has become subject to such disqualification, the question shall be referred for the decision of such member of the House as the House may elect in this behalf and his decision shall be final.

(2) All proceedings under sub-paragraph (1) of this paragraph in relation to any question as to disqualification of a member of a House under this Schedule shall be deemed to be proceedings in Parliament within the meaning of article 122 or, as the case may be, proceedings in the Legislature of a State within the meaning of article 212.

7. **Bar of jurisdiction of courts**—Notwithstanding anything in this Constitution, no court shall have any jurisdiction in respect of any matter connected with the disqualification of a member of a House under this Schedule.

8. **Rules**—(1) Subject to the provisions of sub-paragraph (2) of this paragraph, the Chairman or the Speaker of a House may make rules for giving effect to the provisions of this Schedule, and in particular, and without prejudice to the generality of the foregoing, such rules may provide for—

(a) the maintenance of registers or other records as to the political parties, if any, to which different members of the House belong;

(b) the report which the leader of a legislature party in relation to a member of a House shall furnish with regard to any condonation of the nature referred to in clause (b) of sub-paragraph (1) of paragraph 2 in respect of such member, the time within which and the authority to whom such report shall be furnished;

(c) the reports which a political party shall furnish with regard to admission to such political party of any members of the House and the officer of the House to whom such reports shall be furnished, and

(d) the procedure for deciding any question referred to in sub-paragraph (1) of paragraph 6 including the procedure for any inquiry which may be made for the purpose of deciding such question.

(2) The rules made by the Chairman or the Speaker of a House under sub-paragraph (1) of this paragraph shall be laid as soon as may be after they are made before the House for a total period of thirty days which may be comprised in one session or in two or more successive sessions and shall take effect upon the expiry of the said period of thirty days unless they are sooner approved with or

without modifications or disapproved by the House and where they are so approved, they shall take effect on such approval in the form in which they were laid or in such modified form, as the Case may be, and where they are so disapproved, they shall be of no effect.

(3) The Chairman or the Speaker of a House may, without prejudice to the provisions of article 105 or, as the case may be, article 194, and to any other power which he may have under this Constitution direct that any, wilful contravention by any person of the rules made under this paragraph may be dealt with in the same manner as a breach of privilege of the House.

2 *AIR* (1987) Punjab, p. 263.

3 (1992) Supp. 2 *SCC*, p. 651.

13 THE JAPANESE CONSTITUTION AND REPRESENTATIVE DEMOCRACY

1 The States General was the traditional French system of political representation. It comprised representatives of the First Estate (the clergy), the Second Estate (the nobility) and the Third Estate (the masses).

15 DEMOCRACY AND REPRESENTATION IN THE SPECIAL ADMINISTRATIVE REGIONS OF HONG KONG AND MACAU

1 These themes are explored in Yash Ghai, 'The past and future of Hong Kong's Constitution', *China Quarterly*, 1992, pp. 792–813.

2 Lau Siu-kai, *Decolonisation without Independence: The Unfinished Political Reforms of the Hong Kong Government*, The Institute of Social Studies, The Chinese University of Hong Kong, Hong Kong, Occasional Papers, no. 19.

3 Mr Lee elaborated his views in answer to a question from the author as to why he considered that Hong Kong did not deserve democracy. The answer is reproduced in *Window*, December 1993.

4 The difficulties bureaucrats have in dealing with 'politician' members of the Legislative Council are well set out in a statement by the former Chief Secretary, Sir David Ford, in his statement in the Council of 6 November 1991. See Yash Ghai, 'The Rule of Law and Capitalism: Reflections on the Basic Law, in China, Hong Kong and 1997: Essays in Legal Theories, ed. R. I. Wacks, Hong Kong University Press, Hong Kong, 1993, pp. 310–11. The situation has, if anything, got worse since then, and senior civil servants have engaged in a systematic attack on the more active legislators.

5 Britain had strenuously resisted any Chinese role in Hong Kong before the formal transfer of power. The compromise was an intergovernmental Joint Liaison Group which was to consult on the implementation of the Declaration, discuss matters relating to the smooth transfer of government, and exchange information and conduct consultations on

such matters as may be agreed by the two sides. Britain was able to secure an agreement that the Group 'shall be an organ for liaison and not an organ of power' (Annex II of the Declaration)—a somewhat forlorn hope at it turned out.

6 The memoirs of the man who was for many years the chief of the 'Mafia', Sir Percy Craddock, *Experiences of China,* John Murray, London, 1994, seek to rebut these criticisms but end up, for many readers, confirming them.

7 There is no space to discuss the Patten agenda and reforms. Some of these will be mentioned briefly in the next section. Suffice it to say here that they are of no great significance in so far as democratisation is concerned, but because they were the peg on which China derailed the 'through train', they will leave a deep imprint on the future of democracy in Hong Kong.

8 The existence of the rule of law has been a common explanation for the success of Hong Kong. For references, see Ghai, 'The Rule of Law and Capitalism', pp. 354–6.

A frequent refrain of Patten's speeches is the value of the rule of law to Hong Kong's continued success (implying that British-style administration could alone provide it in Hong Kong and that China did not really understand how to secure it).

9 For these and other criticisms, see Norman Miner, *The Government and Politics in Hong Kong, 5th edn,* Oxford University Press, Hong Kong, 1991, pp. 106–11.

10 A recent incident (December 1994–January 1995) illustrates well both the inability of the administration to come to terms with the politicisation of the Legislative Council and its supposed adherence to advisory and consultative bodies. When a government Bill for redundancy or retirement benefits for workers was successfully amended by the Council on a motion of an elected member, the government withdrew the Bill (having previously warned the member that it would do so if the motion was moved successfully). Its argument was that the Labour Advisory Board (which brings together industry, labour and government) had already agreed on levels of payments. The implication was that the Board was more important than the legislature and that the government would not be frustrated by the legislature. The member of the Council resigned on the issue, precipitating a minor crisis for the government.

11 John Burns, 'China's Governance: Political Reforms in a Turbulent Environment', 119 *China Quarterly* (1989), pp. 480–518.

12 Deng told Margaret Thatcher that he was concerned about the transition—'about man made disturbances'—saying that it was 'very easy to create disturbances' (24 September 1992). He expressed similar fears to Geoffrey Howe on 31 July 1984. He told a delegation from Hong Kong and Macau that China would station forces there to 'prevent disturbances' (3 October 1984) and informed Basic Law drafters that Hong Kong might be used 'as a base of opposition to the mainland under the pretext of "democracy" ', (All the quotations are from Deng, *On the Hong Kong Question).*

13 Deng told the Basic Law Drafting Committee, in an attempt to strengthen anti-democratic forces,

> Would it be good for Hong Kong to hold general elections? I do not think so. For example, as I have said before, Hong Kong affairs will naturally be administered by Hong Kong people, but will it do for the administrators to be elected by a general ballot? We say that Hong Kong's administrators should be people of Hong Kong who love the motherland and Hong Kong, but will a general election necessarily bring out people like that?' (Deng, *On the Hong Kong Question*, p. 56)

'Those who love the motherland' is a code for those who are willing to submit to the will of the ruling authorities on the Mainland.

14 In the absence of a formal mechanism to determine popular views, the government resorts to official surveys of opinion (as with its 1984 proposals for constitutional reform and the Joint Declaration). It is widely recognised that the government fixes results that suit it, and they have enjoyed little public or specialist credibility. See Mark Roberti, *The Fall of Hong Kong: China's Triumph and Britain's Betrayal*, John Wiley, New York, 1994. The 1991 direct elections formed the first test of opposing views, which the United Democrats ('the liberals') won in a convincing fashion.

15 It is perhaps not surprising that the business community's view of governance was derived from the corporate world. Sir S. Y. Chung, for many years its leader, could not accept that a beggar should have the same rights as a wealthy tycoon and believed that elections should be held as in a company, with the largest shareholder getting the biggest say. Another leader, who orchestrated its campaign in the drafting of the Basic Laws, Vincent Lo, was also taken up by business analogies: he thought that a board of directors (the legislature) would monitor the performance of the chairperson (the governor), who would run the company (Hong Kong) to maximise profits for the benefit of shareholders (the workers). This information is derived from Roberti, *The Fall of Hong Kong*, pp. 119 and 176 respectively.

These are not happy analogies for the supporters of democracy, for the Chinese firms are patriarchally run. In regard to corporate law— see Robert Tricker, 'Corporate Governance: A Ripple on the Cultural Reflections', *Capitalism in Contrasting Cultures* eds S. R. Clegg and S. G. Redding, Walter de Gruyter, Berlin, 1990 and are not particularly respectful of the legal regime governing corporations (see report by Price, Waterhouse (Hong Kong), *Eastern Express*, 27 January 1995).

16 I have argued that these firms increasingly see the guarantee of their continued success in close relations with the Chinese authorities, lubricated by personal connections and graft: Ghai, 'The Rule of Law and Capitalism'.

17 Yash Ghai, *Human Rights and Governance: The Asia Debate*, The Asia Foundation, San Francisco, 1994 esp. pp. 15–16.

18 Roberti, *The Fall of Hong Kong*, pp. 211–22.

19 Sau Liu-kai and Kuan Hsin-Chi, *The Ethos of the Hong Kong Chinese*, The Chinese University of Hong Kong, Hong Kong, 1988.

20 The Macau Basic Law also classifies as permanent residents Portuguese who have resided in Macau for a continuous period of seven years and

have taken it as their place of permanent residence—a provision strictly unnecessary since such persons would be covered by another, more general category, but significant for political reasons. In both Basic Laws the relevant article is Article 24.

21 Chinese practice (rather than law) seems to make a distinction between those whose foreign citizenship represents a real link with the foreign country (for example, through a substantial residence there) and those who may have acquired it in Hong Kong, as is the case with those given British nationality under the 1990 UK Nationality Act. The latter may continue to be regarded as Chinese nationals.

22 This distinction was introduced late in the drafting of the Basic Law in Hong Kong, after the UK 1990 Nationality Act under which approximately 150 000 to 200 000 Hong Kong persons would have acquired the right of abode in the UK. The category would also cover those Hong Kong residents who have a Green Card or its equivalent in the US, Canada, Australia, and so on.

23 At present members from Hong Kong and Macau are chosen through the mechanism of the Guangzhou branch of the Communist Party. The Macau members are more closely integrated into the Guangzhou system than those from Hong Kong.

24 No voting age is specified. Hong Kong provided for voting on and after the age of 21 when the Joint Declaration was concluded, and early drafts of the Basic Law had incorporated it. One of Patten's reforms was to lower the voting age to 18. Macau had 18 as the voting age when its Basic Law was enacted.

25 China has opposed the provisions (under the Patten reforms) for the 1995 elections for single-member constituencies as being undemocratic.

26 As part of Patten's reforms for the 1995 elections is that the Election Committee will consist of members of the District Boards, who are themselves directly elected, see *Electoral Provisions (Miscellaneous Amendments) Ordinance*, 1994.

27 The government justified the introduction of functional constituencies as a way of giving

> full weight to representation of economic and professional sectors which are essential to future confidence and prosperity. Direct elections would run the risk of a swift introduction of adversarial politics, and would introduce an element of instability at a critical time (**Green Paper**, *The Further Development of Representative Government in Hong Kong*, **Government** Printer, Hong Kong, July 1984, p. 9).

28 Stanley Moser, 'Seats of **Power**', *Far Eastern Economic Review*, 29 August 1991, pp. 18–20.

29 A government secretary said at a university seminar that Patten was appalled when he first came across functional constituencies, which he likened to 'rotten boroughs'. Initially there was little competition for these seats, but with increasing politicisation in the wake of the Basic Law, there was considerable manipulation of votes and voters. See Moser, 'Seats of Power'.

30 Ian Scott, *Political Change and the Crisis of Legitimacy in Hong Kong*, Oxford University Press, Hong Kong, 1989, pp. 268–73.

31 It is not clear what is the point of recording it. The provision follows the Royal Instructions to the Governor of Hong Kong (para XII), where the purpose is to inform the British government (which does have the power to overrule the governor) of the dispute.

32 However, the citizenship requirements of principal officials are set out in the section on public servants, suggesting that they are to be regarded as such. Principal officials are not mentioned in the comparable section in the Macau Basic Law, perhaps because there are no special citizenship requirements for them; and perhaps also because in Macau principal officials have not always been public servants, an option that was intended to be retained.

33 The matter is complex, but reasons of space prevent its exploration. Suffice it to say that collective responsibility would bind not only the Chief Executive but also his or her officials, who may find it difficult to reconcile with their role as legislators, unless a clear majority is available. Patten has opted against having politicians in his Executive Council, on the basis that this will clarify the respective roles of that Council and the Legislative Councils, and will improve transparency of the policy-making process and sharpen the accountability of the government to the legislature (his address to the Legislative Council, 7 October 1992). However, Patten's own thinking is less than transparent; the British government was accused of having submitted to the Chinese on this, as the United Democrats won most of the geographical constituencies, and the presence of its leader Martin Lee in the inner sanctum of the governor would have been anathema to them.

34 In one sense a weak and fragmented parliamentary system may serve better the purpose of outside intervention, but the considerations of stability obviously weighed heavily with the Chinese.

16 NEPAL'S EXPERIMENT IN REPRESENTATION

1 Jaya Prakash Narayan, *Towards Revolution*, Arnold–Heinemann Publishers, India, 1975.

2 ibid.

Select Bibliography

'A map up here, in the mind,' *The Economist*, 29 June 1991, pp. 16–17.

Agarwal, S. N., *A Ghandian Constitution for Free India*, Allahabad, 1988.

Ali, Sadiq, *Report of the Study Team on Panchayati Raj*, Jaipur, 1962.

Alisjahbana, S. Takdir, *Indonesia: Social and Cultural Revolution*, Oxford University Press, Kuala Lumpur, 1966.

Anderson, Benedict R. O'G., *Language and Power: Exploring Political Cultures in Indonesia*. Cornell University Press, Ithaca, 1990.

Arinanto, Satya, *Hukum dan Demokrasi (Law and Democracy)*, Ind-Hill-Co., Jakarta, 1991.

——, 'Mempersoalkan Kembali Makna Kebebasan Akademik' ('To Rediscuss the Meaning of Academic Freedom'), *Kompas*, 18 December 1993.

——, 'Mencari Esensi "Pers yang Bebas dan Bertanggung Jawab' " ('In Search of the Essence of A "Free and Responsible Press" '), *Kompas*, 2 July 1994.

——, *Pembangunan Hukum dan Demokrasi* [*The Development of Law and Democracy*], Dasamedia Utama, Jakarta, 1993.

——, *Suplemen: Himpunan Peraturan Hukum Tata Negara untuk Perkuliahan 'Hukum Tata Negara' dan 'Lembaga Kepresidenan' (Supplement: Compilation of Constitutional Law Regulations for the Courses of 'Constitutional Law' and 'The Presidency')*, Pusat Studi Hukum Tata Negara Fakultas Hukum Universitas Indonesia, Depok, 1993.

Bone, Robert C., 'Organisation of the Indonesian Elections', 49 *American Political Science Review* (1955), pp. 1067–84.

Bongiwar, L. M., *Evaluation Committee on Panchayat Raj*, Bombay, 1971.

Buch, M. N., 'Panchayat Raj Bill: Constitutional Implications', *Indian Express*, 27 September 1989.

Burns, John, 'China's Governance: Political Reforms in a Turbulent Environment', 119 *China Quarterly* (1989), pp. 480–518.

Chakarvarty, Bijoy, *CLI RSD*, no. 25, col. 206 (13 October 1989).

Chang-ju Ra, 'Jongchijakumbop' ('Political Financing Law'), *Minjokiisong*, October 1986, 142–6.

Chattopadhyaya, P., 'Making Panchayats Work', *Indian Post*, 28 August 1989.

Chen, Mai, 'Remedying New Zealand's Constitution in Crisis', *New Zealand Law Journal*, January 1993.

Chen, Lung-chu & Reisman, W. M., 'Who Owns Taiwan?: A Search for International Title', 81 *Yale Law Journal* (1972), p. 599.

Chow, Y. & Nathan, A. 'Democratizing the Transition in Taiwan', 27 *Asian Survey* (1987), pp. 277, 283–5.

Cooley, Frank L., *Ambonese Adat: A General Description*, Yale University Southeast Asia Studies, New Haven, Conn., 1962.

Craddock, Sir Percy, *Experiences of China*, John Murray, London, 1994.

Dai-Kwon, Choi *Honbophak* (*Science of Constitutional Law*), Pakyongsa, Seoul, 1989, pp. 354–72.

——, 'Jongchikyehyokulwihan myotkaji saengkak (1)' ('Some Thoughts on Political Reforms'), 33 *Seoul Law Journal* 1 (1992), pp. 162–71.

——, 'Jongchikyehyokulwihan myotkaji saengkak (2)' ('Some Thoughts on Political Reforms'), 33 *Seoul Law Journal* 2 (1992), pp. 93–125, 171–80.

Dale, William, 'The Making and Remaking of Commonwealth Countries', 14 *ICLQ*, January (1993).

Das, G., VII *CAD*, p. 523 (22 November 1948).

Das, M., VII *CAD*, p. 308 (8 November 1948).

De A. Samarasinghe, S. W. R., 'Sri Lanka in 1982: A Year of Elections', 23 *Asian Survey* 2 (1983), pp. 158–64.

de Smith, S. A., *The New Commonwealth and its Constitutions*, Stevens & Son, London, 1964.

Deshmukh, P. S., VII *CAD*, p. 252 (5 November 1948).

Dhavan, R., 'Panchayat Raj or Rajiv Raj?', *Indian Express*, 23 July 1989.

Dicey, A. V., *An Introduction to the Study of the Law of the Constitution*, Macmillan & Co. Ltd., London, 1968.

Drake, Christine, *National Integration in Indonesia: Patterns and Policies*, University of Hawaii Press, Honolulu, 1989.

Duffy, Terence, 'Cambodia since the Election: Peace, Democracy and Human Rights?' 15 *Contemporary Southeast Asia* 4 (1994).

Durning, Alan Thein, *Guardians of the Land: Indigenous Peoples and the Health of the Earth*, Worldwatch Institute, Washington, D.C., 1992.

Emmerson, Donald K., *Indonesia's Elite: Political Culture and Cultural Politics*, Cornell University Press, Ithaca, 1976.

Feith, Herbert, *The Decline of Constitutional Democracy in Indonesia*, Cornell University Press, Ithaca, New York, 1964.

Fukuyama, Francis, 'Asia's Soft Authoritarian Alternative', *New Perspectives Quarterly*, Spring 1992.

Gaffar, A., *Javanese Voters: A Case Study of Election Under a Hegemonic Party System*, Gadjah Mada University Press, Gadjah Mada, 1992.

Gandhi, Rajiv, 50 *LSD* (8th series) no. 49, col. 66 (15 May 1989).

Ghai, Yash, *Human Rights and Governance: The Asia Debate*, The Asia Foundation, San Francisco, 1994.

——, 'The past and future of Hong Kong's Constitution', *China Quarterly* 1992, pp. 792–813.

——, 'The Rule of Law and Capitalism: Reflections on the Basic Law', in *China, Hong Kong and 1997: Essays in Legal Theory*, ed. R. I. Wacks, Hong Kong University Press, Hong Kong, 1993, pp. 354–6.

Ghose, S. M., VII *CAD*, p. 523 (22 November 1948).

Government of India's Panchayats at a Glance: Status of Panchayat Rai Institutions in India, 1988–89, Ministry of Agriculture, Delhi, 1989.

Guha, M. A., VII *CAD*, p. 256 (6 November 1948).

Hae-chan Yi, 'I yadanguron jongkwonkyochaemothanda' ('You Cannot Achieve Political Change with these Kinds of Opposition Parties'), *Sindonga*, July 1991, pp. 255–273.

Hanafia, A. Malek, 'The Malaysian General Election of 1986', 6 *Electoral Studies* 3 (1986), pp. 279–85.

Hills, Rodney C., 'The 1990 Election in Tonga', 3 *The Contemporary Pacific* 2 (1991), pp. 357–78.

Himawan, Charles, *The Foreign Investment Process in Indonesia: The Role of Law in the Economic Development of A Third World Country*, Gunung Agung, Singapore, 1980.

Hindley, Donald, 'Indonesia 1971: Pantjsila Democracy and the Second Parliamentary Elections', 12 *Asian Survey* (1972), pp. 56–8.

Ho, Khai Leong, 'The 1986 Malaysia General Election: An Analysis of the Campaign and Results', 16 *Asian Profile* 3 (1988).

Hocking, William Ernest, *Freedom of the Press: A Framework of Principle*, The University of Chicago Press, Chicago, 1947.

Holt, Claire, Anderson, Benedict R.O'G & Siegel, James eds, *Culture and Politics in Indonesia*, Cornell University Press, Ithaca, 1972.

Hong Kong Government Green Paper, *The Further Development of Representative Government in Hong Kong*, Government Printer, Hong Kong, July 1984.

Hong Nack, Kim 'The 1988 Parliamentary Election in South Korea', 29 *Asian Survey* 5 (1989), pp. 480–95.

Indra, H. M. Ridhwan & Arinanto, Satya, *Kekuasaan Presiden dalam UUD 1945 Sangat Besar (The President's Power in the 1945 Constitution is Very Large)*, CV Haji Masagung, Jakarta, 1992.

Institute of Social Sciences, India, *The New Panchayat Raj in Karnataka*, Delhi, 1992.

International Electoral Institute Commission, *Free and Fair Elections—and Beyond, Final Report*, Ministry for Foreign Affairs, Sweden, 1993.

Jain, L. C., 'And soon 68th Amendment? To ban the carrying of night soil', *Indian Express*, 31 July 1989.

Jennings, Ivor, *The Law and the Constitution*, University of London Press, London, 1946.

Josey, Alex, *The Singapore General Elections 1972*, Singapore Eastern University Press, Singapore, 1972.

Joshi, Shuwan L. Joshi & Rose, Leo E., *Democratic Innovations In Nepal*, University of California Press, Berkeley, 1966.

Jupp, James, 'Elections in Vanuatu', 35 *Political Science* 1 (1983), pp. 1–15.

Kahin, Audrey R. ed., *Regional Dynamics of the Indonesian Revolution: Unity from Diversity*, University of Hawaii Press, Honolulu, 1985.

Kahin, George McTurnan ed. *Governments and Politics of Southeast Asia*, Cornell University Press, Ithaca, 1964.

——, *Major Governments of Asia*, Cornell University Press, Ithaca, 1963.

——, *Nationalism and Revolution in Indonesia*, Cornell University Press, Ithaca, New York, 1970.

Kiang, Lim Hng, 'No Need for Opposition Checks and Balances', *Petir*, November/December 1992, pp. 74–7.

King, Daniel E., 'The Thai Parliamentary Elections of 1992: Return to Democracy in an Atypical Year', 32 *Asian Survey* 12 (1992), pp. 1109–23.

King, Peter ed., *Pangu Returns to Power: The 1982 Elections in Papua New Guinea*, Department of Political and Social Change, Canberra, 1989.

Koh, R. C., 'The 1985 Parliamentary Election in South Korea', 25 *Asian Survey* 8 (1985), pp. 883–97.

Kompas (*The Indonesian Kompas daily*), 25 March 1987.

Kompas, 1 December 1988.

Kompas, 26 March 1991.

Kompas, 22 June 1994.

Kondaji Bassapa Report of the Committee on Panchayat Raj, Bangalore, 1962.

Kon Yang, 'Hankukui kukhoeuiwonsonkojaedoui munjaejomkwa ku kaehyokui pangyang' ('Problems in Korean Parliamentary Election System and Suggestions for Its Reform'), 9 *Hanyangdaehak Bophakronchong* (*Hanyang Law Review*) (1992), pp. 99–106.

Kuo, Eddie C. Y., Holaday, Duncan & Peck, Eugenia, *Mirror on the Wall: Media in a Singapore Election*, Asian Mass Communication Research and Information Centre, Singapore, 1993.

Kwang-ung Kim, 'Jongchisonjinhwalulwihan jongchijakum, jongdang mit sonkokwanryonbopjaeui jongbipangan' ('Reform Ideas on Political Funds, Political Parties and Elections Law for Political Advancement'), in *Sinhankukui kukjongkyehyokulwihan bopjaejoligbipanghyang* (*Legislative Directions for Political Reforms of New Korea*), Hankukbopjaeyonkuwon (Korea Legislation Research Institute), Seoul, 1993.

Kwok, Rowena, Leung, Joan & Scott, Ian, *Votes without Power: The Hong Kong Legislative Council Elections 1991*, Hong Kong University Press, Hong Kong, 1992.

Kusnardi, Mohammad and Ibrahim, Harmaily, *Pengantar Hukum Tata Negara Indonesia* (*Introduction to the Indonesian Constitutional Law*), Pusat Saudi Hukum Tata Negara Fakultas Hukum Universitas Indonesia, Jakarta, 1983.

Kye Hi-yol, 'Dangjokpyondongkwa uiwonjik' ('Change of Party Affiliation and the National Assembly Membership'), *Sabophaengjong* (*Justice and Administration*), April 1993, pp. 4–16; May 1993, pp. 37–41.

Kyong-kun Kang, 'Uiwonui dangjokbyongkyongkwa jayuwiimui uimi' ('Change of Party Affiliation by a National Assembly Member'), *Wolkan kosi* (*Monthly Bar Exam*), November 1992, pp. 49–62.

Lal, Brij, 'Before the Storm: An Analysis of the Fiji General Election of 1987', 12 *Pacific Studies* 1 (1988), pp. 71–96.

——, 'Chiefs and Indians: Elections and Politics in Contemporary Fiji', 5 *The Contemporary Pacific* 2 (1993), pp. 275–301.

——, *The Fall and Rise of Sitiveni Rabuka: Fiji General Elections of 1994*, Peace Research Centre, Canberra, 1995.

Lal, Victor, 'The Fiji General Election of 1987', 6 *Electoral Studies* 3 (1987), pp. 249–62.

Liddle, R. William, 'Merekayasa Demokrasi di Indonesia' ('To Engineer the Democracy in Indonesia'), *Kompas*, 6 February 1990.

Lubis, Todung Mulya, *In Search of Human Rights: Legal-Political Dilemmas of Indonesia's New Order 1966–1990*, California University Press, Berkeley, 1990.

MacClancy, J. V., 'The Solomon Islands: First Elections After Independence', 16 *Journal of Pacific History* 3 (1981).

Macdonald, Barrie, 'Elections in Kiribati', 35 *Political Science* 1 (1983), pp. 58–70.

——, 'Tuvalu: the 1981 General Election', 35 *Political Science* 1 (1983).

McPhetres, Samuel, 'Elections in the Northern Mariana Islands', 35 *Political Science* 1 (1983).

Madhav Rao, N., VII *CAD*, p. 386 (9 November 1948).

Madhya Pradesh: Report of the Committee on Panchayat Raj, Bhopal, 1961.

Maisrikrod, Surin, *Thailand's Two General Elections in 1992: Democracy Sustained*, Institute of Southeast Asian Studies, Singapore, 1992.

Mandloi, B. R., VII *CAD*, p. 272 (6 November 1948).

Man-hi Chong, 'Jongdangkukkawa honbopwonriui pyonjil' ('Party State and Transformation of the Constitutional Principles'), *Kosiyonku* (*Bar Exam and Research*), August 1993, pp. 126–39.

May, R. J., 'Elections in the Philippines 1986–87', 7 *Electoral Studies* 1 (1988), pp. 79–81.

Mellor, Norman and Anthony, James, *Fiji Goes to the Polls: The Crucial Legislative Council Elections of 1963*, East-West Center Press, Honolulu, 1968.

Miner, Norman, *The Government and Politics in Hong Kong*, 5th ed., Oxford University Press, Hong Kong, 1991.

Ministry for Foreign Affairs, Sweden, *Free and Fair Elections and Beyond: Conclusions and Suggestions for the Mandate and Tasks of the Proposed Institute for Democracy and Electoral Assistance*, Ministry of Foreign Affairs, Stockholm, 1994.

Moody (Jr), Peter R., 'The Democratization of Taiwan and the Reunification of China', *The Journal of East Asian Affairs*, Winter/Spring, 1991, pp. 144–84.

Moser, Stanley, 'Seats of Power', *Far Eastern Economic Review*, 29 August 1991, pp. 18–20.

Mun-hyon Kim, 'Jonkukkuuiwon sonchulpangbopkwa myotkaji honbopjok munjae' ('The Ways of Selecting the National Assembly Members from the National District and A Few Constitutional Problems'), *Wolkan kosi* (*Monthly Bar Exam*), July 1994, pp. 61–72.

——, 'Kukhoeuiwonui jongdangdaepyosong' ('National Assembly Members as Party Representatives'), *Kosikye* (*Bar Exam Circle*), May 1992, pp. 36–47.

Murthi, Ram, *Report of the Study Team on Panchayati Raj*, Lucknow, 1965.

Naraya, Shriman, *India and Nepal: An Exercise In Open Diplomacy*, Orient Paperbacks, New Delhi, 1971.

Narayan, Jayaprakash, *Towards Revolution*, Arnold-Heinemann Publishers, India, 1975.

Narsimhan, C., *Report on the High Power Committee on Panchayat Raj*, Hyderabad, 1972.

Nasution, Adnan Buyung, *The Aspiration for Constitutional Government in Indonesia: A Socio-legal Study of the Indonesian Konstituante 1956–1959*, Pustaka Sinar Harapan, Jakarta, 1992.

New Zealand Parliamentary Debates (Hansard).

Nordholt, N. G., 'The Indonesian Elections: A National Ritual', in *Man, Meaning and History*, eds Schefold J. Schoorl & J. Tennekes, Martinus Nijhoff, The Hague, 1980.

Norton, Clifford, *NZ Parliamentary Election Results 1946–1987*, Department of Political Science, Victoria University of Wellington, Wellington, 1988.

NSTP Research and Information Services, *Elections In Malaysia: Facts and Figures*, Balai Berita, Kuala Lumpur, 1990.

Oberst, Robert C. & Weilage, Amy, 'Quantitative Tests of Electoral Fraud: The 1982 Sri Lankan Referendum', 5 *Corruption and Reform* (1990), pp. 49–62.

Oliver, Michael ed., *Eleksin: The 1987 National Election in Papua New Guinea*, University of Papua New Guinea Press, Port Moresby, 1989.

Ooi, G. L., *Town Councils in Singapore: Self Determination for Public Housing Estates*, Institute of Policy Studies, Occasional Paper 4, 1985.

Osman, Sabihah, 'State Elections: Implications for Malaysian Unity', 32 *Asian Survey* 4 (1992), pp. 380–91.

Parekh, Rasik Lal, *Report of the Democratic Decentralization Committee*, Ahmedabad, 1960.

Peten, Custaf, et al., *Pakistan, Human Rights after Martial Law: Report of a Mission*, International Commission of Jurists, Geneva, 1987.

Polsby, Nelson, 'Legislatures', in *Governmental Institution and Process*, eds Fred Greenstein & Nelson Polsby, 1975.

Porter, Gareth, *Vietnam: The Politics of Bureaucratic Socialism*, Cornell University Press, Ithaca & London, 1993.

Prakasam, T., VII *CAD*, p. 272 (6 November 1948).

——, VII *CAD*, pp. 521–2 (22 November 1948).

Premdas, Ralph, 'Elections in Fiji: Restoration of the Balance in September 1977', *Journal of Pacific History*, 1979, pp. 194–207.

Premdas, Ralph & Steeves, Jeffrey S., 'National Elections in Papua New Guinea: The Return of Pangu to Power', 23 *Asian Survey* 8 (1983), pp. 991–1006.

Premdas & Steeves, 'The 1993 National Elections in the Solomon Islands', 29 *Journal of Pacific History* 3 (1994), pp. 46–56.

——, 'Vanuatu: the 1991 Elections and the Emergence of a New Order', 343 *Round Table* (1992), pp. 339–57.

Pye, Lucian, *Asian Power and Politics: The Cultural Dimensions of Authority*, Belknap Press, Cambridge, 1985.

Ranga, N. G., VII *CAD*, pp. 350–2 (9 November 1948).

Rashiduzzaman, 'Indirect Elections in Pakistan', 15 *Zeitschrift fur Politik* (1968), pp. 326–36.

Ray, Renuka, VII *CAD*, pp. 356–8 (9 November 1948).

Reich, C., 'The new property', 73 *Yale Law Journal* (1964), p. 733.

Report of the Commission on Centre-State Relations Delhi, 1985.

Report of the Committee on Panchayat Raj Institutions, New Delhi, 1978.

Report of the Electoral Referendum Panel, New Zealand, October 1992.

Report of the Electoral Referendum Panel, New Zealand, December 1993.

Report of the Royal Commission on the Electoral System 'Towards a Better Democracy', New Zealand, December 1986.

Rood, Steven, *Baguio Citizen Response to the February 1986 Snap Election and Revolution*, Cordillera Studies Center, Philippines, Working Paper 4, May 1987.

Rose, Leo E. & Scholz, T., *Nepal: A Profile of a Himalayan Kingdom*, Select Service Syndicate, New Delhi, 1980.

Sachar, Rajinder, '64th Amendment Bill—If Passed a Nullity Ab Initio', *Indian Express*, 18 July 1989.

Saffu, Yaw, 'Papua New Guinea in 1986: preelection mobilization and some nationalism', 27 *Asian Survey* (1987), pp. 264–73.

Sahu, Dinbandhu, *Report of the Gram Panchayats Enquiry Committee*, Bhubhaneshwar, 1958.

Sau, Kiu-kai & Hsin-Chi, Kuan, *The Ethos of the Hong Kong Chinese*, The Chinese University of Hong Kong Press, Hong Kong, 1988.

Saunders, Cheryl & Hassall, Graham (eds), *Asia Pacific Constitutional Yearbook 1993*, Centre for Comparative Constitutional Studies, Unversity of Melbourne, 1994.

Saxena, S. N.,VII *CAD*, p. 216 (5 November 1948).

——, VII *CAD*, pp. 309–10 (6 November 1948).

Scarr, Deryck, 'Fiji and the general election of 1992', 28 *Journal of Pacific History* 1 (1993), pp. 75–92.

Scott, Ian, *Political Change and the Crisis of Legitimacy in Hong Kong*, Oxford University Press, Hong Kong, 1989.

Sekretariat Jenderal MPR-RI, *Ketetapan-ketetapan Majelis Permusyawaratan Rakyat Republik Indonesia Maret 1988 (The Decisions of the People's Consultative Assembly March 1988)*. Sekretariat Jenderal MPR-RI, Jakarta, 1988.

Selbourne, David, 'The Sri Lankan Elections, Oct.–Dec. 1982', 2 *Electoral Studies* 2 (1983).

Seow, Francis, *To Catch a Tartar*, Yale University Press, New Haven, Conn., 1994.

Shah, Rishikesh, *Heroes And Builders of Nepal*, Oxford University Press, London, 1965.

Shuster, Donald R., 'Elections in the Republic of Palau', 35 *Political Science* 1 (1983), pp. 117–32.

Simorangkir, J.C.T. & Mang Reng Say, B., *Around and About the Indonesian Constitution of 1945*, Djambatan, Jakarta, 1980.

Singapore Government, *1984 Constitutional Amendment Act*, No. 16 of 1984.

——, *Group Representative Constituencies: A Summary of the Report of the Select Committee, Ministry of Communications and Information.*

——, *Report of the Rendel Constitutional Commission Singapore 1954.*

——, *Shared Values White Paper*, Cmd.1 of 1991, Singapore Government Printers.

Singh, Bilveer, *Whither PAP's Dominance?*, Petaling Jaya, Pelanduk Publications, 1992.

Singh, Hardyal, *Report of the Committee on Panchayat*, Simoa, 1965.

Singh, Rajinder, *Report of the Study Team on Panchayati Raj*, Chandigarh, 1965.

Singh, R. N., VII *CAD*, p. 240 (5 November 1948).

Singhvi, Shri L. M., 'Why the Amendment?', *Hindustan Times*, 17 May 1989.

Singhvii, L. M., 'The 64th Amendment', *Hindustan Times*, 17 May 1989.

Siu-kai, Lau, *Decolonisation without Independence: The Unfinished Political Reforms of the Hong Kong Government*, The Institute of Social Studies, The Chinese University of Hong Kong, Hong Kong, Occasional Papers, no. 19.

Sivalingam, G., & Peng, Yong Siew, 'The System of Political and Administrative Corruption in a West Malaysian State', 35 *Philippine Journal of Public Administration* 3 (1991), pp. 264–86.

Soepomo, *Undang-undang Dasar Sementara Republik Indonesia, (The Provisional Constitution of the Republic of Indonesia)*. Pradnya Paramita, Jakarta, 1974.

So'o, Asofou, *Universal Suffrage in Western Samoa: The 1991 General Elections*, Regime change and regime maintenance in Asia and the Pacific, working paper no. 10, Research School of Pacific Studies, Canberra, 1993.

Steeves, Jeffrey S., 'Vanuatu: the 1991 National Elections and their Aftermath', 27 *Journal of Pacific History* 2 (1992), pp. 217–28.

Stiller, L. F, *Prithwinarayan Shah in the Light of Dibya Upadesh*, Himalaya Book Centre, Kathmandu, 1989.

Strong, C. F., *Modern Political Constitutions: An Introduction to the Comparative Study of Their History and Existing Form*, Sidgwick & Jackson Limited, London, 1963.

Subramaniam, V., VII *CAD*, p. 525 (22 November 1948).

Suny, Ismail, *Prospek Parpol dan Golkar Ditinjau dari Sudut Hukum Tata Negara (The Prospect of the Political Party and the Functional Group from the Viewpoint of Constitutional Law)*. Paper presented at a Seminar at the Faculty of Law, University of Indonesia, Depok, 22 March 1990.

Suryadinata, Leo, *Military Ascendancy and Political Culture: A Study of Indonesia's Golkar*, Southeast Asia Series No. 85, Ohio University, Athens, 1989.

Tan, Kevin, 'Constitutional Implications of the 1991 General Elections', *Singapore Law Review* (1992).

——, 'The Evolution of Singapore's Modern Constitution: Developments from 1945 to the present day', 1 *Singapore Academy of Law Journal* 1 (1989).

Thayer, Carlyle, *Political Democratisation in Vietnam: Do Elections Really Matter?*, Department of Political and Social Change, Research School of Pacific Studies, Australian National University, Canberra, 1992.

Thio, Li-ann, 'The Post Colonial Constitutional Evolution of the Singapore Legislature', *Singapore Journal of Legal Studies*, July 1993.

Thoolen, Hans ed., *Indonesia and the Rule of Law: Twenty Years of 'New Order' Government*, Frances Pinter, London, 1987.

Tinker, Irene, 'Malayan Elections: Electoral Pattern for Plural Societies?' 9 *Western Political Quarterly* June (1956), pp. 258–82.

Tricker, Robert, 'Corporate Governance: A Ripple on the Cultural Reflections' in *Capitalism in Contrasting Cultures*, eds S. R. Clegg and S. G. Redding, Walter de Gruyter, Berlin, 1990.

Tripathy, K. P., *Report of the Study Team on Panchayat Raj* (Shillong).

Tschol-su Kim, *Honbophakkaeron (Constitutional Law)*, Pakyongsa, Seoul, 1994.

Va'a, Leulu Felise, 'General Elections in Western Samoa, 1979–1982', 35 *Political Science* 1 (1983), pp. 78–102.

Van Trease, Howard, 'The 1991 Election in Kiribati', *Journal of Pacific History* (1992), pp. 66–72.

Wacks, R. W. ed., *China, Hong Kong and 1997: Essays in Legal Theory*, Hong Kong University Press, Hong Kong, 1993.

Ward, Ken, *The 1971 Election in Indonesia: An East Java Case Study*, Monash Papers on Southeast Asia, vol. 2, Centre of Southeast Asian Studies, Monash University, Melbourne, 1974.

Weber, Max, in Guenther Roth & Claus Wittich eds, *Economy and Society: An Outline of Interpretive Sociology*, University of California Press, Berkeley, 1978.

Webster, N., *Panchayati Raj and the Decentralization of Development Planning in West Bengal*, Calcutta, 1992.

Weston, Burns H., Falk, Richard A., & D'Amato, Anthony, *Basic Documents in International Law and World Order*, West Publishing Co., St. Paul, Minnesota, 1990.

Winckler, Edwin A., 'Institutionalization and Participation on Taiwan: From Hard to Soft Authoritarianism?', 99 *China Quarterly* 481 (1984).

Winslow, V., 'Creating a Utopian Parliament', 28 *Malaya Law Review* (1984).

Wol-hwan Ku, 'Jongchijakum, ku hukmak' ('Political Funds, Their Dark Scenes'), *Wolkan Choson*, December 1983.

Wurfel, David, 'The Philippine Elections: Support for Democracy', 2 *Asian Survey* 3 (1962).

Yeh, Jiunn-rong, 'Changing Forces of Constitutional and Regulatory Reform in Taiwan', 4 *Journal of Chinese Law* 83 (1990).

Yon-ju Chong, 'Hyonhaengsonkojaedoui munjaejom' ('Problems in the Present Election System'), *Kosikye (Bar Exam Circle)*, August 1994, pp. 83–98.

Yong-do Pak & In-jae Kim, *Daetongryong kinkupmyongryopgjaedoui komto (A Study on Presidential Emergency Decrees)*, Hankukbopjaey nkuwon, Seoul, 1993.

Yong-song Kwon, *Honbophakwonron (Constitutional Law: A Textbook)*, Seoul, Bopmunsa, 1994.

Zakaria, Fareed, 'Culture is Destiny: A Conversation with Lee Kuan Yew', *Foreign Affairs*, March/April 1994.

Index